— 17

Dominions Diary

RYBURN ARCHIVE EDITIONS

Dominions Diary
The Letters of E. J. Harding
1913 – 1916

edited with an introduction and commentary by

Stephen Constantine
University of Lancaster

Ryburn Publishing

First published in 1992
Ryburn Publishing Ltd
Krumlin, Halifax

Introduction and commentary © Stephen Constantine

ISBN 1-85331-018-2

Composed by Ryburn Typesetting; originated by Ryburn
Reprographics; bound in Edinburgh by Hunter & Foulis

Printed by Ryburn Book Production, Halifax, England

Contents

Dover – Marseilles – Port Said – Suez Canal – Ismailia – Aden –
Colombo – Fremantle – Perth – Adelaide – Melbourne – Hobart –
Bluff – Dunedin – Christchurch – Wellington – Auckland – Rotorua –
Sydney – Brisbane – Toowoomba – Newcastle – Sydney – Canberra –
Melbourne – Hobart – Launceston – Adelaide – Melbourne – Sydney –
Samoa – Hawaii – San Francisco – Grand Canyon – Chicago – New
York – Fishguard

Madeira – Cape Town – Port Elizabeth – East London – Kimberley –
Bloemfontein – Durban – Pietermaritzburg – Pretoria – Johannesburg –
Cape Town – Madeira

Photographic credits

The editor and publisher are grateful to the Royal Commonwealth Society for permitting reproduction of the illustrations which appear on the following pages: 38, 59, 61, 68, 69, 70, 79, 81, 89, 94, 103, 107, 111, 116, 118, 119, 121, 123, 125, 132, 163, 166, 188, 194, 195, 197, 201, 204, 208, 213, 215, 225, 240, 244, 246, 253, 255, 265, 275, 282, 284, 290, 299, 302, 307, 313, 314. For all other photographic illustrations, the editor and publisher are indebted to Professor John M. MacKenzie. The illustrations were scanned by Ian Beesley at Ryburn Reprographics. Harding's sketches have been redrawn by Stephen Constantine and Paul Ferguson who, with Mitch France, also prepared the maps.

List of abbreviations

A.D.C.	Aide de Camp
B.C.	British Columbia
B.N.C.	Brasenose College, Oxford University
C.E.F.	Canadian Expeditionary Force
Cd.	Command paper, published by His Majesty's Stationery Office
C.M.G.	Commander of the Order of St. Michael and St.George
C.N.R.	Canadian Northern Railway
C.O.	Colonial Office
C.P.R.	Canadian Pacific Railway
D.R.C.	Dominions Royal Commission
ft.	feet
G.C.M.G.	Knight Grand Cross of the Order of St. Michael and St. George
G.G.	Governor General
H.E.	His Excellency
ins.	inches
K.C.M.G.	Knight Commander of the Order of St. Michael and St. George
lb.	pound (weight)
£. s. d.	pound sterling, shillings, pence
m.	metre
M.H.R.	Member of the House of Representatives
M.P.	Member of Parliament
N.S.W.	New South Wales
N.Z.	New Zealand
P. & O.	Peninsular and Oriental Steam Navigation Company
P.E.I.	Prince Edward Island
S.A.P.	South African Party

Preface and acknowledgements

The letters which Edward John Harding (1880–1954) wrote home to his father, mother and sister constitute a remarkable diary of a memorable tour at a special time. The writer – who signed himself 'E. J. Harding' even in these personal letters – had been appointed the secretary of the Dominions Royal Commission, in which official capacity during 1913, 1914 and 1916 he travelled around the world on four extensive journeys, visiting Australia, New Zealand, South Africa, Newfoundland and Canada. In January 1913, when he began his first trip, he was merely a 32-year-old Second Class Clerk in the Colonial Office, but promotion and honours followed: from 1930 to 1939 Sir Edward Harding was Permanent Under-Secretary at the Dominions Office (the department made responsible for the affairs largely of the white self-governing societies of the British Empire and the predecessor of the Commonwealth Office).

These are private letters, written to his family, intended partly to entertain and to keep them informed of his whereabouts and activities, but designed also to be preserved for his own use as a record of his experiences. They were handwritten in ink, usually on the official notepaper of the Dominions Royal Commission. Two letters appear to be missing, but the remaining forty-three were found as a collection among his personal effects on his death in 1954. They were deposited in the Library of the Royal Commonwealth Society by his brother-in-law and executor Sir Harry Batterbee. A few historians have made partial use of this source, but the letters are now published in full for the first time. Editorial amendments have been restricted to the omission of Harding's own few deletions, the replacement of ampersands with 'and', the spelling out of abbreviations, some merging of short paragraphs, minor changes in punctuation to clarify the sense and a few corrections of spelling, except in the case of proper names which are printed as written with the correct or more usual versions cited in the notes.

The letters may be read without reference to editorial additions, simply as an almost daily account of a series of long distance journeys by an intelligent and often informed observer with a facile pen and the prejudices and perceptions of his time, his age, his educational background, his profession, his class and his nationality. As such, they have the narrative flow and descriptive virtues of much travel literature.

However, these letters have qualities which have prompted the inclusion of an Introduction and a Commentary on the text. Harding's correspondence provides an unusual and possibly unique account of the operations of a Royal Commission. Probably only such a source could reveal some of the internal mechanics of an official investigation, and certainly only very private letters would contain personal comments by a 'mere' secretary like Harding upon the 'great and the good' who constituted the Commissioners. Moreover, the Dominions Royal Commission was a most unusual body, special in its inclusion of representatives from the overseas dominions of the Empire as well as from the United Kingdom, and unique in the gathering of its evidence not just from staid sittings in London but via extensive and often arduous global inquiries. Editorial additions are therefore intended to explain the origins of the Dominions Royal Commission and add more to Harding's descriptions of its operations and findings. The principal additional sources used for this purpose are the Commission's published reports, Parliamentary Papers relating to the Imperial Conference of 1911, the files of the Colonial Office preserved in the Public Record Office in London, the unpublished letters in the British Library of Sir Edgar Vincent (later Lord D'Abernon) who was the Commission's Chairman, and the diaries of two Commissioners, Sir Henry Rider Haggard and Sir George Foster, the former now in Norfolk Record Office and the latter published as an appendix to W. Stewart Wallace, *The Memoirs of the Rt. Hon. Sir George Foster*, Toronto, 1933.

There are few private accounts of travels around the white dominions of the British Empire in this critical period in its history. These territories were no longer raw settlements but maturing mixed economies and pluralistic societies with internal tensions and growing external interests. Moreover, their national aspirations were not necessarily easy to reconcile with British interests. By 1913 the external security and internal cohesion of the British Empire could no longer be taken for granted, and anxieties already expressed in Great Britain were inevitably intensified with the outbreak of the First World War. The Introduction and editorial notes are therefore also designed to add detail to Harding's descriptions, sufficient to clarify some of the Empire's past history and the current issues with which it was concerned. For these purposes a wide range of additional primary and secondary sources has been consulted, particularly the annual Year Books of Canada, Australia, New Zealand and South Africa, an array of contemporary guidebooks and tourist publications, the Australian, Canadian and South African Dictionaries of Biography, the *Dictionary of National Biography* and *Who Was Who*, A. H. McLintock (ed.), *An Encyclopaedia of New Zealand*, Wellington, 1966, a number of Canadian and Australian encyclopaedias and various editions of the *Encyclopaedia Britannica*. In addition, several academic histories of the United Kingdom, the Empire and the dominions have been used. It is hoped that the information provided on a wide variety of subjects mentioned in the letters will also help recreate the material and cultural world in which Harding was travelling.

To achieve the same end, visual evidence has been added. The illustrations have been selected from material generally contemporary with Harding's visits. Many are picture postcards, often dated by the postmark. Most of the others are official photographs, including several taken by A. Hugh Fisher (1867–1945) on behalf of the Colonial Office Visual Instruction Committee in 1908–09.

In preparing a book of this nature I have accumulated a number of personal debts which it is a pleasure here to acknowledge. Most importantly I am grateful to the Royal Commonwealth Society, to its Library Committee, to its excellent Library staff and especially to two distinguished Librarians: Donald Simpson and Terry Barringer not only supported my suggestion that these letters should be published, but provided freely of their knowledge and time in helping me to find the additional material needed for my Introduction and Commentary. Many of the photographs also come from the remarkable riches of the R.C.S. Library, and for permission to reproduce them in this book I am additionally grateful. I am also conscious of how much I owe to my colleague Professor John MacKenzie. His encouragement for the project included the loan of contemporary guidebooks, the provision of information for my notes and considerable generosity in allowing me to reproduce many illustrations from his remarkable collection of postcards. This book owes much to Wendy Constantine: it was she who prepared a typescript from the original manuscript and it is she who sustained me in my editorial labours. In addition, I have been helped by many people who kindly responded to particular inquiries, including Lee Blond, Dr Ralph Gibson and Dr Marcus Merriman of the University of Lancaster; Dr Kent Fedorowich of Bristol Polytechnic; Ian Warrell of the Tate Gallery and Jacqueline McCormish of the

National Gallery in London; Dr Nigel Dalziel of Lancaster Maritime Museum; Joan Horsley of the National Maritime Museum at Greenwich; Mr M. J. Jones, Secretary of the Institution of Mining and Metallurgy; Dr John Ritchie, General Editor of the *Australian Dictionary of Biography*; Mary P. Bentley, Executive Editor of the *Dictionary of Canadian Biography*; Dr Emma Devapriam of the National Gallery of Victoria; Peter Entwistle of Dunedin Public Art Gallery; Mr A. C. L. Hall of the Wodehouse Library, Dulwich College; Dr T. C. Barnard of Hertford College, Oxford; Dr David Constantine of Queen's College, Oxford; Lady Dagmar Batterbee; Mr W. J. Willcocks and Mr T. H. W. Willcocks; and the staff of the University of Lancaster Library, of Norfolk Record Office, of the Public Record Office, of the British Library and of Rhodes House Library and the Bodleian Library, Oxford. I am grateful to the University of Lancaster for a period of study leave, partly employed to begin my editorial work. Permission to cite extracts from the diaries of Sir Henry Rider Haggard was kindly given by Commander M. E. Cheyne. Finally, the completion of the book and the quality of its production owe a great deal to the staff at Ryburn Publishing with whom it has been a pleasure to work.

Introduction:
E. J. Harding, the British Empire
and the Dominions Royal Commission

When Edward Harding set off from London in January 1913 on the first overseas tour of the Dominions Royal Commission he was still a young man and of comparatively lowly status in the Colonial Office. He was born in St Osyth, Clacton-on-Sea, in Essex on 22 March 1880, the only son of Rev. John Harding (1841–1926) and his wife Laura, née Hewlett. He had two sisters. The elder one was Eleanor Laura (Nellie, died 1950), who in 1909 married Harry, later Sir Harry, Batterbee (1880–1976), a friend from Harding's university years and a close though slightly junior colleague at the Colonial Office and later the Dominions Office: references to 'Harry' occur at intervals in the letters. His younger sister was Evelyn (Eva, died c.1968) to whom he appears to have been particularly close, no doubt because she did not marry but seems to have lived with their father until his death: many of the letters are addressed to her.[1]

This was by tradition largely a family of Anglican clergymen. Not only was his father a clergyman (latterly as Vicar of Christ Church, Beckenham in Kent), but so were three uncles, two great-uncles and his grandfather, Rev. William Harding (1800–1845). However, his great-grandfather, William Harding (1766–1851), had achieved some eminence in public administration, ultimately as the Accountant-General in the Transport Office branch of the Admiralty.

It was natural that someone of Harding's social background would be

---

1. Personal details on Harding and his family are derived from *Who Was Who*, *Dictionary of National Biography*, obituary in *The Times* and letters to the Editor from Mr W. J. Willcocks, 22 Dec. 1987 and Mr T. H. W. Willcocks, 2 Feb. 1988 (second cousins); for lively portraits of Sir Edward Harding and Sir Harry Batterbee see Joe Garner, *The Commonwealth Office 1925–68*, London, 1978, pp.20–2.

educated first at a private preparatory school, the Abbey School in Beckenham, from 1889 to 1893, but it was by no means inevitable that after a brief period at a school in Margate he would become a pupil at Dulwich College from 1895 to 1899.[2] He seems to have enjoyed his time at this prestigious public school, both academically and socially (in his final year he appeared as Socrates in a memorable performance of *The Clouds* by Aristophanes)[3]; later in his life he served for many years as a governor of the school. Dulwich helped him gain entry as a scholar to Hertford College, Oxford, where for four years from October 1899 he studied classics. He obviously relished that experience also, successfully mixing athletics and rowing with his academic work, obtaining a First Class in Moderations in 1901 and a Second Class B.A. in *Literae Humaniores* in 1903. Later he became an Honorary Fellow of the College, to which on his death he left a considerable bequest.[4]

Entrance to the civil service was by competitive examination, and in 1903 Harding was placed 12th.[5] He elected first for a post in the Marine Department at the Board of Trade, but on 31 May 1904 he transferred to the Colonial Office as a Second Class Clerk.[6] The Office at this time was responsible for the affairs not only of the dependent crown colonies but also handled the business of the self-governing colonies of white settlement. These latter territories – Australia, New Zealand, South Africa, Newfoundland and Canada – were normally called the dominions, a distinction formally agreed at a Colonial Conference of premiers in 1907 and marked by the separation of Colonial Office business between the Dominions Division and the Crown Colonies Division.[7] Harding originally worked in the latter, being involved at various times in the affairs of the Eastern dependencies, of East Africa and ultimately of the West Indies. Formal promotion was not rapid, but his abilities seem to have been noticed for on 14 October 1912 he was appointed Assistant Private Secretary to Lewis Harcourt (1863–1922), Secretary of State for the Colonies in the last Liberal Government of 1910–15. In the same year Harding qualified as a barrister, called to the bar by Lincoln's Inn.

---

2. *Dulwich College Register*: he appears to have been first a pupil briefly in 1893–4.
3. There is a review in *The Alleynian*, the school magazine, July 1899.
4. Dr T. C. Barnard, Archivist, Hertford College, to the Editor, 28 June 1991.
5. *Dulwich College Register*.
6. *Colonial Office List*.
7. J. A. Cross, *Whitehall and the Commonwealth*, London, 1967, pp.17–18.

Most of Harding's personal characteristics and cultural interests were by now developed, and many are evident in his letters. He was still single, and indeed did not marry until he was 49. (His wife, Marjorie, was the daughter of Henry Huxley. Her death in 1950 was a terrible blow to him, accelerating his own decline: there were no children.)[8] He seems to have been quite widely read, and he had developed a love of paintings and of music: the family apparently mixed socially and musically with Ralph Vaughan Williams and his sister, and he later became a member of the Council of the Royal College of Music. He also carried with him at least some of his knowledge of classical literature. But perhaps one result of that academic training was a scrupulous care for accuracy in expression and for clarity in thought. This may account for the impatience he showed as a young man towards the indecision and occasional woolly-mindedness of the elderly Commissioners under his care. It was also perhaps later reflected in his attitude towards subordinates in the Dominions Office: a former junior colleague described him as 'a perfectionist ... congenitally incapable of accepting a draft without making some amendment'. To the same observer he appeared 'cold, even distant', with steel grey eyes, no sense of humour, no warmth, no social graces.[9] But that is not entirely the impression generated by the amused tone of many of his letters. It has also been claimed by another former colleague that he had a generous side to his character, apparent 'in many acts of personal kindness'.[10] His sister Eva, recalling the holidays they had together, even described him as 'a delightful travelling companion'. She also believed that 'the tour with the Dominions R. Commission helped to put him "on the map" in the Civil Service'.[11]

The Dominions Royal Commission was appointed on the recommendation of the Imperial Conference held in London over 12 days in May and June 1911. To understand its origins it is necessary to identify the anxieties and ambitions growing in the minds of policy-makers in Britain and in the white dominions from the late 19th century to the period prior to the First World War.

Harding, born in 1880, grew up in a world which might well have induced complacency about the future. Superficially, British global supremacy appeared secure. The economic strength of the United

8. Letter from Evelyn Harding to Donald Simpson, 10 July 1967.
9. Garner, *Commonwealth Office*, p.20.
10. Sir Eric Machtig, writing in the *Dictionary of National Biography*.
11. Evelyn Harding to Donald Simpson, 10 July 1967.

Kingdom remained undeniable. Calculations suggest that between 1870 and 1913 national income grew by 2.3% per annum. Output of manufactured goods and of coal, iron and steel continued to rise up to 1914. Moreover, Britain had for long dominated international trade, responsible, for example, for 32.5% of world exports of manufactured goods in 1899.[12] London was the financial centre of the world: her money markets were the main source of the European capital which was fertilising the economic expansion of the United States and other developing and especially primary-producing countries. As a result the £ sterling was a secure international currency. Moreover, British trade and finance appeared to maintain via the gold standard a fluent system of international exchanges. British emigrants from the British Isles had also over previous generations flowed globally into new settler societies – over 16 million people left the United Kingdom between 1815 and 1914 – and an increasing percentage headed to the Empire.[13]

Most of the world's communications seemed still to centre upon Great Britain. This was perhaps most obvious in the international sea routes from Europe to the rest of the world which British shipping largely dominated: British vessels accounted for nearly 40% of gross registered tonnage in 1913.[14] Harding and the Royal Commissioners were to travel largely, though not exclusively, on British or British Empire vessels. British enterprise was evident too in the development of railway systems, several of which the Commissioners were also going to experience, mainly financed by British investors if not always built by British engineers. It was apparent also in the more recent global spread of the telegraph cables, which appeared to wrap up the world in new tentacles and which Harding found invaluable in his management of the Commission's expeditions: British companies owned 72% of the approximately 190,000 miles of submarine cables laid by 1900.[15] Moreover, English had become by far the most common language of international communication. In addition, these structures and influences appeared to be protected by the invincible arm of the Royal Navy, certainly the most powerful fleet of its day: its overseas bases at

12. M. W. Kirby, *The Decline of British Economic Power since 1870*, London, pp.143, 145.
13. Stephen Constantine (ed.), *Emigrants and Empire: British Settlement in the Dominions between the Wars*, Manchester, 1990, pp.1–2, 18.
14. William Woodruff, *Impact of Western Man*, London, 1966, p.255.
15. Daniel R. Headrick, *The Tools of Empire*, New York and Oxford, 1981, p.162.

the turn of the century commanded strategic sea routes and the oceans of the world, from Gibraltar to Alexandria, from Aden to Trincomalee, from Singapore to Hong Kong, across the Pacific, in the South Atlantic and around the West Indies.[16]

Intimately connected with these indicators of power was the British Empire. While external British economic and political interests had always extended beyond the formal Empire, its red presence on the maps was the most visual indication of British global supremacy and certainly the most vigorously emphasised feature in official and unofficial propaganda from the end of the 19th century. In addition to the white settler dominions, there was, of course, a huge Indian Empire, supervised by the India Office, and a vast array of dependent colonies and protectorates, many only recently acquired especially in the tropical regions of Africa, Asia and the Pacific, creating additional responsibilities for the Colonial Office.[17] Although the formal British Empire even by 1913 was absorbing no more than 35% of British exports and providing only 20% of British imports,[18] not surprisingly the Empire was generally taken to be an asset of exceptional value, either actual or potential, since it seemingly covered a quarter of the world's surface and included about the same proportion of the world's population. Harding on his travels was to note both the current output of agricultural and mineral products in the dominions, some signs of manufacturing expansion and the potential for further economic development.

But there were reasons too for concern. Great Britain by the end of the 19th century was no longer the only industrial nation, and the country was beginning a relative decline. European and American competitors had bitten into her lead. For example, already by 1900–04 the United Kingdom was responsible for only 15% of world steel production, Germany for 22% and the United States for 41%.[19] Their production also of iron, coal and manufactured goods restricted the growth of British sales in their home markets and challenged British producers even in Britain. Signs of sluggish trade persuaded many of the need to improve production, marketing and supplies of raw materials.

---

16. Paul M. Kennedy, *The Rise and Fall of British Naval Mastery*, London, 1976: there is an informative map of bases and cable routes on p.207.
17. The affairs of some territories, like Egypt and the Sudan, were supervised by the Foreign Office.
18. I. M. Drummond, *British Economic Policy and the Empire*, London, 1972, graphs on pp.19 and 21.
19. Donald Read, *England 1868–1914*, London, 1979, p.389.

There were, however, additional aspects of *fin-de-siècle* Great Britain which, in conjunction, some observers regarded with disquiet, including the expansion of trade unionism, the growth of socialism and even the women's suffrage movement. Then there were revelations about poverty and ill-health, exposed by sociological inquiry and confirmed, apparently, by the large numbers of volunteers for the South African War of 1899–1902 who were found to be quite unfit for military duties: the poor quality of the manpower (and indeed womanpower) of the United Kingdom seemed a weak base upon which to maintain population growth, prosperity and international authority.[20] Meantime, external military dangers had also increased. Friction with France eventually declined after the creation of the Anglo-French entente in 1904, but the equivalent deal with Russia in 1907 had not dispersed all concerns. Moreover, the development of an American navy had added to the complexities of global defence. At least the Japanese, with their new navy, had been adopted as a useful ally in 1902. But there seemed no ready solution to the challenge of Imperial Germany in Europe: the funding of their expanded and modernised fleet from 1898 had severely, and expensively, provoked another cycle in the arms race.[21]

Contemplating these difficulties, Joseph Chamberlain (1836–1914), Secretary of State for the Colonies, addressed the prime ministers of the white settler societies at the Colonial Conference of 1902: 'The Weary Titan staggers under the too vast orb of its fate. We have borne the burden long enough. We think it is time our children should assist us to support it.'[22] Such appeals, not always so patronisingly worded, were expressed by British ministers seeking especially military contributions at several of the Colonial and Imperial Conferences held first in 1887 and repeated in 1897, 1902, 1907 and 1911. There was, in addition, a special Imperial Defence Conference in 1909.[23] These were also the occasions when imperial pressure groups in Britain, like the British Empire League,

20. For reviews of these issues see *ibid.* and B. B. Gilbert, *The Evolution of National Insurance*, London, 1966.
21. P. M. Kennedy, *The Realities Behind Diplomacy*, Glasgow, 1981; Aaron L. Friedberg, *The Weary Titan: Britain and the Experience of Relative Decline 1895–1905*, Princeton, 1988.
22. Julian Amery, *The Life of Joseph Chamberlain*, vol.4, London, 1951, p.421.
23. Their history is reviewed in J. E. Tyler, 'Development of the Imperial Conference, 1887–1914', in E. A. Benians *et al* (eds.), *The Cambridge History of the British Empire*, Vol.3, Cambridge, 1959, pp.406–37 and J. E. Kendle, *The Colonial and Imperial Conferences 1887–1911*, London, 1967.

redoubled their agitation, trying to drive heads of state into embracing their particular panacea.[24] This was never likely to be easy.

At the Conferences, representatives of the United Kingdom met ministers from the self-governing parts of the Empire. Since the 1840s, these colonies had all acquired so-called responsible government, beginning with the Canadian colonies (formed into the Dominion of Canada in 1867) and followed by Newfoundland (not fused into Canada until 1949), the colonies in Australia (federating into the Commonwealth of Australia in 1900), New Zealand (keeping herself distinct from that federation), and the territories in South Africa (becoming another federated state as the Union of South Africa in 1910). The concession of responsible government transferred to these colonies most of the characteristics of Westminster-style government: local ministries were politically dependent not upon the approval of the Governor or Governor-General, who represented the Crown, but upon majority support in their locally-elected assemblies. As a result, of course, local interests tended to determine the policies of colonial governments. Moreover, these were pluralistic societies, and governments had to navigate warily if they were to maintain the range of support needed for political stability in their often divided societies. For example, tensions between English and French Canadians echoed those between Boers and Britons in South Africa. In Australia and New Zealand, urbanisation, the spread of manufacturing and the organisation of labour created different conflicts, discernible also in other parts of the Empire. Although most prominent colonial politicians, like the majority of their electorates, expressed loyalty to the imperial connection, there were few who would risk unqualified commitment. Rather they felt obliged to protect or enhance perceived national self-interest in their discussions with British ministers.[25]

In practice that meant firstly achieving some better recognition of their status within the imperial system: the adoption of the term 'dominion' in 1907 and the establishment of the Dominions Division in the Colonial Office helped distinguish these territories from the autocratically run Indian Empire and the dependent crown colonies and protectorates. Since they remained, however, possessions of the Crown, the determination of foreign policy and the power to declare war still

---

24. See, for example, John M. MacKenzie, *Propaganda and Empire*, Manchester, 1984, pp.148–68.
25. Nicholas Mansergh, *The Commonwealth Experience*, London, 1969; W. D. McIntyre, *Colonies into Commonwealth*, London, 1966.

remained vested in London. Not surprisingly, most prime ministers from the dominions wanted at least to be kept better informed of British policy-making: representation on the Committee of Imperial Defence, created in 1902, and the airing of such matters at Conferences were further gains. But the price could be British demands for practical assistance in the implementation of policy, especially in the form of naval assistance in cash or in kind. Conscious of domestic opinion, this reciprocal concession was not always readily forthcoming, especially from Canada and South Africa who suffered from fewer security anxieties than citizens of Australia and New Zealand. Then there were economic interests to negotiate. The dominions had control over their own domestic economic developments and over their external trade. Canada, Australia and to a lesser extent New Zealand had developed by 1900 significant manufacturing sectors, partially protected even against British producers by tariff barriers: such protection they would not readily abandon, although they might impose lower duties on British imports or, more likely, higher ones on foreign goods. But at the same time they were all primarily exporters of food, minerals and other primary products, and in a competitive international market they were very anxious to obtain privileged access to the large domestic market of the United Kingdom through special import tariff preferences.

Whereas British ministers from both the Conservative and Liberal parties were generally ready to concede status to the dominions and to open up avenues for consultation on foreign and defence matters, preferably in return for dominion assistance, there was a much more divided British response to the idea of preferential tariffs. Such a move meant abandoning the policy of free trade adopted early in the 19th century, which many believed had been responsible for British growth and prosperity. It would require the imposition of new taxes on imports of food and raw materials from non-Empire suppliers particularly in Europe and the United States, with a consequent risk of a rise in the cost of living and in the production costs of British industry. Joseph Chamberlain was willing to pay this price, but when he publicly launched his tariff reform campaign in 1903, he split the Conservative ranks. By contrast he generated among Liberals a new-found party unity and helped their sweeping victory in the general election of 1906. Not surprisingly, the Liberals thereafter stuck to the talisman of free trade, a commitment made clear in 1907 when Liberal ministers hosted their first Colonial Conference and repelled demands upon them.[26]

The 1911 Imperial Conference reviewed some of these issues once more.[27] Amongst a lengthy agenda, clogged, for example, with schemes for imperial postal orders and for action over cables, emigration and the navy, was the idea of an Imperial Council recommended by the New Zealand Prime Minister, Sir Joseph Ward (1856–1930). This hinted at a greater degree of imperial political unity: it was, accordingly, rebuffed by other dominions leaders, sensitive to the prejudices of many of their domestic constituents. It was particularly unacceptable to Louis Botha (1862–1919), a former Boer commando leader but the first Prime Minister of the new Union of South Africa, and to Sir Wilfrid Laurier (1841–1919), the first French-Canadian Prime Minister of Canada. Since the United Kingdom's Liberal government remained committed to free trade, and indeed had just had its mandate renewed, after a fashion, at two general elections in 1910, there was also obviously going to be little progress in terms of creating through tariff reform any greater imperial economic unity.

It was in this context that the idea of a Royal Commission to investigate the trade and natural resources of the dominions emerged. The Australian government, led by Andrew Fisher (1862–1928), introduced a resolution for discussion by the Conference at the session held on 16 June which piously urged members to make every effort to bring about co-operation in commercial relations. This might be interpreted as a coded plea for a scheme of imperial preference. If so it was not realistic politics. This was not just because of the attitude of the British government, but because the Canadian government had recently secured a reciprocity treaty with the United States which encouraged freer trade outside the Empire across their border. However, Laurier remained keen to explore additional if compatible commercial opportunities inside the Empire. He therefore expressed general sympathy for Fisher's objectives, but proposed an alternative resolution:

> That His Majesty should be approached with a view to the appointment of a Royal Commission representing the United Kingdom, Canada, Australia, New Zealand, South Africa, and Newfoundland, with a view of investigating and reporting upon the

---

26. G. S. Graham, 'Imperial Finance, Trade and Communications, 1895–1914' in Benians, *C.H.B.E*, pp.451–3; R. Hyam, *Elgin and Churchill at the Colonial Office*, London, 1968, p.342.
27. British Parliamentary Papers, *Imperial Conference 1911, Précis of the Proceedings*, Cd 5741, 1911 and *Minutes of Proceedings of the Imperial Conference 1911*, Cd 5745, 1911. See also I. R. Hancock, 'The 1911 Imperial Conference', *Historical Studies*, vol.12, no.47, Oct. 1966, pp.156–72.

natural resources of each part of the Empire represented at this Conference, the development attained and attainable, and the facilities for production, manufacture, and distribution, the trade of each part with the others and with the outside world, the food and raw material requirements of each, and the sources thereof available, to what extent, if any, the trade between each of the different parts has been affected by legislation in each, either beneficially or otherwise.

It was difficult to find fault with such a proposal (apart from its punctuation). It had always been generally agreed that the resources of the dominions were as yet incompletely recognised. Although there had been many years of settlement, investment and exploitation, openings for further development seemed likely, bringing rewards to producers and to consumers both locally and elsewhere in the Empire, including the United Kingdom. Moreover, this appeared to be a practical if modest suggestion, and not merely an empty aspiration, and it was praised as such. It was also politically safe. No one could really object to a mere commission of inquiry, especially since it did not commit ministers to any subsequent action. Just to make sure, Harcourt, the Secretary of State, proposed an additional clause to safeguard his government's free trade commitment:

> and by what methods, consistent with the existing fiscal policy of each part, the trade of each part with the others may be improved and extended.

This addition was accepted by the dominions prime ministers without murmur, though in their hearts in some cases not perhaps with enthusiasm. Prime Minister Asquith (1852–1928), however, speaking for the British government and claiming to speak for all, endorsed it strongly, declaring that 'every self-governing State in the Empire must pursue such a fiscal policy as in the opinion of the majority of its citizens was for the time best suited to the requirements and conditions of their own country'.[28] It proved to be an important amendment, because the Conservative government in Canada, which succeeded Laurier's Liberal administration shortly after the Conference, attempted unsuccessfully to get the restriction removed.[29]

---

28. Cd 5745, pp.339–45.
29. Harcourt's refusal is recorded in Public Record Office file CO 886/5, pp.246–8, 252–4, 256–7.

In due course, after the Conference dispersed, the Royal Commission was drawn up. The terms of reference followed almost precisely the words of Laurier's amended resolution.[30]

The next step of course was to appoint the Commissioners. Fisher had spoken of the need to select men of 'high standing'. It proved to be unexpectedly difficult to organise a settled team. There were to be six representatives from the United Kingdom and one from each of the five dominions. The Colonial Office on 27 July 1911 asked the Governors of New Zealand and Newfoundland and the Governors-General of Canada, Australia and South Africa to choose their representative, on the recommendation, naturally, of their ministers.[31] Meanwhile, the British members were being selected. However, several months elapsed before the first formal appointments to the Royal Commission could be made on 15 April 1912. Further difficulties then followed.[32]

The first Chairman appointed was Lord Inchcape (1852–1932), formerly a member of the Legislative Council of the Viceroy of India and a major figure in the world of imperial shipping and commerce (and the author of a remarkably extensive and boastful entry in *Who is Who*), but he had scarcely accepted the post before he felt obliged to resign for urgent business reasons.[33] He was replaced on 31 August 1912 by a new appointment, Arnold Morley (1849–1916), a former Liberal Chief Whip and Postmaster-General from 1892 to 1895. Sadly, owing to the death of his wife (whom he had only married the previous year) and his own ill-health, in October 1912 he too resigned. On 26 November 1912 the office of Chairman eventually devolved upon one of the other Commissioners, Sir Edgar Vincent (1857–1941). He retained the position until the whole business was completed, although he did not accompany the Commission on its 1914 and 1916 tours of Newfoundland and Canada. He had once been in the Coldstream Guards but resigned to develop a distinguished career in the Balkans and Middle East in a variety of financial and administrative posts, at one time as Governor of the Imperial Ottoman Bank in Constantinople, and from 1899 to 1906 as a Conservative M.P. He was appointed Chairman of the Central Control Board to restrict the drink trade during the First

---

30. *First Interim Report*, Cd 6515, 1912, pp.2–3.
31. CO 532/34/CO23509 and CO886/5, p.233.
32. See CO files especially CO532/48/CO10435.
33. Personal details of the Commissioners and others are mainly from volumes of *Who Was Who, Dictionary of National Biography* and obituaries in *The Times*.

World War and was later a notable Ambassador to Berlin 1920–26, Chairman of the Medical Research Council 1929–33 and even for a while Chairman of the Lawn Tennis Association. He became Baron D'Abernon on 2 July 1914, in part at least for his services on the Dominions Royal Commission, and he was promoted to G.C.M.G when it was all over in 1917.

To maintain the correct number of United Kingdom representatives on the Commission after the resignation of Morley, Sir Alfred Edmund Bateman (1844–1929) was appointed on 17 December 1912. He had joined the Board of Trade as a young civil servant in 1865 and eventually became Comptroller-General for Commerce, Labour and Statistics. His statistical expertise, further emphasised as Chairman of an Advisory Committee on Commercial Intelligence and as President of the Royal Statistical Society, would be much valued by the D.R.C. in its wrestling with such issues. He had also acquired considerable experience of international economic negotiations, and had already served on a variety of Royal Commissions and official inquiries. But he was 68 years old when he set out on the first overseas tour and, as Harding put it, 'getting rather tottery'. One other early drop-out from the Commission was Lt-Col. Sir Charles John Owens (1845–1933), who had eventually chosen a business career and had become General Manager of the London and South-Western Railway in 1890, but he withdrew from the Commission when in 1912 he became Director.[34] Railway expertise was valued, so he was replaced on 15 November 1912 by Joseph Tatlow (1851–1929), who had spent all his working life in the business, from 1890 until 1912 as General Manager and thereafter Director of the Midland Great Western Railway of Ireland: in 1920 he published his memoirs, *Fifty Years of Railway Life in England, Scotland and Ireland*.

One of the original appointments was William Lorimer (1844–1922), who could draw upon a long career in the locomotive industry, latterly as Chairman of the North British Locomotive Company, and also in the steel industry, as Chairman of the Steel Company of Scotland. Along the way he had acquired a knowledge of, indeed a passion for, mineral-mining. He also acquired, in 1913, a second wife, who was one of the personalities (and problems) of the 1914 tours. Sadly he was also rather deaf, although apparently energetic in spite of his age. His work for the

---

34. It is also reported that one of the Commissioners resigned because his wife objected to him going on 'distant tours': W. Stewart Wallace, *The Memoirs of the Rt. Hon. Sir George Foster*, Toronto, 1933, p.170.

Commission brought him a knighthood in 1917. Probably the most widely known Commissioner was Sir Henry Rider Haggard (1856–1925), appointed not, one trusts, for his qualities as a writer of popular fiction but for his considerable expertise as a practical farmer (in Norfolk), his extensive researches into agriculture in Britain and in Europe (leading to such publications as *Rural England* in 1902 and *Rural Denmark* in 1911), his membership of several previous official inquiries (including a recent Royal Commission on Coastal Erosion and Afforestation), and for his commitment to imperial causes (not least when on the staff of Sir Theophilus Shepstone in the Transvaal in 1877 and subsequently as a prominent member of the Royal Colonial Institute). He seems to have been hurt that he, along with some other members of the Commission, received no additional honour for his efforts on the Commission.[35] The remaining United Kingdom representative was Tom Garnett: although his name is absent from the usual biographical reference books, he was evidently a cotton manufacturer from the North of England and the director of an engineering company.

Selecting and maintaining the representation from the dominions also proved tricky. The Colonial Office were told in August 1911 that the Liberal government of Canada had chosen Peter Charles Larkin (1856–1930), a businessman (known as the 'Tea King of America'), a Liberal and a future High Commissioner. But when Laurier's ministry was replaced by the Conservative government of Sir Robert Borden (1854–1937) in October 1911, the new administration chose instead a more congenial representative, George Eulas Foster (1847–1931), their own Minister of Trade and Commerce. A Colonial Office clerk noted that 'he is, of course, a strong Imperialist, protectionist, and advocate of Imperial preference'.[36] He had been a Conservative member of the Canadian Parliament with only one break since 1882. He remained on the Commission until it had completed its work, occasionally acting as Chairman, but because of the demands of domestic politics he missed the tour of South Africa. The reward for his efforts was a knighthood in 1914, and to his greater pleasure he was made a member of the Privy Council in 1916. He remained a minister until 1921 and then served as a Senator until 1931.[37]

---

35. D. S. Higgins (ed.), *The Private Diaries of Sir Henry Rider Haggard*, London, 1980, p.107.
36. CO 886/5, pp.234, 237–8, 247; CO 532/35/CO39570 and CO 532/37/Gov6963, minute of 6 March 1912.
37. Wallace, *Foster*, pp.167–74, 185–6 and, for his 1913 journal, 228–57.

South African representation was even more troubled. Sir David Pieter de Villiers Graaf (1859–1931) was the first choice, Minister of Posts and Telegraphs in the first Union government from 1910 and a South African delegate at the Imperial Conference in 1911. But when the Commission was about to begin its work in 1912 he was ill and detained in South Africa. His replacement on 5 July 1912 was the man closest to hand, Sir Richard Prince Solomon (1850–1913), South Africa's first High Commissioner in London. He had previously been in London as Agent-General for the Transvaal, and before that he was a member of Cape Colony's House of Assembly and also involved in the reconstruction of the Transvaal after the Boer War. He attended those sessions of the D.R.C. which were held in London, but did not join the overseas tour to Australia and New Zealand. And then he died on 10 October 1913. His replacement, on 12 February 1914, was Sir Jan Willem Stuckeris Langerman (1853–1931). He was a member of the Union's House of Assembly as well as President of the Rand Chamber of Mines and Managing Director of the Robinson Group of Mines: as a member of the D.R.C. on its South Africa tour and later in Canada he was able to offer informed though not disinterested advice on mining operations in the Empire.

New Zealand representation began rather badly. In March 1912 it was announced that the choice was Sir Joseph Ward, the former Liberal prime minister who had attended the 1911 Imperial Conference and had only resigned his premiership after the general election later that year. The Liberals maintained office under a new leader into 1912 with a bare majority of one, and Ward decided that because he could not risk an election by resigning his seat as M.P. he would have to abandon the D.R.C.. ('No great loss', minuted a Colonial Office clerk.)[38] His successor, appointed on 5 July 1912, was John Robert Sinclair (1850–1940), a lawyer by profession and a member of New Zealand's upper house, the Legislative Council. He was knighted in 1918. He was one of the few members of the D.R.C. who thereafter worked steadily through all the tours and sessions.

This was unfortunately not true of the Australian representative, Donald Campbell (1866–1945). He had been a journalist and an engineer and was something of an authority on river navigation. His experience of working at the Broken Hill mines in New South Wales must also have been useful to the Commission. He had been a Labor member of the South Australian legislature from 1906, but his defeat in

---

38. CO532/38/Gov17739, 10 June 1912.

the election of 1912 released him for duty with the D.R.C. However, the work of the Commission was suspended with the outbreak of the First World War, and when attempts were made to revive it in 1915 the Australian delegate was removed and was never returned. Maybe that was why he received no formal honour for his labours.[39]

While these comings and goings continued, the man from Newfoundland stuck to his task. Edgar Rennie Bowring (1858–1943), knighted for services rendered in June 1915, represented a small and to be frank rather poor community: his qualities included considerable business experience in the Bowring family firm (a shipping company trading in Britain and the United States as well as in Newfoundland), political knowledge derived from membership of the Newfoundland Legislative Council, and his acceptance of the Newfoundland Government's request that he should pay all his own expenses. He later served as his country's first High Commissioner in London.[40]

The Commission would also need administrative support. The Treasury naturally took a keen interest in appointments, salaries and claims for expenses. The most important selection was that of Secretary. The first choice was not Harding but a senior colleague, W. A. Robinson (1874–1950), a First Class Clerk in the Colonial Office which he had joined in 1897. He was currently being paid a salary of £725 a year (on a scale rising from £600 to £800 – a top working-class wage at this time was around £160): as Secretary of the D.R.C. he was entitled to an extra £300, but to his annoyance the Treasury insisted that he should be restricted to a maximum of £1000. However, he could claim travel expenses and also subsistence costs, rising when abroad up to £2 per night on land and 10 shillings per night (50p) on ship.[41] Robinson was responsible for the establishment of the secretariat, for negotiating financial arrangements, for organising with the Commissioners the collection of evidence in London during 1912, for drafting the Commission's *First Interim Report*, for the publication of its first volumes of evidence and for beginning the preparations for the tour to Australia and New Zealand. But in November 1912 he transferred to another government department. Indeed, he then moved through a sequence of senior posts at the Office of Works, Air Ministry, Ministry of Health and Ministry of Supply, becoming Sir Arthur Robinson along the way.

39. CO886/5, p.247; despatches on CO532/77, especially Gov13305; *Australian Dictionary of Biography*.
40. CO886/5, pp.244–6; David Keir, *The Bowring Story*, London, 1962.
41. CO532/47/Treas14264.

Harding was still not chosen as the successor. Dougal Orme Malcolm (1877–1955) initially took on the job, a First Class Clerk in the Treasury but formerly from 1900 at the Colonial Office and then private secretary to the Governor of the Transvaal 1905–10 and to the Governor-General of Canada 1910–11. However, he had been installed barely a month before he too resigned, crossing to the private sector to become a director of the British South Africa Company and in 1937 its President, where in 1938 he picked up a knighthood.[42] Only after his departure was the post of Secretary to the Dominions Royal Commission offered to Edward Harding, with effect from 9 December 1912. The Treasury made a saving on the replacement, because Harding's basic pay as a Second Class Clerk was lower. (The starting salary on such a grade was £200.)

By the time he took over, other parts of the bureaucracy had been put in place. An Assistant Secretary from the Board of Trade, W. J. Glenny (1873–1963), had been appointed at an additional salary of £150 a year plus appropriate expenses. Glenny served the D.R.C. both at home and on tour in South Africa and Newfoundland, but with the outbreak of war the Board of Trade insisted upon his return to their office.[43] Because of the important statistical work he did, Harding insisted upon a replacement: A. E. Mitchell, a Staff Clerk in the Treasury, was appointed in November 1914.[44] Another early recruit was Alfred E. Bridgman (born 1860), Assistant Superintendent of Printing in the Colonial Office since 1900, to act as a shorthand clerk. This was not yet a feminised trade, but it already paid badly, for poor Bridgman was restricted to extra pay of only 35 shillings a week (£1.75) on top of his current salary of £300 a year, and his subsistence allowance when abroad was only half that of the Secretary. Harding complained after the tour to Australia and New Zealand that in practice it was impossible to fix him up with different, cheaper hotel accommodation (except, oddly enough, in Melbourne).[45] One other recruit was a private secretary for the Chairman, who was to be paid £250 a year plus expenses. The man appointed was C. Brodie Bass, formerly secretary to the City of London Free Trade Committee, who also

---

42. CO532/47/Treas37587 and CO532/448/CO10435.
43. CO532/46/BT7919, CO532/47/Treas14264; he was temporarily loaned back on a part-time basis when Harding late in 1915 departed on military duty, CO532/81/BT55815; he became Inspector-General at the Department of Overseas Trade 1925–29 and pitched up as Commercial Counsellor to H.M. Legation in Stockholm, 1929–34.
44. CO532/73/BT25019, BT45810, Treas36890.
45. CO532/47/Treas18333, Harding to Just, 22 Aug. 1913.

undertook work compiling statistical tables, accompanied the Commission on its tour of Australasia, remained in London when the Commission went to South Africa and Newfoundland, joined the Yorkshire regiment on the outbreak of war, and was killed in action in 1915: the Commissioners paid tribute to him in their *Final Report*. Finally, 'it has been found necessary also to engage the services of a lady typist at a cost of 25/3 a week' (£1.26).[46] The Dominions Royal Commission was fixed up with its own office in Scotland House on Victoria Embankment in the heart of Westminster, and its own headed notepaper was printed.

Decisions on the proper allocation of costs between the respective governments had also been made. It was agreed that Commissioners would receive no financial remuneration, but each government would pay the personal expenses of its own representative (six of them in the case of the British government). The United Kingdom Commissioners, for example, were to receive 4 guineas a day (£4.20) for subsistence plus travel expenses. The British Treasury also agreed to pay the whole cost of office accommodation. But following the principle agreed by the prime ministers at the Imperial Conference, all other general expenditure, including secretarial salaries, ought to have been shared equally between the six governments. However, Newfoundland, although already saved some expense by Bowring's generosity, argued that since most benefits from the Commission's work would accrue to the larger dominions, general costs should be allocated in proportion to population. Eventually the Colonial Office persuaded the Treasury to allow Newfoundland's costs to be limited to a maximum of £500 per year and for the British government to pick up any extra bills.[47] After each financial year, the Treasury calculated the cost of divisible expenses: for example, after the tour to Australia and New Zealand, the total for 1912–13 (minus items not yet in the accounts) was calculated to be £1638 1s 6d, and each government was billed for £273 0s 3d (including Newfoundland).[48] The total bill for 1913–14 had, however, risen markedly to £5024 7s 8d or £837 7s 11d per government (but presumably less for Newfoundland).[49] Costs fell again in 1914–15 to £2022 13s 6d or £337 2s 3d each, and for 1915–16 only £849 2s 6d had to be divided.[50]

---

46. CO532/49/MO38609.
47. CO532/37/Gov3112, CO532/47/Treas5943, CO886/5, p.241.
48. CO532/61/Treas33254 and 44388.
49. CO532/73/Treas51143, CO532/81/Treas54730.
50. CO532/88/Treas13119; CO532/103/Treas16522 and CO532/103/Treas46749.

Once appointments and basic arrangements had been made, the first preliminary gathering of the United Kingdom representatives was held on 16 April 1912. The Commission had its first full meeting, after the overseas members had assembled, on 13 June 1912, when it finalised its bureaucratic structure, decided upon its programme and resisted one last effort by Foster, the Canadian representative, to include tariffs in its terms of reference.[51] Memoranda were framed for despatch to official bodies in Britain and overseas seeking statistical answers to questions about production, trade and migration and information about commercial law, ports and railways.[52] At the same time arrangements were made for the questioning of the first witnesses in London. These sessions were held in the D.R.C's offices over 26 days from 9 October to 21 November, when representatives from a wide variety of official and unofficial organisations appeared. Questions and answers together with submitted documents were later published in full.[53] This record-keeping, typical of Royal Commissions, was repeated for all the formal sessions overseas. Meantime, on 28 December 1912 the Commissioners signed their first brief *Interim Report*, devoted largely to explaining why an investigation of migration was relevant to their inquiry and how and when they proposed to gather further evidence.[54]

The original schedule envisaged for the rest of the investigation included a tour of New Zealand and Australia from February to April 1913, the gathering of further evidence in London later that year, a visit to South Africa in December 1913 and a tour of Canada and Newfoundland in the autumn of 1914. The Final Report should be ready for the Imperial Conference expected in 1915.[55] The overseas tours obviously required considerable preparation, and the Secretary relied on an official contact in each dominion whose task it was to propose an itinerary, to collect data and to organise witnesses. Commissioners were understandably interested too in the quality of their accommodation and transport. The Secretary was also expected to keep down costs, for example, by wheedling free rail passes.[56]

---

51.   CO532/48/CO20495; Wallace, *Foster*, p.169.
52.   CO532/48/CO20495, CO532/66/Gov4986.
53.   *D.R.C. Minutes of Evidence Taken in London, Part 1, Migration*, Cd 6516, 1912, and *Part 2, Natural Resources, Trade and Legislation*, Cd 6517, 1912.
54.   Cd 6515, 1912.
55.   CO532/49/MO38609, memo by Malcolm, 6 Dec. 1912.
56.   CO532/40 especially Gov37567 and CO532/52/Gov21106.

Thus equipped, the D.R.C. departed for Australia and New Zealand in January 1913, to South Africa in February 1914 (behind the original schedule) and to Newfoundland and Canada in July 1914 (slightly in advance of first plans). As Harding's letters reveal, prior arrangements still left a great deal of organisation to be completed on the spot, and much tidying up after the event, including the submission of regular accounts to the Treasury[57] and, of course, the preparation of evidence for publication and the drafting of reports. As Harding's letters show, this last labour for the Secretary began on his voyages home, followed by revisions after discussions with the Commissioners at meetings in London.[58] The 65-page *Second Interim Report: Australasia* was signed on 16 January 1914, six months after his return,[59] and the *Third Interim Report: South Africa*, 60 pages, was completed on 25 June 1914, just two months after the trip.[60] Meanwhile, the Commission had held further short sessions in London over 3 days in November 1913 and 9 days in January 1914.

Progress was then abruptly checked when King George V, speaking for the entire British Empire, formally declared war on the Central Powers on 4 August 1914. As Harding describes, the news seriously upset the Commissioners, by then in Nova Scotia, but the decision to suspend the Royal Commission was taken not by them but by the Secretary of State for the Colonies in consultation with the Chairman, who was still in London, without seeking the advice of the governments of the dominions.[61] The Commissioners returned and only reconvened to sign on 9 December 1914 their short, 27-page, *Fourth Interim Report: Newfoundland.*[62] Then they dispersed.

The revival of the D.R.C. was largely the work of Foster, but he could draw upon the strategically placed support of Harding in the Colonial Office. Canada, of course, was the one dominion not yet investigated, and her representative was probably the most committed of the overseas members: Foster had clear views as to the kind of imperial development programme he wished the Commission to recommend. But by the time he tried to resurrect the inquiry in April 1915, the Australian government had already decided that the Commission had become an irrelevance and had withdrawn its representative. There were objections

---

57. CO532/47/Treas14264.
58. See entries in Higgins, *Haggard Diaries*, and Wallace, *Foster*.
59. Cd 7210, 1914.
60. Cd 7505, 1914.
61. CO532/75/MO29715.
62. Cd 7711, 1915.

also from some senior staff in the Colonial Office. Long delays followed while obstacles were dealt with and the availability of Commissioners investigated, until the prospect of not arriving in Canada until the onset of winter weather led to a further postponement.[63] Following this setback, Harding departed for military service on 20 November 1915, becoming a Second Lieutenant in the Royal Garrison Artillery.[64]

However, the determination to complete the inquiry remained and in the summer of 1916, all the dominions, except still the Australians, agreed to its resumption. D'Abernon had persuaded the new Secretary of State, Andrew Bonar Law (1858–1923), that the Canadians remained insistent; the argument that it would be politically unwise to cause offence seems to have prevailed. Enough Commissioners were collected, Harding was released from his military duties by the War Office, the Board of Trade was grudgingly persuaded to release Glenny part-time, and in August the last journey began.[65] The *Fifth Interim Report: Canada*, 61 pages, was signed on 31 January 1917, two and a half months after the completion of the tour.[66]

By this time, the volume of evidence collected by the Commission was enormous. The official record calculated that formal sessions had been held on 157 days, to which the investigations conducted by various sub-committees could be added. Alongside its five interim reports, the Commission published fifteen volumes of minutes of evidence and papers plus three volumes of its own memoranda, tables and statistics. Making sense of this data for a *Final Report* intensely occupied Harding, the Chairman and those Commissioners available in the New Year: the report was signed on 21 February 1917.[67] The Chairman was not content with this achievement. He reckoned that the report's recommendations were, or ought to be, a matter of widespread public interest, and he persuaded the Secretary of State, Walter Long (1854–1924), that a cheap edition, lacking the deterrent appearance of an official 'blue-book', ought to be published at a subsidised price. Some Colonial Office staff were aghast at this unjustifiable expense ('the most absurd waste of public money that I have ever heard of'), but Harding was instructed to press

---

63. Despatches and minutes on CO532/77 and 78; see also CO532/81/ Treas4131 and CO532/82/MO35482.
64. *Colonial Office List*; CO532/83/MO52861.
65. CO532/84 and 89 contains most of the relevant files, but see also CO532/88/BT54569 and BT58555.
66. Cd 8457, 1917.
67. Cd 8462, 1917. It includes a list of all the other publications.

on. The Treasury finally agreed to the printing of 3000 copies in the new format, at a selling price of 1s 6d. Since they cost 2s 6d each to produce, the Treasury were perhaps only reconciled by insisting that the extra cost should also be shouldered by the dominions.[68]

What impact did the Dominions Royal Commission have on subsequent Empire developments? During the course of its long deliberations the Commissioners delivered themselves of many proposals. Some of these were offered privately, such as the suggestion to the British Cotton Growing Association that they should consider Australia as territory fit for their activities.[69] More substantial were the formal recommendations which concluded each of the interim reports. They dealt, for example, with the population needs of Australia and New Zealand, the organisation of South Africa's mining industry, ways of improving the cod fisheries in Newfoundland and shipping services to Canada. Most of these major items were, however, revisited in the *Final Report*.

This remarkable document, of 199 folio pages, discussed at length the external trade of the dominions, their natural resources, how products had been mobilised for war, how they might be conserved and developed for future use, the role of scientific research in their exploitation, the complex problems of migration, the nature and extent of overseas communications, the subjects of product distribution and marketing, and such topics as commercial legislation, trade intelligence and the adequacy of statistics. As *The Times* enthusiastically concluded, 'the report constitutes the most complete record of any Imperial investigation that has yet been carried out'.[70]

Taken separately, many of the proposals made reasonable sense, and it is possible to follow their traces into subsequent discussions and indeed into legislative and administrative action. For example, ignorance about the natural resources and trade opportunities in the dominions could be partly redeemed, as suggested, by the appointment of more Board of Trade Commissioners in Empire countries and by improvements in the gathering of statistics: the positive responses which followed were noted with approval by the Imperial War Conferences meeting in April 1917 and in June–July 1918. Similarly suggestions on the need to deepen harbours, cheapen freight rates and improve the mail

---

68. CO532/96/CO15316, CO532/103/Treas35329 and Treas37951.
69. CO532/63/MO12247 and MO16220.
70. 27 March 1917, p.7

and cable services received further sympathetic attention.[71] There is also no doubt that the D.R.C's recommmmendations on migration matters fed directly into such legislation as the (abortive) Emigration Bill of 1918 and the creation of the Oversea Settlement Committee and the scheme for ex-servicemen's emigration to the dominions.[72]

But cumulatively the *Final Report* of the D.R.C. was flawed. It bore to begin with too heavy an imprint of Sir George Foster and his particular brand of Canadian Conservative opinion. Almost uniquely, he began the investigation believing that out of it should emerge a tighter imperial economic unity, forged through a mutual interest in economic development and security. As indicated, in normal circumstances such a programme, inevitably leaning towards imperial tariff preferences, was not practical politics in the United Kingdom. However, the shock of the war had shaken many in Britain into a sense of how vulnerable the nation had become by allowing herself to be tied through free trade to world suppliers who might prove in wartime to be hostile.[73] Susceptible to these worries, the Commissioners themselves concluded that 'It is vital that the Empire should, as far as possible, be placed in a position which would enable it to resist any pressure which a foreign Power or group of Powers could exercise in time of peace or war in virtue of a control of raw materials and commodities essential to well-being'.[74] To achieve such security they went on to recommend the establishment of an Imperial Development Board, manned by representatives of the dominions as well as the United Kingdom, India and the Colonial Empire, paid for by all governments, though based in London, and investigative and advisory in its duties, although perhaps only initially.[75]

---

71. Resolutions V on Trade Commissioners and XIII on the Imperial Mineral Resources Bureau, *Imperial War Conference, 1917: Extracts from Minutes of Proceedings*, Cd 8566, 1917, and Resolutions VIII on Conference of Statisticians, XIV on cable communications and XXIV on the supervision of shipping, *Imperial War Conference, 1918: Extracts from Minutes of Proceedings*, Cd 9177.
72. See especially the chapters by Keith Williams and Kent Fedorowich in Constantine (ed.), *Emigrants and Empire*.
73. For these responses and subsequent reactions see W. K. Hancock, *Survey of British Commonwealth Affairs*, vol. 2, *Problems of Economic Policy*, part 1, London, 1940, pp.94–110 and Stephen Constantine, *The Making of British Colonial Development Policy 1914–1940*, London, 1984, pp.30–61.
74. *Final Report*, para 735.
75. Foster was particularly behind this plan, for which he continued to lobby: CO532/104/MO8389, CO532/102/BT38110, minute by Harding, 2 Aug. 1917.

This was precisely the kind of centralised imperial body which some dominions governments before the war had become shy of endorsing. Moreover, it conjured up the prospect of state intervention in economic affairs which traditionally had been viewed uneasily by most economists, businessmen and ministers in the United Kingdom. It also clashed uncomfortably with the ideals of those Colonial Office staff who regarded their duties as being passively to protect rather than actively to develop imperial territories. This central D.R.C. recommendation therefore met with a cautious official reception. And then, when the urgency of the 'economics of siege' passed with the approach of military victory, it faded largely from view. It had been symptomatic of anxiety, and the ending of the war allowed relief to flood in, or at least different problems to take over.[76] Prominent among new concerns was the determination of the dominions to assert still more their independence of the so-called Mother Country by becoming separate signatories of the Treaty of Versailles: they may not individually have declared war in 1914, but they were determined to make their own peace. The pre-war trajectory of developments in British relations with the dominions was restored.

This was a post-war process in which Harding too was to play a principal part. In its *Final Report* the Commissioners praised 'the exceptional capacity and remarkable powers of work of our Secretary.... We consider that Mr Harding's qualifications mark him out as destined to render notable services to the Empire'. This sounds like more than the required formal compliment. It was a conclusion endorsed by the Secretary of State: 'I am well assured that Mr Harding widely deserves the tribute paid him by the Commissioners.'[77] He was also awarded a C.M.G. in 1917. But perhaps the least ambiguous sign of immediate and continuing approval was promotion, to First Class Clerk in June 1916, to Acting Principal Clerk in 1919, to Principal Clerk in 1920 and Assistant Secretary in 1921. His work for the Commission and the knowledge of people and places he had gained in his travels naturally ensured that henceforth his expertise would be employed within the Dominions Division of the Colonial Office. It also followed that when in 1925 those duties at last became the responsibility of a quite separate department of state, the Dominions Office, Harding would be transferred with them, and to the enhanced status of Assistant Under-Secretary. In 1930 he

---

76. Suzann Buckley, 'The Colonial Office and the Establishment of an Imperial Development Board: the Impact of World War 1', *Journal of Imperial and Commonwealth History*, vol.2, 1974, pp.308–17.

77. Cd 8462, para.738; CO532/104/MO8389, minute of 22 Feb. 1917.

became its official head as Permanent Under-Secretary. He was knighted in 1928 and awarded a G.C.M.G. in 1939. And then in 1940 he took up an appointment as High Commissioner in South Africa. Ill-health led to his temporary retirement in 1941, but from 1942 until his final departure from the service in 1944 he remained in Cape Town as a representative of the new High Commissioner.

Reviewing his later career, it is apparent that the role which Harding then played deviated in spirit from the tenor of the *Final Report*. The reaction against the centralising aspects of the Commission's recommendations as well as the personal knowledge of the dominions he had gained in its wanderings may have helped him in handling the remarkable evolution of Empire into Commonwealth which was completed between the wars. He was deeply involved, for example, in the negotiations which led to an enhanced definition of dominion status at the Imperial Conference in 1926 ('autonomous communities ... equal in status ... and freely associated') and to the passage of the Statute of Westminster in 1931. One colleague claimed that 'No state servant played a greater part in bringing about these epoch-making and far-reaching developments'.[78]

Sir Edward Harding seems to have kept few private papers. It is perhaps indicative of the understanding he gained while acting as Secretary to the Dominions Royal Commission that the letters he wrote home from its overseas tours should alone have been preserved.

---

78. Machtig in *Dictionary of National Biography*; see also Mansergh, *Commonwealth Experience*, Garner, *Commonwealth Office* and R. F. Holland, *Britain and the Commonwealth Alliance 1918–1939*, London, 1981.

S. S. Ventura.

June 5ᵗʰ (B) 1913.

Nearing Pago Pago —

My dear Eva

I must really begin a letter this evening, even if I don't get very far with it, as it is probably the only time in my life when I shall be spending two Thursdays in one week. This fact, you will see, is duly marked on the heading to this letter. We have crossed the 180ᵗʰ meridian, (I think that is the proper term), which means that we are half way round the world. Consequently we have gained 12 hours, and we shall have gained another 12 before we get home. To day, therefore, is "thrown in".

I foresee interesting controversies with the Treasury, who count one's allowance by nights, when I send in a claim for 31 nights in June!

Having got so far, I fear I must stop. We are due at Pago Pago, the American part of Samoa, early to morrow morning. I must get out a camera and a sun hat in view of emergencies, & then go off to bed.

Page of Harding letter, dated 5 June 1913.   *Harding Manuscript, f.181*

First Journey

To Australia and New Zealand, January–July 1913

Dominions Royal Commission
Jan. 17th 1913

My dear Eva,

If I am to keep a diary letter it must clearly be written up daily – so I will begin this evening. Not that there is very much to record up to now.

We had a good send off at Victoria, quite a number of C.O. people there, also Rowntree and Jack, and we had an entirely uneventful journey to Dover and in fact to Marseilles.[1] The French train was luxurious, but rather jolty, and it crawled round Paris at a snail's pace without going right in. I made up my mind that another time (if there is another time!) I would go by the ordinary train to Paris and the ordinary night train to Marseilles. Which incidentally is cheaper.

I always thought of waking up to blue skies and a bluer sea. But the real view of the Mediterranean was nothing of the kind. There were lowering skies, and a very dingy sea, and all along the little bit of the

---

1. P. & O. ships to Australia left London every alternate Friday. First-class fares cost between £71 10s 0d and £82 10s 0d, second-class from £41 16s 0d to £46 4s 0d. The voyage was scheduled to take 32 days to Fremantle and 41 days to Sydney. However, since the sea journey to Marseilles took 7 days and the passage of the Bay of Biscay could be rough, many travellers preferred to cross France by train (first class, P. & O. Express, £9 9s 11d), leaving London at 11.00 a.m. on Thursday and arriving at Marseilles at 7.10 a.m. on Friday. There, they boarded the ship which sailed at 10.00 a.m. Dover, with a population of 43,645 according to the census of 1911, was a garrison town and an important Royal Navy depot as well as the major port for Cross-Channel ferries. The development of Marseilles had been accelerated by the French conquest of Algeria in 1830, the opening of the Suez Canal in 1869 and the consequent expansion of Mediterranean traffic. It had become a city of 421,116 people by the time of the 1906 census.

Gibraltar, the Dry Docks and Ships of War.   *Postcard dated 21 September 1910*

coast to Marseilles there were factories and half-made roads. Finally we crawled into the docks to find no porters to speak of – and had to drag our own despatch boxes etc. through a shed and over gunnybags or something of the kind to the *Medina*.[2]

Once arrived, matters, and the day, improved. We found all the 'more experienced' of the travellers lamenting their doings in The Bay. They had a very bad Saturday and Sunday, and it was so rough that they couldn't land at Gibraltar.[3] Even the Purser admitted to the fact of bad weather.

---

2. *Medina*, 12,400 tons, 550 feet long by 63 feet wide, was built for P. & O. by Caird on the Clyde. She could carry 660 passengers. She was launched in 1911 and served first as a royal yacht to carry King George V and Queen Mary to the Delhi Durbar. She began regular P. & O. services in June 1912. She was sunk by a German submarine on 28 April 1917: this was not the only vessel upon which the Commissioners sailed which later suffered such a fate. The Peninsular and Oriental Steam Navigation Company, originally formed in 1837, had already by mid-century greatly extended its range, particularly for the shipping of mail, from the Iberian peninsula into the Mediterranean and on to India, then Australasia and the Far East. By 1910 P. & O. operated a fleet of 64 ships. Gunnybags were hard-wearing fabric sacks for cargo, usually made from jute.
3. Gibraltar was a British crown colony, valued especially as a strategic naval base, commanding the entrance to the Mediterranean. It had been captured in 1704 during the War of the Spanish Succession and ceded by Spain to Great Britain by the Treaty of Utrecht in 1713.

But we have had none of that today. The sea has been almost smooth, and we spent the first hour or so passing quite close to the French coast which looked rather arid but otherwise delightful.

Since then we have been out of sight of land, and I have been unpacking, getting to work in the 'Study Cabin' (which is most comfortable and will be most useful)[4] and making the acquaintance of the rest of the party.

As I don't know much of them yet, I won't go into details.[5] I will only say that the Misses Lorimer don't come up to their Father (nor to the sister who called with a packet of letters a day or so before we left) and that Mr. Campbell, the Australian member, whose acquaintance I make for the first time, has an accent you could (with difficulty) cut with a knife. We have a special table for meals which is eyed with some awe (or more likely amusement) by the other passengers. I feel sure that boredom will descend upon me shortly if I have to sit there for every meal. The Commission party isn't exactly what you would call entertaining.

Saturday, Jan. 18th

This has been a quite uneventful day and a very few lines will describe it. I have spent most of the day in working in the 'Study Cabin' which is really extraordinarily useful. The only drawback that appears at present is that the Commissioners use it a great deal, and interrupt continued work somewhat. However, one picks up a great deal of miscellaneous information which may be useful later on, and after all the Cabin wasn't made for me only! Incidentally I have discovered that Mr. Campbell, his accent once got over, is quite interesting and even entertaining.

The rest of the day (I am writing just before dinner) has been occupied in meals and occasional exercise round the decks. I haven't made any further acquaintances yet as I have been too busy and most of the passengers are getting off at Port Said and it doesn't seem worthwhile to cultivate them. But no one looks wildly exciting. We went

---

4. For this facility the Commission were charged an extra £25.
5. The Commission party with Harding consisted of Vincent, Bateman, Garnett, Lorimer, Tatlow (representing the United Kingdom) and Campbell (Australia), plus Bridgman, Bass and sundry wives and daughters. Haggard (U.K.) would join them in Colombo, Sinclair (New Zealand) in Dunedin, Bowring (Newfoundland) in Wellington and Foster (Canada) in Auckland. There was no representative from South Africa on this trip.

through the Straits of Bonifaccio last night or early this morning and so saw nothing of them, and have been out of sight of land (and ships) all day.[6] The sea is fairly calm – but the *Medina* seems to 'lollop' along (I think that is the right word) i.e. there is always more or less of a roll.

Sunday, Jan. 19th

Since I wrote last night – there has been eventful monotony. First of all, about 9 p.m. we passed comparatively quite near Stromboli.[7] It rises in a cone shape right out of the sea but, unfortunately, the night was rather cloudy, and we couldn't see the top. (We passed the Straits of Messina some hours later on, but I didn't stay up to see them.)[8] Secondly, this morning there was a parade of the crew. I was on the 'Lascar' side (the white crew were on the other side of the deck) and very curious they looked – with a variety of coloured sashes and Company's uniform.[9] Apparently this review is a weekly function so another time I must try to get a photograph.[10]

Thirdly, it is getting warmer, and the sun has been shining all day – the first we have seen of it since Marseilles. And fourthly, I have been discovering acquaintances. There is one Cullen – whom I knew slightly and I think 'tubbed' at Oxford.[11] He is now on the Stock Exchange and going out to Egypt for a holiday. There are Mr. and Mrs. Bray – who used to live at Beckenham and are now at Walton Heath.[12] He, curiously enough, is a member of the firm who effected all my insurance policies.

---

6. The Straits of Bonifacio lie between Corsica and Sardinia.
7. In the Lipari or Aeolian Islands, north-east of Sicily, rising to 924 m.
8. Between Sicily and the Italian mainland.
9. Lascar, probably derived from the Urdu word *lashkar* meaning army, was the term invariably used by the British to describe non-European seamen, usually East Indians.
10. Harding refers several times to taking photographs. These are, alas, now lost. Hand-held cameras were readily available by 1913. George Eastman (1854–1932) began to market the first Kodak roll-film camera in 1888.
11. Tubs, at Oxford University, were pairs rowing boats, often used for training crews for eights.
12. Beckenham and Walton Heath were being absorbed as suburbs by 'the capital of the British Empire'. Greater London, the largest city in the world, contained a population of 7¼ million in 1911. David Lloyd George (1863–1945), then Chancellor of the Exchequer in the Liberal government, also had a house at Walton Heath: it was dynamited by suffragettes on 19 February 1913.

They are also going to Egypt.[13] And finally, I have been talking this evening to Mr. Randell who is 'supernumerary' Chief Officer, and a friend of Frank. He is a cheery person, and I liked him very much. He offered me a seat at his table after Port Said. But I had to say that I couldn't be certain. I would like to, but it would require tact successfully to evade the Commissioners!

Otherwise there is nothing much to record. I have been working a certain amount, and walking about – and that completes the story. No – I have left out the service which the Captain conducted this morning in the Cabin. It was short and stuffy (I mean the saloon atmosphere was stuffy). The music was excruciating – a harmonium and violin which were at discord with each other and the congregation. The chief feature was the collection which realized some £14!

Monday, Jan. 20th

I must close up this letter tonight as we are due in at Port Said tomorrow, and I shan't have much time then.

This morning opened with a view of Crete which lasted for some little time. There were snow mountains – one, we were told, nearly 8000 feet high – which looked most gorgeous. A holiday there, from the point of view of say 30 miles away, seemed a very desirable thing.[14] Since then, and till this evening, nothing much has happened. I have been working on and off and taking exercise in the intervals. It has been another gorgeous day – but rather a cold wind.

I moved my table at dinner (one of the Commissioners, Mr. Garnett, who has been seedy since we left Marseilles turning up for the first time, so that we were one too many) and found myself next to a much

---

13. Because of the volume of English tourists, Cairo was already being described by 1899 as 'a suburb of London'. The firm of Thomas Cook (1808–92), which began in 1841 with a railway excursion to a local temperance meeting, had conducted its first tour to Egypt in 1869.

14. Mount Idhi, rising to 2456 m., was the highest point in Crete. This was probably not yet a good time for a holiday on the island. The prolonged retreat of the Ottoman Empire from Europe made the Eastern Mediterranean an unstable area, to the concern of major powers like Great Britain. Crete had escaped from three hundred years of Turkish control in 1897 and obtained autonomous status, but not the union with mainland Greece which most Greeks wanted: this was secured only after the First Balkan War, beginning in October 1912, and by the Treaty of London, accepted by the defeated Turks in May 1913.

betravelled person going out to Australia for the 'n'th time who enlivened me with lurid stories of the Red Sea in the hot months. Since dinner I have been talking to a parson from Vancouver with strong Imperial ideas – an interesting (though somewhat verbose) person who unfortunately is getting off at Port Said. However, he has presented me with a card and hopes to see us at Vancouver. Last of all there has been excitement in the shape of a wireless message[15] from Prince d'Arenberg (the President of the Suez Canal) who wants to know how many of the Commission are coming to see him at Ismailia.[16] Ismailia is in the middle of the Canal and the *Medina* doesn't stop there. Nor indeed anywhere after leaving Port Said till Aden – not even Suez. The only alternatives, therefore, seem to be either to have a launch down to Ismailia from Port Said and back again in the evening – or to sleep there, I suppose under Prince d'Arenberg's roof!, and pick up the *Medina* next day. The latter involves coming off in the pilot boat, and the Captain, to whom I have just spoken, does not recommend it for some of the somewhat decrepit Commissioners! It remains to be seen what Sir E. Vincent settles. But for that you may have to wait till I can write from Aden.

> My remembrances to all and sundry
> Your affectionate brother
> E. J. Harding

---

15. Wireless telegraphy, developed in Britain especially by the Marconi Company, had recently become well-established in commercial shipping. The messages leading in July 1910 to the identification of Dr Crippen in mid-Atlantic and his subsequent arrest in Canada and those transmitted by the sinking *Titanic* on the night of 14–15 April 1912 attracted publicity to the new technology.

16. The Suez Canal was constructed under the direction of the French engineer Ferdinand de Lesseps (1805–94) and was opened in 1869. Its commercial operations were controlled by the Suez Canal Company, in which the British government, thanks to Disraeli (1804–81), had bought 44% of the shares for £4 million in 1875. Prince d'Arenberg (1837–1924) served as the third president of the company from 1896 to 1913. The company's operational headquarters were at Ismailia, named after Ismail, the Khedive of Egypt who had sponsored and invested heavily in the canal. His bankruptcy in 1876 was followed in 1878 by an Anglo-French Dual Control over his government's finances. In 1879 he was deposed and replaced by his son, the Khedive Tewfik. In 1913 over 60% of the shipping passing through the canal, some 12 million tons, was British; nevertheless this represented a decline from the overwhelming British predominance of the later 1870s to the early 1890s when almost 80% of the traffic had regularly been British. (By 1955 less than 30% was British.)

Port Said, View of the Port.   *Postcard franked 19 September 1912*

DOMINIONS ROYAL COMMISSION
At Port Said
Wednesday, Jan. 22nd 1913

My dear Father,

I think I left off (on Monday night) with the arrival of a telegram from Prince d'Arenberg asking how the Commission were going to get to Ismailia. Finally, Sir Edgar Vincent settled to send a telegram that six would come down but wanted to get back to the ship in the evening, leaving it to the authorities to settle how to get the party there and back. This I duly sent by Marconigram. The sequel will come presently. Yesterday (Tuesday) was a most exciting day, quite in contrast to the preceding ones. It started with the bustle on board of passengers preparing to leave at Port Said. There were 180 of them – and they certainly won't be much loss. The ship was far too crowded

Then about 11 a.m. palm trees and dahabeahs (the Egyptian boats) began to make their appearance.[17] Lunch was put forward and got through quickly, and by 1 o'clock we were into Port Said. I can't say it was very attractive externally. The shipping, of course, was interesting (we have seen so little lately) and so was the mole, which runs out to

---

17. Dahabeah were long, light-draft, sailing vessels, particularly common on the Nile.

show the entrance, and the statue of Ferdinand de Lesseps. But the town, at a first appearance, looks rather like a second rate French watering place, and the Mediterranean tails off in a row of breakers quite after the fashion of Trouville.[18]

However, we didn't have to wait long for excitement as among the crowd of boats coming off was a very smart steam launch with a number of distinguished French officials – practically all having the ribbon, which means the Legion of Honour.[19] To these we were formally presented in the Saloon by Sir Edgar Vincent (who by the way speaks French like a native), and they proceeded to take us off – by us I mean four Commissioners, myself and Bridgman – on a tour round the harbour.[20] We went all round and very interesting it was. There are lots of new works going forward – including provision for oil storage which interested me a good deal[21] – and we also landed at the fresh water tanks, which supply the shipping. There is a subtropical garden close by the tanks with bougainvillea growing wild.[22] I forgot to say that the day was quite hot,

18. Port Said was first developed by the Suez Canal Company in 1859 at the Mediterranean entrance to the canal. It was named after Said Pasha. The population of 50,000 included 10,000 Europeans (census of 1907). The statue of de Lesseps by the French sculptor Fremiet had been unveiled in 1899: with its pedestal it stood 57 feet high. It was pulled down by Egyptian nationalists in 1956. Trouville, on the Normandy coast of France, had become a popular holiday resort and place of retirement for members of the better-off English middle class.
19. The Legion of Honour had been founded by Napoleon in 1802.
20. Although Harding notices the French role in the Company's operations at Port Said, he does not mention that the French had been politically excluded from Egypt following a British 'peace-keeping' military invasion in 1882 and the establishment of a British protectorate. The British consul-general – in 1913 Lord Kitchener (1850–1916) – exercised enormous influence over the Khedive. French resentment was eased only when they were assured of an equivalent control over Morocco as part of the Anglo-French Entente signed in 1904.
21. Oil was beginning to replace coal as fuel for ships, but it powered only 3.4% of total world tonnage by 1914. Oil supplies raised new strategical problems following the Royal Navy's construction of oil-powered vessels shortly before the war.
22. This vivid and robust climbing shrub, originally from South America, was named after Louis Antoine de Bougainville (1729–1811), sailor, soldier, scientist, mathematician, diplomat, author and Fellow of the Royal Society. His reputation as a successful French explorer of the South Seas in 1767–69 has suffered in comparison with that of Captain James Cook (1728–79), at least in the English-speaking world.

Port Said, Offices of the Suez Canal Company and *Medina*, dressed as a Royal Yacht en route to the Delhi Burbar, 1911.   *Postcard*

but the wind cold – so that a greatcoat was quite acceptable.

The harbour tour completed we changed to a much bigger launch, very fast – about 20 knots – and fitted with comfortable deck chairs. There ensconced, and with the officials to talk to, we started down the Canal.

Steamers are only allowed to go down at about 5 miles an hour – but the launch went at least four times as fast. The wash was tremendous, and we had to slow down quite often in order to avoid upsetting a row boat or hurting the new stone slopes where the Canal is being widened. Even so we got down to Ismailia (which is half way down the Canal) in about 2½ hours. We shall take 8 hours or so today. (I am writing just before we sail.)

I think I will leave over saying anything of the Canal till I have been down the second time today – and go on at once to Ismailia.

Just as the sun was setting we came out into one of the smaller lakes, turned off to the right and made straight for what looked like a big grove of palm trees. A little nearer and one could see a big bathing station, and nearer still there appeared a landing stage with Prince d'Arenberg, more officials, and two motor cars waiting.

More presentations and touring. Then the party (being pleased to find themselves on shore) proceeded to leave the motor cars to crawl behind at a respectful distance and to walk through the gardens which have been planted right round the European quarter of the town.

The gardens are quite the most marvellous thing I have seen yet. They are elaborately irrigated with water which comes down in a canal from the Nile (which canal incidentally supplies Port Said and Suez with its drinking water). And there are groves of immense acacias, palms and some kind of conifer which look as though they might never have heard of the vicinity of sand. This to say nothing of the flowers which I really can't attempt to describe. Add to this a most perfect afterglow, and you can possibly begin to imagine the sensation the gardens produced. Finally, there were very curious Egyptian sculptures which had been found in the desert close by and transplanted for further adornment of the gardens. These, which were at the furthest point of the gardens, could hardly be seen as the light had nearly gone, and at that point, therefore, we took to the motor cars.

They conveyed us to the Suez Canal Company's offices (the head-quarters of which are at Ismailia), part of which has apparently been fitted up as a private house for Prince d'Arenberg. Here there were more officials and, of course, 'the mixture as before'. Then there was desultory conversation for an hour or so – which would have been amusing but for the strain of endeavouring to find subjects which would suit the officials' (somewhat limited) English and our (much more limited) French. And there followed an elaborate dinner (preceded by a serious conversation with me by one of the officials as to what the order of precedence among the Commissioners was!).

Dinner was followed by more talk (of the same kind as before). Then the motor cars to the station, and return by train, right through the desert, to Port Said. The Company's kindness extended to a reserved compartment (in the name of Sir E. 'Finclet'), carriages from Port Said Station to the quay and a launch out to the *Medina*. Altogether it was an experience worth having. I hope all our 'beanfeasts' will be similar. With difficulty I evaded a pressing invitation to the Commissioners to go down again to Ismailia today, have more launches and another dinner, and be put on board the *Medina* as she goes by Ismailia! Finally I got off on the plea that, while it would be easy to put on board one Commissioner (Sir E. Vincent stayed at Ismailia for the night), the Captain might be annoyed, with some justification, if he had to stop the ship for a party.

I ought to add, 'to complete the record', that I found out the main officials to be the Chief Engineer of the Canal, the 'Marine Superintendent' (and a predecessor – now retired), the Chief Agent at Cairo, and the General Manager at Paris, down on a visit.

I fear this description isn't what it should be but, as I write, the mail bags from the *Osiris* are being shot on board just over our heads and the row is terrific.[23]

Thursday evening, Jan. 23rd
In the Red Sea

We got off about noon from Port Said yesterday, and proceeded to move down the Canal in a leisurely way at the head of a string of four steamers half a mile apart.

But I am very glad to have been down slowly, as one had time to look at things and also one could see much further from the deck of the *Medina* than from the launch. By the way, we had another high official of the Canal on board who explained to the two Commissioners in particular who hadn't been down the Canal, and to such of the rest of us as cared to listen, anything of interest.

The Canal goes perfectly straight for the first 25 miles (there are no locks) and then bends somewhat till it gets to Ismailia. What it does after that I don't know as we came through by night. But it isn't in the least dull, as the railway from Port Said to Cairo runs alongside for most of the way, and by the Canal a path of some description, and on the path are little encampments and passing Arabs and sometimes camels and goats. Then on the other side there stretches unending desert, at least so it appears. And on that side there is a 'permanent' mirage of cliffs and trees and lakes – whereas really there is nothing but sand! There are occasional encampments on that side too, and about half way down the 'straight', if one can call it so, there is an Arab village, through which goes the old trade route from Asia to Africa. There is a ferry there for people and beasts, and we saw a large caravan waiting to come over – there must have been 100 camels I should think. The village is a simple affair – a tiny mosque and a clump of mud huts, with a sand bank round the whole (I suppose plastered up with mud) in order to keep off the worst of the sandstorms. What the people live on I really can't imagine. However, they seem happy enough, and come down to the bank to salute the steamer with shouts for 'backsheesh'.

At night time the effect is even more wonderful. All the steamers have to put up powerful searchlights in the bows, so that they shan't get out

---

23. *Osiris*, 1750 tons, 330 feet by 37 feet, was built for P. & O. and launched from Caird's shipyard on the Clyde in 1898. With her sister ship *Isis*, she earned a remarkable reputation for speed and reliability, sailing every Sunday from Brindisi in Southern Italy, carrying mailbags and 78 first-class passengers and connecting two days later with the P. & O. steamers at Port Said. In 1914 both ships were requisitioned by the British Admiralty.

of the channel. To see four of these big steamers all lighted up and with searchlights in front apparently moving slowly along the desert is an amazing sight. I can't think of anything more calculated to point the contrast between the ancient world and the modern.

We had a small excitement in the evening in seeing Sir Edgar Vincent being put on board at Ismailia. He had spent the whole day seeing more of the Canal and going right down to Suez. And he brought with him a huge bunch of roses (fancy roses in the middle of the desert) grown in the gardens at Ismailia and sent by Prince d'Arenberg to the ladies of the party.

Altogether I shan't soon forget my experience of the Suez Canal. I ought to put in before stopping a few words about Port Said. We had a walk through it between 7 and 8 in the morning. But it isn't worth much description – being a compound of a second rate French watering place (I think I said that before) and a fourteenth rate Eastern town. The most attractive parts of it were the children in various stages of costume from half a nightshirt to what one is accustomed to see, and the goats taking round the morning milk. They bring it to the door and are milked into bottles.

Today has been quiet by contrast. We woke to find ourselves in The Gulf of Suez, and have been steaming down it and the Red Sea all the rest of the day. I always imagined there was nothing but sand banks in the Gulf – but there are really high granite mountains on each side. One is supposed to see Sinai, but I can't say I did. But the coast looks very inhospitable, and barren in the extreme. The less serious of the party discuss the probable effect in Arabia of a smallholdings scheme and a progressive land tax.[24]

A few games on deck, a gradual increase in acquaintances (people are much more friendly since Port Said) and the usual work make up the rest of the story. It is getting not a little hot, and I am writing this evening in shirtsleeves.

Saturday evening
Jan. 25th 1913

We are due into Aden tomorrow so I must finish up this letter this evening. I didn't write yesterday as there was really nothing to record – save heat increased to an almost uncomfortable extent, and various essays in deck games as a relief from Commission work (which extend one's acquaintances, but otherwise are of no particular interest especially if one enters for competitions, as I did, without previous practice).[25]

Today has been like yesterday, only that the heat was more so – at least it was last night and this morning, but this afternoon we struck a head breeze which cooled things very considerably.

I haven't been able to escape from the Commission's clutches at meals, so the Chief Officer still goes without my company. However, we have a table on the cool side – so perhaps it is for the best.

There is a fancy dress dance on the ship tonight which I ought to watch though I don't propose to dance! So I must stop.

> Ever your affectionate son
> E. J. Harding

> DOMINIONS ROYAL COMMISSION
> Gulf of Aden
> Monday, January 27th 1913

My dear Eva,

I rather fancy that before this week ends (we aren't due at Colombo till Saturday) there will be various days intermitted as I shall be working – that is, if there isn't a storm – and probably not doing much else.

But that is no reason for not going back to the past and telling you about Aden. We got into sight of land late on Saturday evening, and found ourselves that night seeing various lighthouses, and passing by the islands known as the 'Twelve Apostles'.

By Sunday morning we were just in the Straits of Bab-el-Mandeb and going by Perim (which, in case you don't know, is an island lying almost in the middle of the Straits) and all the morning we were well in sight of land making up towards Aden.[26]

It is an extraordinary coast – either there are immense stretches of sand with mountains well behind or else very rugged cliffs, rather like

---

24. Smallholdings and land taxes were currently hotly debated political topics in Britain. They were to feature in Lloyd George's Land Campaign, launched in October 1913.

25. Yet according to John Arlott (ed.), *The Oxford Companion to Sports and Games* (1976), deck games organised for passengers date only from the 1920s. In a letter written on board ship to his wife, Sir Edgar Vincent was to confess that he had sprained his wrist playing cricket.

26. Perim Island at the southern entrance to the Red Sea had been briefly occupied by the British during the Napoleonic Wars and was formally annexed and fortified as a strategic asset in 1857. It was governed as a dependency of Aden.

Tyrol mountains, coming straight down into the sea. What the formation is I don't know, but it is all extremely desolate, and there is no vegetation and hardly a sign of life.

By two o'clock we were getting into Aden – and here is the place to mention two (possible) tragedies on board. The first happened to the printer, making his first voyage, who succeeded in bursting a blood vessel and had to be taken to the Aden Hospital. (What will happen to him I can't think – I should be very sorry to be in his place – but the only result to us is that the dinner menus are no longer printed!)

The second happened, and I fear is happening still, to an Indian army officer who was returning to his regiment – Alexander by name. He had been on sick leave through malaria and had applied for an extension, but was refused it. On the voyage out he had another attack, and was so bad by Aden that it was very doubtful whether he could be moved to the Bombay steamer. Fortunately his wife was travelling out with him, and finally the 'transfer' was successfully carried out. But I am very sorry for him. He was the man (I don't know if I mentioned this before) whom I found at our table at tea the first day on board, and who confided to me with awe that we were 'trespassing' on a Royal Commission! Both he and his wife were particularly nice.

Now to return to Aden.[27] We finally anchored about 4 p.m., and after tea went off on shore on a launch (the agent's launch) thoughtfully provided by the Captain! So is our path made easy.

Aden consists of a series of rocky and cindery hills with houses at various altitudes (and a very occasional shrub) and at the bottom, between the hills and the sea, a native town with shops etc. The atmosphere is dazzlingly clear, and it is somewhat trying to be out in the sun. But we were lucky to chance on a good day. The temperature was perhaps eighty something, and I heard someone say that it was the coolest day they had known for years.

There are the usual 'hangers on' about the landing stage whom we evaded with difficulty but, once past them, the population is extremely entertaining. There are natives from Somaliland (just across the Gulf), Arabians, Indians, a few obvious Jews, and a heterogeneous lot of others. Their costumes are anything from nothing to the gaudiest of

---

27. Aden's strategic and commercial value on the route to and from India largely explains the British expedition which captured the town and seaport in 1839. The Political Resident who governed the territory was responsible to the Government of India.

Aden, the Landing Pier.   *Postcard*

clothes and turbans. I saw one man whose costume, apart from a cloth
or two, was a headgear bearing an extremely good resemblance to the
Royal Standard. There are quite a lot of camels – vicious-looking beasts
who look as if they would spit at you. One particularly attractive sight
was a Red Cross British waggon (there is, of course, a garrison in the
place), drawn by a camel at full trot.

After we had inspected the shops and I had bought your present
(which by the way was only got with the aid of Mrs. Tatlow, the wife of
one of the Commissioners, and after protracted haggling which reduced
the price to nearly one half of the original amount demanded), Bass and
I pursued our investigations into the region of the barracks which lie on
the side of the hill. We discovered a sentry mounting guard clad in a shirt,
shorts and putties. Thus does red tape surrender to the exigencies of
climate. We talked to some of the Tommies,[28] who seemed fairly
contented (but then they haven't had a summer in Aden yet!) and who
showed us a path which led over the hills and back to the town through
the native quarter. It was getting dark by then (there had been a gorgeous
sunset over the harbour), and we had an amusing walk. All the

---

28. Rudyard Kipling (1865–1936) had popularised the term as the generic name
for British soldiers in 'Tommy', one of his *Barrack Room Ballads* published
in 1892: 'Then it's Tommy this, an' Tommy that, an' "Tommy 'ow's yer
soul?" / But it's "Thin red line of 'eroes" when the drums begin to roll'.

population inhabit the streets (at which I am not surprised judging by the look of the houses), and they all take a deep interest in passing strangers.

We came back to the *Medina* by the launch and spent the evening watching the lights of the town and the *Salzette*, the other P. & O. boat, which was waiting to take the passengers and mails to Bombay.[29] She is painted white, and looked very jolly. Also I believe she is very fast (in fact the fastest boat anywhere in the East) and has a great reputation for rolling.

Really it is an experience worth having to come down this way if only to realize the extraordinary 'Britishness' of this particular route. One sails on comfortably for three or four days and then, when things are perhaps becoming a trifle monotonous, one finds a relaxation in the shape of a port very British-looking (in all but the houses and population) and with all the necessary appliances for buying Kodak films, Whisky, Picture Postcards and other British delights. I think it ought really to be called 'The Imperial Piccadilly'.[30]

We left Aden early this morning, about 1.30 I think, but I was asleep and only just woke up for a minute or two to see the land slipping away.

Today we have been in the Gulf aiming for Cape Guardafui and Socotra – the former of which we shall, I suppose, pass tonight.[31] It is still quite cool (comparatively speaking) and there has been a good breeze, with uninterrupted sunshine. In fact clouds for the last week have been rarities to be much admired. I wonder if you can say as much in England!

Thursday, Jan. 30th 1913
Indian Ocean

As I rather expected, nothing happened on Tuesday or Wednesday worth recording, and indeed nothing has today, but I had better write a little this evening as I shall be busy tomorrow with official letters to be

---

29. P. & O. had run a weekly mail service to Bombay since 1868. Since the 1890s ships on the Australian service had carried the mail to Aden for transhipment. *Salsette*, 5850 tons, 440 feet by 53 feet, had been specially built for this service in 1908, by Caird on the Clyde: she was the fastest P. & O. ocean vessel of her day. She was sunk by a German submarine on 20 July 1917.

30. Plain postcards were widely used for commercial purposes from the 1870s, but they became a hugely popular form of communication during the 1890s when pictures were added. In 1914 an estimated 880 million cards were posted in Britain alone.

31. Cape Guardafui is on the coast of Somalia, a territory partitioned in the late 19th century into French, British and Italian colonies. Socotra, in the Arabian Sea, was another strategic island controlled by Great Britain, from 1876.

sent off at Colombo. It has been damp the last few days, and rather hot, but not unduly so, and I really anticipated something a good deal worse going through the tropics. However, it is said on all hands that this is a particularly cool trip.

Our study cabin, however, *is* very hot and I don't go there if I can help it after the morning – despite its two electric fans, three portholes and large skylight. I take up my abode instead in my cabin, which is right in front and gets any breeze there is. (I am in fact sitting on my bunk now to write this letter.) I suppose I mentioned that I changed my quarters at Port Said – but, in case I didn't, do so again. The change is very much for the better, but I am told that there are grave disadvantages in a gale, as it is impossible to get to any other part of the ship without going out on deck! However, we haven't had a sign of a gale yet.

There have been deck sports the last two days, but I didn't enter as I find that I have much too much work to do, and it needs all day practically – till dinner time – to do it. But I hope I got a photograph this afternoon of one of the most amusing – a pillow fight between two men sitting opposite one another on a spar over a large canvas bath with 3 feet of water in it. The loser is the one who falls in first under the force of the other's blows – the contest usually lasts about 10 seconds.

The only other episode which seems worth mentioning is the gradual disappearance of the north star (it is very low on the horizon now) and the appearance of the Southern Cross. If the one I have been shown is the right one, it is very disappointing – rather like the Great Bear with one pointer missing. But perhaps I have got hold of the wrong constellation, or else it may get brighter as it rises higher in the sky.

My fountain pen, I find, is empty so I shall have, perforce, to stop![32]

Friday, Jan. 31st

We aren't due at Colombo till 3 p.m. tomorrow but I think I had better finish up this letter tonight, and perhaps I can send a card to say that we actually have arrived when we do so. But it has been 83 in the shade today – and damp heat at that – and I was persuaded this evening to dance a set of lancers, so you mustn't expect much.

---

32. Fountain pens were one of those life-enhancing 19th-century inventions. The first patent was taken out in 1809, but such pens only became popular following the production of a truly practical design by L.E. Waterman of New York in 1884.

The event of today has been passing the Southern Maldive islands – low shores with a lighthouse, and nothing but trees, so far as one could see, inland. I pity the lighthouse keepers, but from a distance the islands looked very fascinating.[33]

The only other incident is the fact, which I heard to day, that a Somali boy who was helping to coal, or tranship mails, or something, got left on board at Aden, and has had to be taken on to Colombo. His total outfit for the trip is a loincloth. He can't speak a word of anything but Arabic, and opinion is divided as to how he will fare at Colombo. The purser told me that he might be locked up as a stowaway – but that probably it wouldn't be worth it!

A lot of the passengers tranship at Colombo for Calcutta and the East, so that there will be comparatively an empty boat from there. However, some of the nicest people go on, so perhaps we shan't lose very much. I must try and tell you something of the passengers in the next letter. The 10 days to Freemantle should afford some scope. You won't, of course, expect to hear for 3 weeks or so after getting this.

Ever your affectionate brother
E. J. Harding

Dominions Royal Commission
Nearing the Equator
Monday, Feb. 3rd 1913

My dear Father,

I always pictured the neighbourhood of the Equator as a calm region with the bluest of skies and the hottest of heats. Instead we have been beating along all day under a cloudy sky with occasional torrents of rain – to the accompaniment of a strong wind and the consequential rolling and pitching.

Besides all that it has been most horribly damp and everyone has been either sea sick or limp in the extreme. I belong to the latter band.

However, this evening there is less sea, and I must force myself to write about Colombo, damp notwithstanding.[34] By tomorrow morning we expect to have crossed the line – but they have no ceremonies now, so I hope for an undisturbed night when I have finished writing.[35]

We 'made' Ceylon about midday on Saturday, and earlier in the morning sent off a wireless message to Stubbs (who was acting Governor)[36] to tell him that ten of the party wanted to get up to Kandy if they could and to stop the night there.[37] He had promised to send them up if it could be managed.

When we got inside the breakwater (the ships lie just inside, about half a mile from the shore) off came the Government launch, with an A.D.C. on board, one Captain Beatty Crozier who sought me out and told me that they had had 100 inches of rain or so in the last month and that they couldn't guarantee the railway if there were another night's rain. So (feeling that we couldn't take the risk of upsetting a continent by failing to arrive in New Zealand at the appointed time!) we abandoned Kandy and arranged instead that the ladies should drive round in the Government motor car in the course of the afternoon, and that some of the Commissioners should have dinner at Queen's House (that is, Government House in Colombo) in the evening.

As everyone was keen to sleep on shore, if possible, they all packed bags and arranged to take rooms at a hotel known as the Galle Face about a mile along the sea front.[38] The bags were duly delivered over to the Hotel porters (at least we thought they were), and the A.D.C.

---

33. The Maldive Islands in the Indian Ocean were annexed as dependent territories of Ceylon (now Sri Lanka) following the British occupation of Ceylon during the Napoleonic Wars.

34. Colombo, with a population of 211,274 in 1911, was the administrative capital of the British Colony of Ceylon. The first Europeans to occupy the island were the Portuguese in the 16th century. They were expelled by the Dutch in the 17th century, and they in turn were ousted by the British in 1796. The seaboard formally became British territory at the Treaty of Amiens in 1802, and the hinterland was conquered and annexed in 1815. A secure harbour was constructed 1872–82. There was a major Royal Navy base at Trincomalee on the other side of the island.

35. Passengers and crew crossing the equator for the first time were traditionally treated to a shipboard cermony, sometimes rather rough, presided over by 'King Neptune'.

36. R.E. Stubbs (1876–1947), later Sir Edward Stubbs, was the Colonial Secretary of Ceylon and acting Governor. He had joined the Colonial Office in 1900, where he had been a colleague of Harding, but then moved into the Colonial Service, serving first in Ceylon until 1919 and later as Governor of Hong Kong, of Jamaica and of Cyprus before returning to Ceylon where he remained until his retirement in 1937.

37. Kandy, the capital of the former Sinhalese monarchy, lies in the central mountains. Harding's companions would have wanted to see the Dalada Maligawa, the temple built in the 16th century to honour and protect the tooth of Buddha.

38. The capital's most prestigious hotel, opened in 1864. It stood (and stands) beside the promenade and green, known as the 'Hyde Park of Colombo', provided in 1859 'for the ladies and children' by Governor Sir Henry Ward (1797–1860).

Colombo Harbour, Ceylon.   *Postcard*

instructed a Queen's House servant at the Quay to see them at once through the Customs.

Once arrived at the quay (it was very hot and sticky there), all the rest of the party but myself packed themselves up in the motor car or in 'rickshaws' and set out for the hotel. I stayed with the A.D.C. to explain to him who the Commissioners were, and what he ought to talk to them about at dinner – and it ended by my going with him straight up to Queen's House, where we were saluted by sentries and (after a refreshing wash) I was taken to tea with 'H.E.'.

Really it was too ludicrous for words, and I was hard put it to prevent myself upsetting the dignity of the situation.

There were two men, the A.D.C. and the Private Secretary (both about two years younger than Stubbs if that), talking of him as 'H.E.' and addressing him as 'Sir', and when he came in to tea, the proper procedure was to let him sit down first, and motion to someone (it was me – for that occasion) to come and sit down beside him.

Then there were the surroundings – a vast house with punkahs going and State portraits of Queen Victoria and King Edward and Queen Alexandra on the walls[39] – and, as I said, saluting sentries and all the rest of it, enclosing Stubbs whom one knows as a person of caustic tongue and no respect whatever for institutions (except perhaps himself!). *Quantum mutatus* etc. etc. etc.[40]

Colombo, Galle Face Hotel.   *Postcard*

I escaped, in due course, from 'the presence', and with the help of the A.D.C. found out by telephone that the Galle Face Hotel was full, and that the Commission party had had to go elsewhere for rooms. So I thought it high time to go in search of my bag, hired a 'rickshaw' and set out in search.

A rickshaw is a two-wheeled and very light vehicle with shafts drawn by a native who trots all the way except when the road is uphill. I hope to have got a photograph and so of some to show you presently. You sit in it with legs comfortably outstretched, and try to look as dignified as possible. Only there is an uncomfortable feeling at the back of one's mind that it is rather bad luck on the coolie pulling the conveyance.

I won't weary you with all the incidents of the search for the luggage. The upshot of it was that some of it had never left the ship at all. Some more of it (including my own bag) had gone up to the Galle Face Hotel and was returned after I had spent a hot (and very cross) half hour on the wharf looking for it. Some more got up to the Hotel and stayed there.

---

39.   Where were King George V and Queen Mary? Victoria had died in 1901 and her son, Edward VII, in 1910. His wife, Queen Alexandra, lived until 1925.

40.   'Quantum mutatus ab illo / Hectore qui...': 'How changed from that / Hector who...': Virgil (70–19 B.C.), *The Aeneid*, book 2, lines 274–5.

The result was that two Commissioners never got their bags in time to change for dinner and had to give up Queen's House. Two more slept at a hotel (Mount Lavinia) 7 miles out of Colombo, and only got their bags 10 minutes before it was time for them to start. I, possibly, was the luckiest of all, for I found my bag in time to engage a bathroom to change in at another hotel – and even managed to secure a bath before dressing.

Dinner was a repetition of tea – only more so. But it was quite interesting, for I got next to the A.D.C. and next to him was the acting Colonial Secretary, both of whom were quite entertaining. There was a tragedy, though, behind the latter, for he was a (very) disappointed applicant for the post which was given to Stubbs. I wondered what his feelings were as he sat and looked at Stubbs across the table.

Dinner over I chartered a boat and got rowed out to the *Medina* – as it was quite hopeless to try and get a room in the town. But I paid the penalty in the shape of a horrible din all night. They were loading cargo just outside my cabin, and you can imagine that I got very little sleep, and there were dusky forms lying asleep all along the deck in the intervals of coaling!

Tuesday evening, Feb. 4th

This is the evening of the 'Sea Symphony'. As it is about 11 p.m. here and we are about 5½ hours in front of you, I suppose the preparations are just beginning and I am wondering how it will go off. But I doubt whether Walt Whitman was ever in the tropics. Doesn't the poem end up with 'following' and if so, does it mean following wind? I can't remember and haven't the words here.[41] But if it *does*, it is the last thing to be cheerful about. We have had such a wind, or something like it all day, and the consequence is that there is no air, and even my cabin is hot.

---

41. The Sea Symphony of Ralph Vaughan Williams (1872–1958), a setting of poems by Walt Whitman, was first performed in Leeds in 1910. Its first London performance by the Bach Choir (of which Eva Harding was probably a member) took place on 4 February 1913. The poem in the third movement does, indeed, end with the word 'following'. The Harding family and the Vaughan Williams family were near neighbours in Surrey and probably friends; the Hardings lived at Coldharbour, a hamlet near Dorking, about 50 kilometres from London, and Eva was a member of the Coldharbour Choir, which was conducted for many years by Margaret Vaughan Williams (1871–1931), the composer's sister.

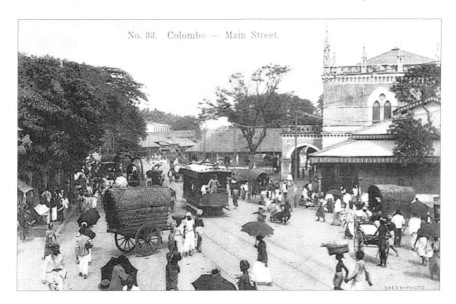

Colombo, Main Street.   *Postcard*

However, to return to Colombo. We weren't due to sail till 1 p.m. and early on Sunday morning Mr. Campbell, the Australian member, Bridgman, Bass and I chartered a boat to take us ashore again for a drive round the town.

Just by the harbour the place is rather European, and there is the usual gang of loafers on the look out for making money. But once out of the vicinity and the place becomes most fascinating. There is a curious mixture of the West and East, for there are good metalled roads and tramcars and on each side native houses and shops with a great babble of noise going on.

Most of the traffic is in bullock carts – rather reminiscent of carriers' vans in England, but with a bullock to draw them instead of a horse. And there are, of course, the usual variegated costumes or the lack of them. Up to the age of 5 or so it is quite *comme il faut* to have a costume of a string of beads and an anklet. After that there is great scope for variety of taste. Some of the people (and all the indoor servants at Queen's House I think) wear tortoiseshell combs at the back of the head. And most of the natives anoint their heads with coconut oil. It is said to keep the heat off (I hope it does, for a good many have no head gear at all) and also to be good for the hair.

We drove right through the native quarter, then through (apparently) a European suburban quarter, and reached our furthest point in the famous Cinnamon Gardens. We dismounted there, and slowly walked round with a sort of Park Keeper as escort. The gardens are most beautiful, with all sorts of trees, shrubs and flowers growing in them. I came away with a cocoa bean, a pod of cotton, some cinnamon bark and cinnamon root in my pocket, and I was also persuaded to buy (for 1/– after 8/– had been asked for it first) a necklace of flaming red cinnamon seeds.[42] I don't quite see its use at present (possibly Wendy Cowell might like it), but anyhow it is very jolly to look at.

The vegetation is, of course, wonderful in Ceylon, and even 'at the fringe' it was splendid. The banyan trees are as interesting as any. They let drop roots from branches say 20 feet up, which form into independent trees, so that there is a small grove, where there was one tree, after a few years. But also it is certainly exciting to the newcomer to see coconut trees with great clusters of fruit.

We couldn't stay too long in the gardens, for fear of missing the launch. As a matter of fact the *Medina* left punctually at one – so it was perhaps as well that we didn't attempt Kandy.

Sir Rider Haggard turned up safely at Colombo, so I was able to send off the prearranged telegram to the Treasury (I wonder if you have heard of its arrival by now) announcing the readiness of all the various members of the party to draw their appropriate allowances. As the party is now complete I think I shall have to try a few character sketches before we get to Freemantle, but I may as well wait a few days, so as to get a better impression of Rider Haggard.[43]

We are past the Equator now: it is comforting to think that damp heat may soon be diminishing.

Sunday, Feb. 9th

The sun doesn't set now till well after 6. I observed that fact yesterday and comforted myself with the thought that we were well out of the tropics. But we haven't got out of either the heat or the damp yet. Everything is wringing wet today, and it is as stuffy as can be. However, there can't be very much more of it now – at least I hope so.

---

42. The Cinammon Gardens had been an area preserved by the Dutch for the cultivation of cinammon bushes, but by 1913 this had become largely a high-class residential area whose streets were named after former British governors of the colony. '1/–' represents one shilling (5p.)
43. Haggard had been in India, visiting his second daughter, Dolly, and her husband.

A week at sea, without a vestige of land (and we have had that now), is not particularly exhilarating. We didn't even see the Cocos Islands (the home of one Ross who is known as 'The King' and reported on annually by someone from the Straits if he can get there).[44] But we got into touch by wireless telegraph, and I got through a telegram to Perth saying that Sir E. Vincent wanted to see the Governor of Western Australia while the *Medina* is at Perth. It arrived safely as we got an answer this morning.

It occurs to me that you are probably rather tired of hearing of these various telegrams. I can only answer that they are practically the only incidents to mention.

There is one more, though, to put down with the record of this last week. That is that on Friday and yesterday we had quite a heavy sea, so much so that on Friday night I could really hardly sleep for the pitching. However, matters didn't go so far that I couldn't get out in the morning!

Everybody with the Commission party turned up to breakfast in the morning (I think, as a matter of fact, that we were the only complete breakfast table), but there was a general feeling that it would be wise to postpone the informal meeting of the Commission (the first on the voyage) which had been arranged for 10 a.m. However, the sea quieted as the day went on, and we had the meeting after tea. It (the meeting) isn't worth writing about. Will not (or may not) the results be handed down to oblivion when the Commission reports?[45]

So I have, after all, to turn to character sketches. I had better begin with 'acquaintances' on board – but I haven't made very many really as I have been busy working most of the time.

There is a small Semitic contingent – Aarons, Cohen etc. – who seem quite pleasant, but are much given to bridge. I have, as I told you I should, started to play a little since Colombo – but my path hasn't run across theirs yet.

---

44. The first European to discover the Cocos Islands in the Indian Ocean was William Keeling (d.1620) in 1609. The Ross family settled there in the 1820s, and a British protectorate was formally established in 1856. This was later supervised by the government of the British colony of the Straits Settlements, territories which had themselves been acquired by the British at various dates during the 19th century, the most important, Singapore, in 1819.

45. Vincent wrote at this time: 'The Commission is happy and friendly: we have divided up the various subjects – and each one sits immersed in a different Blue-book'.

Then there is a person who 'travels in millinery' – i.e. she purchases French hats for some large Sydney House. She must be well over 50, to be kind, but dresses after the fashion of 22 and has caused much amusement by informing the ship that she had had her character told at Port Said, and was told that she would get stout when she grew old.

There is also a designing widow (at least there is no husband on board) with a designing daughter, who (I mean the widow) is said to have made careful inquiries after leaving Marseilles as to the financial status of all the young men on board, and – just before reaching Colombo – to have congratulated one man on his engagement to the daughter. He (who was transhipping there) hastily replied that he hadn't heard of it before, but that, anyhow, he already had a black wife.

I tell you all this, so that you may see the kind of stories afloat – they are amusing to relieve monotony!

Of more attractive people I haven't found many. But there is a boy at Eton – one Gibb – (who, I find, is in Mr. Stone's house) who is pleasant enough.[46] He is travelling with a grandfather and an aunt, and I have discovered that the said grandfather, or his father, I am not sure which, took Minnickfold for 3 months about 4 years ago.

On the whole the pleasantest people are a certain Professor Allen and his family. He is Dean of the Faculty of Medicine at Melbourne and a very clever fellow, I should say.[47] His wife is nice, but somewhat unduly talkative. There are three daughters, all born in Australia, and just returning from a first year in Europe. They deal rather in superlatives – especially in talking of England – but are otherwise quite interesting. I am still heartwhole, though!

Of the Commission party, Sir Edgar Vincent strikes me as altogether exceptional. He is very handsome and extremely rich – therefore a very good figurehead – but also extraordinarily quick, and very fertile in ideas. In fact he has so many that he sometimes forgets one and takes up another while one is still struggling with the first! But if this Commission is to do any good (about which, I find, everyone has the greatest doubt!) it will be largely his doing. Sir A. Bateman is getting rather tottery, he is also 'reminiscently' official. But, for the purposes of the Commission,

---

46. Eton College (founded 1441) was the prestigious English public school which rivalled Harrow (1571) and Dulwich (1606), where Harding was educated.
47. Professor Harry Allen (1854–1926) was a distinguished Professor of Pathology at the University of Melbourne 1906–24: he was knighted in 1914. Vincent warmed to him also: 'a fine rugged type of mind and honest heart....'

this will be all to the good – he will serve as a useful check to Sir Edgar Vincent if the latter's schemes grow too wild. Otherwise he is very jolly, and has a good sense of humour.

Mr. Lorimer remains delightful. He is a glutton for work, and has spent hours at the mass of stuff which there is to read. So much the better for me. He has the strongest possible common sense – which is applied invariably if he can hear what is said to him. But he is very deaf. My natural speech is growing permanently louder in the effort to make him hear.

Mr. Garnett and Mr. Tatlow – quite nice but nothing exceptional. Mr. Tatlow is the stolid successful railway manager. Mr. Garnett is the prosperous cotton manufacturer, but, being a typical North of England type, is interested in all sorts of things outside his work. He hunts and plays golf, both pursuits which he hopes to follow in New Zealand and Australia. He is very widely read, and has his own ideas about things. Incidentally he is a Director of the Company which constructs the screws for all the P. & O. ships.

Both these have their wives with them. Mrs. Tatlow, like Mr., is ordinary. Mrs. Garnett, I like very much. She is large, domestic, and motherly. The Garnetts have 10 children – the eldest of whom is married to the Editor of the Melbourne *Age* (with whom she will stay most of the time in Australia)[48] – and Mrs. Garnett would clearly be quite pleased to bring up as many more.

Mr. Campbell, I think, I have described already. Finally there is Sir Rider Haggard. I suspend judgment on him. I think he is of the temperament which has very ordinary Imperial ideas, and thinks they are extraordinary. Perhaps that is the result of being a novelist with a really keen imagination.

This is so long a letter that I will leave out Bass and Bridgman, particularly as there is nothing to say about either.

And, lest this letter should fall into the hands of any of the party, I will close it up now and send it off.

Ever your affectionate son
E. J. Harding

---

48. The Garnetts' son-in-law held a prestigious post: the *Age* had become a politically influential newspaper under the editorship from 1859 to 1908 of David Syme (1827–1908).

Monday, Feb. 10th

I didn't, after all, close this up last night and will add one word this morning – that is that in the Southern Hemisphere the sun doesn't, as I had vaguely imagined, rise in the west – or do something curious of that sort. What it does do is to travel from west to east via the *north*.[49] I daresay I could have worked this out at home, and no doubt you could – but here is the phenomenon visible, so perhaps it is worth mentioning.

DOMINIONS ROYAL COMMISSION
Australian Bight
Feb. 13th 1913

My dear Eva,

The Bight, despite its reputation, has been very kind to us so far, and I can write quite in peace this evening to tell you of our doings at Fremantle.[50]

We had been telegraphing there in the usual way for a day or so beforehand, but it wasn't till we got into the harbour that we found there was a 'beanfeast' already going on which quite overshadowed us. (Observe how my head is beginning to swell already!) The fact was that Wednesday Feb. 12th had been fixed for the cutting of the first sod of the West Australian end of the Transcontinental Railway (the other end is at Port Augusta in South Australia), and a lot of Federal legislators with the Prime Minister at the head of them had come over from Melbourne to take part in the ceremony.[51] They arrived at Fremantle by the Orient Boat which got in just ahead of us.

---

49. Harding, of course, means from east to west.
50. The Great Australian Bight, a notoriously rough stretch of water, extends from Albany in Western Australia to Adelaide in South Australia. The Commission was about to begin a short preparatory visit to Australia: the collection of Australian evidence was properly to begin on their return visit late in March.
51. Melbourne was the seat of the Federal government in 1913. From 1 January 1901, the separate British colonies had combined in a federation to form the Commonwealth of Australia. The constitution established an Executive Council and a Legislative Assembly made up of a Senate and a House of Representatives. A Governor-General representing the Crown was Head of State. The total population of Australia was 4,872,059 in 1913, plus an estimated maximum of 100,000 surviving aborigines. Considerable powers were retained by each State government, which had its own ministers, Parliament and Governor. Western Australia was the largest but least

However, we had quite enough ceremony as it was – the usual A.D.C. to the Governor, the President of the Chamber of Commerce, and the Acting Premier of Western Australia (with another Minister or so). Add to these the reporter for whom fortunately we prepared in advance. We gave him the little account of the Commission which you read perhaps in the *Daily News* which I sent you (by the way – will you please keep that and any others I may send home as I may like them later) and also little biographies of the members culled from *Who's Who* or else supplied by the members whose names were not there already.

They (by whom I mean the West Australian Government) certainly did us very well in spite of their preoccupation, for they provided 5 or 6 motor cars to take the party up to Perth (which is about 12 miles from Fremantle), the capital. The Governor had organized a lunch in honour of the Federal Visitors, and he swept in the Commission as well.[52]

I succeeded in getting off all the rest of the party first, and then had time to deal with our letters and telegrams of which there were a lot. (The proposed arrangements for our two days at Melbourne are positively horrifying – but I won't anticipate them now.) The result was that Bass, Bridgman and I (the other two had stayed to help me out) had a motor car all to ourselves. We had a very jolly Scotch chauffeur who had been out just two years from Glasgow, was very pleased with the country and hadn't the slightest intention of returning. From him we learned a good deal.

First impressions are always mixed, but on the whole mine of Australia more than fulfilled expectations. Fremantle itself is just an English-looking port. The railway runs down to the wharf, and behind

---

populated of the Australian states. It started as a military and convict settlement in 1826, partly to pre-empt the French, but free settlement began in 1829. Development was slow, and dependent from 1850 to 1868 upon imported convict labour, until the discovery of the Coolgardie and Kalgoorlie goldfields in the 1890s and the expansion of pastoralism and arable farming. The colony was granted responsible government in 1890, and by 1913 the population had reached 320,684. The construction of the Transcontinental Railway had been a precondition for Western Australia agreeing to join the federation, but construction did not begin until 1912 and the line was not finished until October 1917.

52. The Governor of Western Australia was Sir Harry Barron (1847–1920). After retiring in 1907 from a career in the Royal Artillery, he was appointed Governor of Tasmania in 1907 and moved to Western Australia in 1913, where in spite of his lack of political experience he navigated some tricky constitutional issues.

Fremantle Harbour, Western Australia, Wheat Exports.

Photograph dated 1910

the station, rather difficult to get at, is the town. Thus.

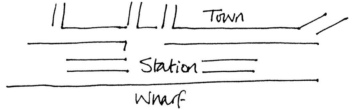

And the town itself is new and rather shoddy-looking.[53] Also the road to Perth, at any rate the first part of it, was very bumpy and stony.

But, in spite of these drawbacks, I was very much taken with the country. White Australia is very apparent from the outset. Most of the

---

53. Fremantle, at the mouth of the Swan River, was established in 1829, and named after Captain Charles Fremantle, the commander of the first expedition of free settlers. The opening of its improved harbour in 1897 allowed it to become Western Australia's principal port. By 1911 it had a population of 14,499.

Perth, Western Australia, from King's Park.   *Photograph dated 1909*

way from Fremantle to Perth has a sprinkling of houses, and there were the children coming out of school, and playing about on their way home, just as it might be in England.

There was something invigorating in the air, in spite of the heat and glare (for it was well over 90° in the shade), and particularly as one got near Perth and away from the sandbelt near the coast the country got quite pretty and there were glimpses of hills (the Darling range, I suppose) beyond. The authorities have laid out a most beautiful park the last 2 miles or so of the way from Fremantle. We drove right through the park and stopped at the top of the hill above the city to get a good look at it. Perth lies, like Truro, at the head of an estuary, which broadens out as it gets higher up. And the city comes down almost to the water's edge. It looked an ideal place for sailing.[54]

We drove to the Bank, where I got some money, and then on to Government House (at least I did – the other two weren't going). And there I made my first acquaintance with the Australian Labour Party. To our ideas they don't look like legislators, anyhow in outward appearance (most of the Labour Government which now runs West Australia consists, I believe, of ex-Cornish miners) but I, at least, found them

---

54. Perth, further up the Swan River, was first settled in 1829 and became the state capital. In 1913 the population of Perth's metropolitan area reached 121,700. The 1000 acres of King's Park crowned the summit of Mount Eliza. Truro is in Cornwall, England.

Perth, Hay Street.   *Photograph c.1910*

most interesting when I came to talk to them.[55] I found myself, at lunch,
as a matter of fact, next to a member of the opposition in the Federal
House of Representatives.[56] He had a large estate somewhere up in
Victoria with sheep by the thousand, and was obviously a Protectionist
by policy not conviction.[57] Next to him was the West Australian
Minister of Mines and Railways and, across, the Lieutenant-Governor
of Western Australia, one Sir Edward Stone.[58] So, it wasn't wholly a
'Labour' atmosphere.

I won't go into details as to the lunch except to say that there were no
speeches, and that everything was over by about 2.45. After that the
whole party walked (if they felt equal to it) in Government House
garden, and anyhow talked on the verandah. I escaped to send off
telegrams and to have a talk with someone from the Government
Statistician's Office who wanted to see me.

We left Perth about 4.30 and came back to Fremantle by a steam
launch. That was most delightful. The estuary winds about in all
directions and there are woods coming down to the banks very often.

We were landed at the wharf, got back to the *Medina* and sailed at 7
p.m. One line more – to show something of Australian manners. We have

had to take on to Adelaide some 60 tons of cargo intended for Fremantle. The dockers there knocked off at 6 p.m. and wouldn't come back till 9 on any consideration and it wasn't worthwhile keeping the ship till then.

Feb. 16th 1913
Between Adelaide and Melbourne

I have been very busy all day preparing to get off the boat, and I doubt if I have much time for writing in Melbourne, so I will finish up this letter this evening, and hope for another chance when we have left for New Zealand.

Nothing particular happened between Fremantle and Adelaide except a violent scare that there was a case of smallpox on board. The rumour went round like wildfire, of course, and as the Australian law still provides for strict quarantine, all the passengers would have been detained at a quarantine station for a fortnight at least if the case had been really smallpox.

Wouldn't New Zealand (or rather the authorities concerned) have been put out? – and I can picture the Commissioners speechless with rage.

Fortunately it turned out to be a measles case, so we breathe again. But I thought with melancholy over the difference between a Dominion and a Colony governed from Downing St. In the West Indies we abolished 'strict quarantine' years ago.

---

55. The Australian Labor Party developed out of trade unionism. Its first representatives were elected in 1891, in New South Wales, and it formed its first (brief) government in 1899, in Queensland, the first Labor government in the world. Labor held power in Western Australia from October 1911 to July 1916.

56. Labor was also in power in the Federal government. It had formed its first brief Federal administration in 1904 and a second in 1908–9. It governed more securely, with Andrew Fisher (1862–1928) as Prime Minister, from April 1910 to June 1913 and again from September 1914, first under Fisher and then under William Morris Hughes (1864–1952), until the party split in 1916 over military conscription. Labor's emergence fused the other parties into an opposition coalition which eventually called itself the Liberal Party.

57. Liberals in Australasia showed none of the dogmatic loyalty to the principles of Free Trade which characterised the British Liberal Party: protection against foreign, even British, imports was regarded as a means of assisting national economic expansion as well as of raising government revenue.

58. Sir Edward Stone (1844–1920) had been Chief Justice for Western Australia from 1901 before becoming Lieutenant-Governor in 1906.

Adelaide lies about half way up a big gulf – as you come up it there is a long ridge of hills on the right. Adelaide itself lies just under the hills about seven miles from the sea.[59] The intervening miles are low lying – alluvial very likely. Then comes Port Adelaide and after that the 'Outer Harbour', where there is a wharf at which the ships lie. I will draw another small picture at the side to explain matters. We got alongside about 10 a.m. on Saturday morning, got some more letters (one saying that our berths on the New Zealand steamer were all right) and then had to face more reporters. Fortunately Rider Haggard is used to them, and, though he would disclaim it, obviously rather likes them. And Sir Edgar Vincent also submitted. So I wasn't much bothered.

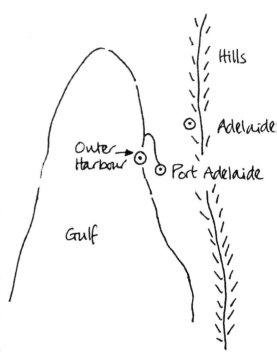

The Government were as kind as the West Australian one (there is a Liberal Government, by the way, not a Labour one, in power in South Australia, and incidentally the Liberal victory there a year ago, gave the Commission its Australian member – for Mr. Campbell, who was a member of the Labour party, lost his seat).

They gave us the Government car to take us from the harbour to Adelaide, entertained us at lunch at one of the hotels, and afterwards took such members of the party as would go for a motor drive round the hills behind the city – i.e. the hills I have tried to show in my sketch map.

59. Adelaide, at the head of the Gulf of St Vincent, was first settled in 1836 and named after the wife of King William IV. By 1913 the metropolitan area contained a population of 201,000. It was the capital of South Australia, the only Australian state not to have been a penal settlement. The territory was first entered by Europeans in 1802, it became a chartered colony following an Act of 1834 and a crown colony in 1842. It obtained responsible government in 1856. Wheat-growing and mineral-mining stimulated its development. The population of the state in 1913 was 440,047.

Really, Adelaide and its surroundings are most beautiful. The city is well laid out and well built. It has good public buildings, wide streets and delightful public gardens. And all the way round the city proper, about half a mile broad, is a belt of parkland, which is never to be built over, cutting off the inside part from the suburbs.[60] Not that the suburbs are at all inclined to be 'slummy' – and just as in West Australia the children were a great feature and all looked the picture of health.

But the most astonishing part came when we left city, suburbs and plain, and began to climb the hills. They run to 2000 ft, or a little more, and are either bare – like the South Downs – or rather higher up covered with various trees. Gum trees, *the* great Australian tree, are most in evidence, but there were also orchards, vineyards, and at the top, pine trees. The whole countryside in fact was quite like Surrey, or perhaps rather Mortain, on a larger scale.[61]

And when we got to the top (our destination was the house of one Sir Landon Berny Thom who was giving us tea) I really thought I was home again.[62] The house had a view for 50 miles or so over Adelaide and the sea (and other ways too, I believe, only it was misty and we couldn't see much) and just below it were terraces full of rhododendrons.

We had to have a hasty tea, and scuttle down to Adelaide at a pace well over the limit, for fear of losing the train. But certainly it was a most delightful afternoon.

---

60. Adelaide's attractiveness owed much to Colonel William Light (1786–1839), the Surveyor-General for South Australia from 1836 until his death: he chose the site, and his city plan guided most subsequent development. The 1900 acres of surrounding parkland were described in 1914 as 'the lungs of the city'. Its most impressive buildings at that time were Government House (1838), the cathedral (1878), the public library (1884) and Parliament House, with its imposing marble columns, whose construction began in 1883.
61. The South Downs are in Sussex, about 70 kilometres from the Harding home in Surrey. Mortain is in Normandy, France.
62. One of the occasions when Harding's ear for proper names fails him. Sir John Langdon Bonython (1848–1939) – the name was originally Cornish – had been born in London, son of a builder, but with his family he emigrated to South Australia in 1854, where he eventually grew rich through successful speculations in mining shares. He then became editor and owner for 45 years of the Adelaide *Advertiser*, a member of the House of Representatives 1901–6, a defender of the interests of the small business and landholding middle class, a supporter of Liberal progressive policies, and a major public benefactor, particularly in the area of education.

Our particular cicerone was a certain Colonel Weir, who commanded one of the Adelaide regiments, a most enthusiastic Australian, full of all kinds of information.[63]

We had also a chauffeur addressed as 'Charlie', said to be equally at home with camels, four in hands, and motor cars.[64] Certainly he was very much at home with the latter.

We returned to the *Medina* to find on board a man specially entrusted by the New South Wales Government to come down to Adelaide and travel to Melbourne in order to discuss with the Commission their tour in New South Wales – so you can imagine that what with him and packing to do, I have had a pretty busy day. However, we have succeeded in collaborating a tour which sounds promising if rather excessive – and I am very glad he came, as it will ease matters a lot presently.

I shall be very sorry to leave the *Medina*. Certainly we have been extraordinarily favoured by the weather. We haven't had one day which has really been *very* rough. But still, in spite of her tendency to roll on small provocation, she is very comfortable and all the people have been particularly kind. I don't think there is much to add about the passengers, except that I find that the Gibbs – the people who were at Minnickfold – are going on to New Zealand which will be pleasant.

> Ever your affectionate brother
> E. J. Harding

---

63. Over 16,000 Australian troops came to the aid of the Imperial mother country in the Boer War in South Africa 1899–1902: greater demands were made in the Great War which lay just ahead. Colonel (later Brigadier-General) Stanley Weir (1866–1944) was commissioned in 1890, became a colonel in 1913 and commanded a battalion at Gallipoli in 1915.
64. Camels were used in the Australian interior from the 1860s to the 1920s for exploration and the transport of goods: their drivers, usually from north-west India, were colloquially called Afghans or Ghans.
65. There is probably a letter missing before this one, covering a short visit to Melbourne and the sea crossing to Tasmania, Monday 17 February to Thursday 20 February 1913. Just before sailing, Vincent had written: 'The immediate prospect ... fills me with gloom. Something like an Atlantic voyage on a Channel Steamer and an old one at that'.
66. The Union Steam Ship Company had been founded in Dunedin, New Zealand, in 1875 and developed services first to Australia and then to the Pacific Islands, India, Canada and, from 1910, to San Francisco. In 1913 the company operated a weekly service each way from Melbourne via Hobart to New Zealand. *Warrimoo*, 3350 tons, 360 feet by 42 feet, was built by Swan Hunter on the Tyne and launched in 1892, originally for the

Dominions Royal Commission
S.S Warrimoo
South Pacific Ocean
Feb. 23rd 1913

My dear Eva,

I hope to post this tomorrow, when we get off this boat – and very thankful we shall be to be off her.[65] Fortunately, so far, we have had an extraordinarily good passage from Hobart (it is said to be one of the worst seas in the world) – no wind to speak of and only a heavy swell. But it is bitterly cold, so that for the first time since Port Said I have got out thick clothes, and almost wish I had thicker, and also everyone is thoroughly sick of the *Warrimoo*. Quite apart from the 'company' which I mentioned in my last letter, she is dirty, stuffy and uncomfortable. There is nowhere really attractive to sit in, and very little space to walk in. The Agent of the Union Company at Hobart, who came on board obviously to receive compliments, must have been surprised at his reception. He went away depressed, and, I hope, wiser.[66]

We have petroleum forward, and calcide of carbium (I think) just over my cabin.[67] The Commissioners unanimously suggest burning the ship in the cause of humanity! This is but a poor ending to a good voyage.

It is pleasanter to go back to Hobart where (on Friday) we had really a jolly day.[68] There were no particular formalities, but the Chief Secretary (one Dr. Butler)[69] came down in the morning with two motor

---

Canadian–Australian Line's trans-Tasman trade: the company, the route and the ship were taken over by the Union Company in 1901.

67. Probably calcium carbide, used for lighting and acetylene equipment: like most men from his social and educational background, Harding's knowledge of science and technology was limited.

68. Abel Tasman (c.1603–59) called the place he sighted in 1642 Van Dieman's Land. It was annexed by New South Wales and used by the British as a dumping ground for convicts from 1803 until 1853, when the practice ceased and the name was changed to Tasmania in an effort to remove the 'stain' of its reputation. It became a separate colony in 1825 and obtained responsible government in 1856. Mineral-mining, forestry and apple-growing eventually created a modest prosperity. In 1913 the population of the state was 201,675. Hobart, the capital, was named after Robert Hobart (1760–1816), Secretary of State at the time of its first settlement in 1804. It had developed from a prison to a metropolitan district of 40,000 people by 1913. Along the way, all the aborigines had disappeared.

69. Dr Gamaliel Henry Butler (1854–1914) combined a medical and a political career: he became a member of Tasmania's Legislative Council in 1896 and served as Chief Secretary in Tasmania's Liberal governments 1909–14.

Hobart, Tasmania, Part of the Wharves.   *Postcard*

cars, and took such of the party as were willing to go, half way up the mountain (Mount Wellington) which lies at the back of Hobart.

It is quite high, well over 4000 ft, and the road winds up through woods – mostly gum trees, and a good many of them just burnt stumps because of forest fires. Then, half way up, at a place called Springs there is a little wooden hotel, like a Swiss Mountain Hotel, from which you can look up to the top of Mount Wellington and down to Hobart and the sea.

We couldn't scale the mountain – it would have taken too long (I must hope for a chance when we come back). But we stayed 20 minutes or so to 'admire the view' and could see what a wonderful situation the town has. It lies about 12 miles or so up a very deep river with low hills on each side of it, so that there is a perfectly safe anchorage. And then behind it is this gorgeous mountain which must be snow covered in winter.

From the Hotel we could see right down to the river and all the inlets which stud the coast. If Glengarriff[70] were multiplied by ten, it would rather resemble the South Tasmanian Coast, so you can imagine from that how beautiful it is.

We drove back to Hobart, had a small 'circular tour' on the other side, and got back in time for lunch. After lunch the Premier[71] came to call on Sir Edgar Vincent. There is no 'divinity hedging' statesmen in this part of the world.[72] He just came up the gangway, spoke to me for a minute or two, and then sat down and talked to a group of Commissioners for half an hour or so (he was within earshot of the remarks to the Agent about this ship).

Nothing else happened except the visit of the usual reporters. It all seemed quite quiet after Melbourne, and was therefore much more enjoyable. As a matter of fact most of the members of the Government were away in the interior, opening irrigation works or something of that kind. I wish they could always be correspondingly removed.

So now we have had a glimpse of all the Australian states but two, and New Zealand is just beginning operations. We had a wireless message of welcome last night.

It crossed one from the Commission asking for a special train to take them from Bluff to Dunedin tomorrow, so that they could carry out their programme and start work on Tuesday. It remains to be seen what will be the result. (The reason for the train is that the boat is late and won't be in time for us to catch the ordinary train.)

I don't think there is anything more worth recording, save that the Gibbs (I mean the people who were at Minnickfold) have come on this boat, so that we aren't dependent on new acquaintances. As a matter of fact, I have hardly spoken to anyone 'new' on board except the Captain and Purser. Our chief amusement is the interchange of as cutting remarks as we can think of on the deficiencies of the *Warrimoo*, and a little bridge in the evening.

> Ever your affectionate brother
> E. J. Harding

I forgot to add, as a third recreation, watching the albatrosses of which there are heaps.

---

70. In Bantry Bay, Co. Cork, Ireland.
71. Albert Edward Solomon (1876–1914) was first elected as a Liberal in 1909 and held several posts in the Government of Tasmania before becoming Prime Minister in June 1912. His government had a majority of just one seat, and it is said that the strain of maintaining office with such a margin accounted for his death on 5 October 1914, aged 39.
72. 'There's such divinity doth hedge a king ...', William Shakespeare (1564–1616), *Hamlet*, IV, v, 123.

Bluff, Post Office and Railway Station, and (facing page) Wharf.   *Postcards*

DOMINIONS ROYAL COMMISSION
Grand Hotel
Dunedin
Feb. 26th 1913

My dear Father,

I foresee that I shall have very considerable difficulty in keeping up a long diary letter now that we are really arrived and hard at it: however, I expect you will want me to try – so I must try to put in odd moments. This one is 11.15 p.m., and I have been hard at work since 7.30 this evening so you mustn't expect much.[73]

We didn't after all get in to Bluff without a tossing. On Sunday night we had had a wireless message saying that they had arranged a special train but 'weather at present unsuitable for tug' – so we imagined that there was something in store. (I ought to explain that Bluff is a port into which you can't get except at a particular state of the tide, and we knew that, unless we got a tug, we should have to lie outside for several hours.)[74]

The imagination proved right; we woke on Monday (at least I did) to find my cabin trunk shooting from under the bunk, and all my papers pouring on to the floor, and the deck had a tilt of at least 15 degrees.

The actual sea didn't last very long as we got into the shelter of the land by 9 o'clock but the tilt continued till we got into port and even then. Something must have happened to the ballast tanks, I think. Anyhow it was another count against the *Warrimoo* which, as I think I said before, we were heartily glad to leave.

All the morning we were quite close in to the New Zealand coast, and very jolly it looked – high cliffs and hills, and an occasional snow mountain behind. Unfortunately we only had just the glimpse of the latter, as the country between Bluff and here and all round Dunedin is hilly but by no means mountainous.

We duly 'hung outside' Bluff for a couple of hours, and got in about 5 p.m. to find the special train waiting, and therewith Malcolm Ross – the man appointed by the New Zealand Government to do the local work of the Commission (to whom of course I had been writing from

---

73. The Commission was about to begin in New Zealand its formal gathering of overseas evidence. New Zealand became a British colony in 1840, following the signing of the Treaty of Waitangi by Maori chiefs and by Captain William Hobson (1793–1842), representing the Crown. The New Zealand Company and its derivatives organised much of the initial immigration and the establishment of settlements in North and South Islands. Responsible government was secured in 1856. The constitution originally left each of the provinces with considerable local powers, but a unitary state was created in 1876, with a House of Representatives, a Legislative Council and a Governor representing the Crown. The Maori population of New Zealand fell severely until the late 19th century but then began slowly to recover: according to the 1911 census there were 52,723 Maori, mainly in the North Island, and 1,005,585 Europeans.
74. Bluff was first settled by Europeans as a whaling station about 1836. It developed as a port particularly for immigrants and to service Invercargill and Southland. Its population in 1911 was 1780.

England) – and also one Hislop, Under Secretary for Internal Affairs in New Zealand (a sort of 'Permanent Under Secretary of State' no doubt). He used to be Private Secretary to Sir Joseph Ward and was in England for the conferences of 1907 and 1911.[75] We had the warmest of welcomes from both – and, better still for the moment, found that they had brought along a sort of 'Office Keeper' to look after our luggage. This meant that all our baggage got shifted very quickly into the train, and we were off by 5.30. The first thing, of course, was the inevitable President and Secretary of the local Chamber of Commerce – by local I mean Invercargill, which is a biggish town in the south of N.Z. of which Bluff is the port.[76] But they didn't worry much, and we had a comfortable dinner in the train and were in to Dunedin at 11 p.m.

Unfortunately it got dark so soon that we couldn't see much of the country, but what we could see was very pleasant English-looking country. The only obvious differences are that the houses here generally have corrugated iron roofs, that the railways are unfenced at the road crossings, and that *phormium tenax* grows wild wherever there is water. Probably you will have forgotten what *phormium* is so I had better explain that it is the hemp we have been trying with indifferent success to grow commercially in St. Helena.[77] Hence its interest for me. I must certainly stop at this point and go to bed – leaving our Dunedin experiences as a further instalment.

---

75. Malcolm Ross (1862–1930), the Commission's New Zealand agent, was well-known as a journalist and confidant of politicians: he was also a mountaineer, pioneer explorer of New Zealand and founder of the New Zealand Alpine Club. James Hislop (1870–1932) joined the civil service in 1885 and served as under-secretary at the Department of Internal Affairs 1912–28. Sir Joseph Ward (1856–1930), a former mayor of Bluff, was Prime Minister 1906–12 and 1928–30.

76. The land upon which Invercargill was founded was purchased from the local Maori in 1853, and the town was named after Captain William Cargill (1784–1860), co-founder of the settlement at Dunedin and Superintendent of the province of Otago. Its prosperity relied upon pasture farming, it became the capital of a new province of Southland founded in 1861, and it boasted a population in 1911 of 15,858.

77. St Helena, most famous as Napoleon's final place of exile, lies 1800 kilometres from the coast of Africa in the South Atlantic. Discovered by the Portuguese and then occupied by the Dutch, the island fell under the control of the English East India Company before becoming a formal crown colony in 1834. The development there of flax-growing, with the encouragement of the Colonial Office, was intended to increase empire production of a valuable commodity and also to offset some of the administrative costs of crown colony administration.

Dunedin, Town Hall and Octagon.   *Postcard*

Christ Church
Sunday, March 2nd

My surmise at the beginning of this letter has proved too true. I haven't had a minute till this evening to go on with this letter, and here are we at Christ Church, and in fact half way through our time here. However, I must go back to Dunedin.[78] Tuesday, Wednesday and Thursday were mostly spent in taking evidence there, and I hadn't very much time to look about. As the evidence won't interest you, and anyhow will be published later, I suppose, I won't go in to that, and will only say that the actual sittings were at the City Corporation Chamber in the Town Hall (quite a good building)[79] and were as dull as sittings

---

78. Dunedin is the old Gaelic name for Edinburgh. The first organised British settlers were mainly Free Church Presbyterian Scots, brought in by the Otago Association in 1848. The town grew rapidly after the discovery of gold in the province in the 1860s and the developing use of the adjacent Port Chalmers. By 1911 the population of Dunedin was 64,237.
79. The town hall was designed by the Scottish-born Robert Arthur Lawson (1833–1902) and built 1878–80. Lawson settled in Dunedin in 1862 and was responsible for many other public buildings, churches and private houses, particularly in Otago.

generally are. The most exciting witness was one William Belcher, Secretary of the Seamen's Union, who talked about shipping questions. He was a 'navvy' person with an obvious predilection for the bottle and was so interested in the Commission that he came to see us off at the station. There he made an apparent effort to steal my despatch box containing the cash box. At least I found him conveying it up to the carriage door. But perhaps it was only kindness.[80]

Probably a little about Dunedin itself and our 'private' doings there will interest you more. I shall have to start again with a little map to show you how it lies (next page for this). It lies at the neck of a promontory which runs parallel with the main coast line. The hills come down to within half a mile or so of the water, and the town is built on the intervening space and up the hills. Dunedin isn't so very big, but it is well laid out, and from the hills it looks rather a fine city. There is really no difference 'internally' between it and an English provincial city except that the buildings are newer.

The Grand Hotel, where we stayed, was intensely Mid-Victorian – stuffy smell in the dining room, flues under the beds, chandeliers and all the rest of it.

Now for our private doings. On Tuesday afternoon, after the sitting was over, I was taken for a walk round the town by one of the witnesses – the Secretary of the 'Dunedin Expansion League' (which exists to attract immigrants to it and the surrounding districts).[81] On Tuesday evening we all went to a big dinner party at the Dunedin Club given by Mr. Sinclair, the New Zealand member of the Commission. I found myself next to a certain Mr. Joachim, a director of a big coal company,[82] whom, about half way through dinner, I discovered to be immensely interested in pictures. So having talked coal for the first part of dinner,

---

80. William Belcher (d.1926) had become Secretary of the New Zealand branch of the Australian Federated Seamen's Union in 1908. The Commissioners questioned 18 witnesses in total during their three days of formal sittings in Dunedin, February 25–27.

81. Otago was losing to places in North Island its former pre-eminence as the most prosperous and populous region of New Zealand, and it was anxious to attract more immigrants and investment.

82. George Joachim (1842–1920), Managing Director of the Westport Coal Company from 1877 to 1920, later gave evidence to the Commission. The West Coast of South Island was New Zealand's most important coal-mining district, responsible in 1910 for 60% of national production, and Westport, a borough established in 1873, was a major centre.

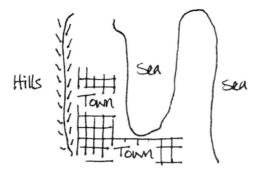

we devoted most of the rest to Pre-Raphaelite art! He (Joachim) was very keen on getting for New Zealand some of the spare Turner drawings in London. So I put him on to the Chairman who is a Trustee of the National Gallery.[83]

On Wednesday afternoon we had a half holiday and were taken out in motor cars (provided by the Chamber of Commerce) to the Taieri plain – a perfectly flat plain lying about 10 miles behind Dunedin and surrounded by hills. There we had tea with a quite delightful Scotch farmer called Blackie and an equally delightful wife. The land is, I imagine, very rich from a farmer's point of view. Anyhow, he seemed to do well out of it. We came back by way of a woollen factory in the same plain (one of the biggest in New Zealand), and walked through it, so that any of the Commissioners versed in such subjects might compare its conditions with English ones.[84] I, having no knowledge of the kind, was

---

83. Joachim became president of the Otago Art Society and a trustee of the Dunedin Public Art Gallery. His wife, Susanna White Wimperis (c.1843–1915), her two sisters Fanny (1840–1925) and Jenny (1838–1927) and her brother Edmund (1835–1900) were all talented watercolour painters whose New Zealand work is represented in the Hocken Library in Dunedin. J. M. W. Turner (1775–1851) left over 20,000 watercolours and 300 paintings to the nation on his death. Most are now in the Tate Gallery in London; the records in London and in Dunedin show that nothing came of this proposal to transfer part of the bequest to New Zealand. Frances Hodgkins (1870–1947), perhaps New Zealand's most distinguished artist, was born and spent her early life in Dunedin.
84. Haggard's diary confirms that this was the Mosgiel Woollen Mill, the first in the country, established in 1871 by Arthur Burns (1830–1901), a grand-nephew of the poet Robert Burns. The expansion of manufacturing in New Zealand and its protection with customs tariffs were controversial proposals at this time, with implications for industrial exports from Great Britain.

mainly concerned with the noise which was terrific, and the fact that all the hands, mostly women and girls, looked thoroughly well and thriving. Of course, all their hours are regulated by law (the Government regulates most things here) but, apart from that, the conditions all round are very good, lots of fresh air, and plenty of room.[85] The inspection ended with the usual speeches and 'tribute' in the shape of a rug made in the factory, which was presented to Mrs. Tatlow.

Thursday was mainly evidence and packing, but in the evening I went out to dinner, again at the Club, with a Round Table group. The Round Table is an institution in London which runs a quarterly (a very interesting one too) and exists to foster Imperialism (or however else you like to term the same thing). The Editor of the quarterly, whom I had been introduced to in London by Malcolm, had given me a letter of introduction to his various correspondents in New Zealand, and I daresay I shall see a good many of them as they are inclined to be very friendly.[86] Anyhow, the people at this particular dinner were, and I had a very interesting evening. The most enlightening was, I think, Holdsworth, the General Manager of The Union Steamship Company.[87] (He, by the way, had suffered much at the hands of several of the Commissioners on account of their experiences in the *Warrimoo* which belongs to the said Company!)

Friday began by my seeing the Whitworths – Mr., Mrs. and Miss – who, as I expect you will remember, are the relations of the Andersons. He is Traffic Superintendent for the whole of the South Island of New Zealand – which, I imagine, must be rather an important post, anyhow much more important than that of carpenter on an estate. Mrs. is quite like Mrs. Anderson (I should almost have recognized her from the likeness). Miss is an ordinary Colonial girl – or perhaps rather out of the ordinary since she seemed rather shy, which I imagine most of these girls are not. Anyhow, she had a certain air of primness about her which,

---

85. The first Factory Acts in New Zealand date from the 1870s. Comprehensive codes followed the creation of the innovative Department of Labour in 1892, especially under the energetic direction of its first Secretary, Edgar Tregear (1846–1931), and its first Minister, William Pember Reeves (1857–1932).

86. The movement and its journal were founded in 1910 by enthusiasts seeking closer imperial unity and greater co-operation. The editor of *The Round Table* from 1910 to 1916 was Philip Kerr, later Lord Lothian (1882–1940).

87. Charles Holdsworth (1863–1935) was a director of the company until his death: he was knighted in 1926.

I don't know why, reminded me rather of Miss Furnival. I took a photograph of the family in one of the Dunedin gardens – thinking that the Andersons would be pleased if it turned out well.

Which reminds me that the fame of the Coldharbour Choral has reached even to these parts. The Whitcombs, I found, knew all about Eva and the famous quartet banner.

The rest of Friday was spent in the train coming up from Dunedin to Christ Church. We left at 11.15 a.m. and got in just after 7 p.m. – and it is about 230 miles. So you will realize that travelling is not too fast here. Still, it is only a single line railway and also a rather narrow gauge.[88] I was working most of the day, and didn't look out very much, but the country was decidedly interesting. The first part hilly, till about 60 miles or so north of Dunedin. All the rest the Canterbury plains, where most of the frozen meat comes from.[89] They are perfectly flat, but cut in various parts by the rivers coming down from the Alps on the western side of the island. The rivers are rather depressing, at any rate this time of year, as the water is low, and the beds, which are very wide, are full of stones. Of course, the rivers coming down from the Swiss Alps are just the same.

Two incidents broke the monotony of the journey – first, more tribute in the shape of a 14 lb river trout which someone put on board,[90] and secondly an almost if not quite unprecedented thing in the shape of a sitting of the Commission on board the train.

The President of the Harbour Board at one of the ports we passed – Timaru, a great shipping place of frozen mutton – boarded the train, and explained to such members as could hear him for the noise the

---

88. New Zealand railways were short and local before Sir Julius Vogel (1835–99), the Colonial Treasurer and subsequently Prime Minister, initiated in 1870 a massive national programme of loan-financed public works (and immigration). By 1879 more than 1600 kilometres of new track had been laid, including the 620-kilometre stretch from Bluff to Christchurch, to a 3 ft. 6 in. gauge. (The standard gauge in Great Britain was 4 ft. 8½ in.)
89. The first shipment of 130 tons of frozen meat from New Zealand to Great Britain left Port Chalmers on 15 February 1882. The voyage took 98 days. The meat arrived in good condition and was sold at a profit for 6½d (2½p) per lb.
90. British settlers found New Zealand's indigenous fish unsuitable for sport: brown trout were imported from 'home' and were first released successfully near Dunedin in 1869. Acclimatisation societies, formed largely in the 1860s and 1870s, introduced many species of European flora and fauna into New Zealand, with often devastating effect upon indigenous stock.

potentialities of the harbour.[91] The more 'precedent-bound' of the Commissioners – particularly Bateman – viewed the proceedings with grave suspicion, and sat in a corner listening under protest. But it strikes me as an admirable idea.

I will leave over Christ Church till the next letter, and end with an impression or two more. The first that, even after a week in New Zealand, one feels distinctly in a home atmosphere. The people are all British, the customs are practically identical, and the institutions – down to the Public Library and the Bar Parlour of a Public House – are on exactly similar lines.

What does strike one, of course, especially in travelling, is the extreme emptiness of the country. I am not sure whether, if it weren't for the village churches and the hedges, one mightn't say the same of most English countrysides. But anyhow, the want of people is very apparent between the towns where the express stops.

The second impression is the general prosperity of the people, and the third the, to me, extremely attractive democratic feeling. Class distinctions seem practically non-existent. That, at any rate, is the idea I have at present.

> Ever your affectionate son
> E. J. Harding

> DOMINIONS ROYAL COMMISSION
> Wellington Club
> Wellington
> Saturday, March 8th 1913

My dear Eva,

My last letter went off last Sunday and from then till now I really haven't had a minute to begin another letter. The fact is that practically the whole time the Commission is sitting, I am either writing letters, or talking to prospective witnesses, or arranging interviews for single Commissioners with various people. Consequently the whole of the

---

91. Timaru, 200 kilometres north of Dunedin, was first established as a whaling station in 1837, was resettled in 1852 and had become a town of 11,280 people by 1911. Construction of an artificial port on the exposed coastline was difficult. The first stage began in 1878, but the extension which made the harbour safe in all weathers was not completed until 1906: hence the desire of the Harbour Board to impress their success upon the Commissioners.

particular work I have – that of seeing that the evidence is properly collected for publication has to be left till the evening, and that can't always be done because one has to go out to dinner. Anyhow, I find my usual hours are bed at midnight and up soon after 7, so you may imagine life is not too easy.

Moreover, difficulties develop as the work proceeds which are amusing to think of afterwards but are somewhat trying at the time. The first is that it is almost impossible to get the Commissioners to make up their minds to do anything. They will not say whether they will or will not go to some particular factory, or accept some particular invitation, and they have to be 'coaxed' in the best way available. Fortunately for me, most of that particular work falls on Ross, the New Zealand man who has been put onto the work – so I escape a good deal. But I feel it somewhat. However, the idiosyncracies of the various members afford good scope for amusement, and on the whole we get on pretty well. And I daresay one gets used to it.

The other main difficulty is old Lorimer. He is cruelly deaf, and even with the aid of his acoustikon (the batteries of which have hitherto consistently failed to work!) hardly ever hears what a witness is saying.[92] Consequently he repeats other members' questions to their extreme boredom, and we have to try to devise means of getting him work by himself. Fortunately he is very keen and really most effective at getting to the bottom of things, and quite willing to talk for hours to any expert he can get hold of on the subjects which interest him – mainly minerals.[93]

So we have now started a system of getting 'tame experts' to talk to him alone – a process which the Chairman describes as 'locking up the elder with an expert' (Lorimer is an elder of the Presbyterian Church) – and that bids fair to work well. But it landed us, at the start, with quite another problem. I put on Bridgman, the shorthand clerk, to take a shorthand note of the proceedings but, after a shot or two, he has struck, complaining that a conversation between Lorimer, with a pipe in his mouth and surrounded by maps and papers, and an expert whom he can hear most imperfectly

---

92. Electrical hearing aids began to replace the ear trumpet from the early 20th century. Alexander Graham Bell (1847–1922), a teacher of deaf-mutes as well as an inventor, devised an aid on the principles of his telephone, combining a carbon microphone, a battery and a magnetic earphone. This system was widely adopted until displaced by valve amplifiers around 1935.
93. Partly due to Lorimer's efforts, the D.R.C. in its *Final Report* reviewed at length the mineral resources of the Empire and recommended methods to increase production.

is no fit subject for the best of transcribers – which he doesn't profess to be. I am, therefore, reduced to suggesting to Lorimer that he should have his conversation and afterwards dictate a note of the results, which he has accepted. I can't help thinking, though, that I must have wounded his feelings pretty badly in the course of these processes.

The other Commissioners view the proceedings with much amusement! This is rather a lengthy preliminary, but no account of this 'peregrination' would be anywhere near complete without a reference to our troubles. I haven't got to the stage, anyhow, where they are big enough to spoil the interest of the proceedings.

Sunday, March 9th

So I will go back to where I left off last time – that is, I think, to the day on which we arrived at Christ Church.

Christ Church is a great contrast to Dunedin.[94] It lies on a perfectly flat plain – the Canterbury plain indeed, where all the lambs come from: historically it is an English settlement as compared with Dunedin which is Scotch: and it has a semi old-world appearance, with a beautiful river winding through the city, a park, and a cathedral (not a good one though) in the central square.[95] The hotel where we stayed – Warner's – was an improvement on the Dunedin one. But it was inclined to be noisy, as the trams were just outside, and it suffered from what all the hotels (and houses too for that matter) suffer in this country – that is stuffiness. They never seem to open any windows if they can help it.

There was rather a good place for the sittings in Christ Church – the old Provincial Council Chamber, which must be at least 40 years old, antique for this country.[96] But there was nothing of particular interest in

94. Christchurch was founded in 1850 as a Church of England settlement by the Canterbury Association. It was named after the Oxford University college of its first leader, John Robert Godley (1814–61). Sheep farming on the Canterbury plains secured its future, and by 1911 it contained 75,353 people.
95. The building of the cathedral, to an English Gothic design of Sir George Gilbert Scott (1811–78), began in 1864, but the nave was not ready for use until 1881 and the transept and chancel were consecrated only in 1904.
96. Built in timber and stone in Gothic style between 1859 and 1865: this was the seat of the Canterbury provincial government until the abolition of the provinces. It was designed by Benjamin Mountfort (1824–98), who trained in England under Sir Gilbert Scott, emigrated to Christchurch in 1850 and became the province's principal architect. Here the Commission questioned 14 witnesses on Saturday, Monday and Tuesday, March 1, 3 and 4.

Christchurch,   *Postcard, issued by the New Zealand High Commission*
Cathedral Square.   *Emigration Department, received 13 October 1914*

the sittings at Christ Church, so I won't stay over them, and will go on
as I did in writing about Dunedin to 'private and personal' doings.

Our first day there (Saturday) was pretty slack. There was 'evidence' in
the morning, and I had to work for most of the afternoon. But after an
early tea Bridgman and I put ourselves on a tram car and were conveyed
to New Brighton, a little seaside place about 5 miles away. If New
Zealand had 5 million inhabitants instead of one, as it certainly should
and no doubt will, New Brighton would become a great seaside watering
place.[97] It has as fine a stretch of perfectly hard sand as I have ever seen,
and you can gaze away to mountains on both sides – the big New Zealand
chain on the left and the Lyttelton Peninsula on the right. We had some
beautiful views of both, and a most glorious sunset to set them off.

We came back by another tram, which went by way of the race course
(where they have a 'totalisator' instead of the usual 'bookie' enclosure –
a paternal Government allows the former and takes a share of the

---

97. New Brighton was developed in emulation of Brighton back 'home' in
    Sussex. An entertainments pier 210 m. long was opened in 1894 (and
    survived until 1965). In June 1991 New Zealand's population was reported
    to be 3,427,796.

proceeds)[98] and a small farm, where there were wild nasturtiums. I had a talk with the mistress of the said farm, who came from Derbyshire, but had been out here 50 years. The farms, by the way, are rather misleading to the uninitiated. You think at first they are 'shanties' as they have the usual corrugated iron roofs and look rather dilapidated. Then one remembers that most of the town houses are just the same, so that they aren't much below the standard.

Sunday brought a rest by way of a change. I went to the cathedral in the morning (the music was good and the preacher bad) and in the afternoon had quite a long walk up into the hills in the Lyttelton Peninsula. The tram out of Christ Church takes you a good way up, but we had a walk of 3 or 4 miles further and got to a point where we could look right down into a beautiful inlet – called Governor's Bay and beyond it to Lyttelton, which is the port of Christ Church, and the open sea.[99] In Lyttelton harbour was lying the *Terra Nova* – the unfortunate Scott's ship. We thought we got a glimpse of her from the hills (and did certainly on the Tuesday evening when we left by steamer for Wellington). Everyone in New Zealand is, of course, intensely interested in the fate of the expedition, as Scott sailed for the Pole from Lyttelton, and lots of the people knew him.[100]

We got back at six, and in the evening I went out with Ross to supper with some people with whom his son was staying. He (Ross) is a man of over 50 (and looks about 35) and has a son aged 23. I can't remember the name of the people – not that it matters much – but it was interesting to see a New Zealand home. It wasn't anything much unlike the ordinary English house – but the most interesting part was the very obvious lack of servants. All the householders are crying out for servants and have to do with makeshifts of any kind they can get or, as happens in most cases, to do the work themselves. There is great scope for the

---

98. Harding was perhaps aware that controversial legislation in 1910 had recently excluded bookmakers from racecourses.

99. Permanent European settlement began in the bay in the 1840s. The port was named in 1858 after the chairman of the Canterbury Association, Lord Lyttelton (1817–76). In 1911 it had a population of 4058.

100. Captain Robert Falcon Scott (1868–1912) left Lyttelton for the Antarctic on 26 November 1910 and died on his return from the South Pole on 29 March 1912. The *Terra Nova* returned to Lyttelton on 11 February 1913. 'We landed to find the Empire ... in mourning', recorded Apsley Cherry-Gerard. A statue of Scott, sculpted by his widow, Kathleen Lady Kennett, was erected in Christchurch on the bank of the River Avon in 1917.

Commission there – if they can find means to solve the problem, without making it harder for the irate heads of households at home.[101]

Monday saw the rush of work begin again, but we got off fairly early in the evening and I explored the river in a boat with Ross and subsequently the Park and Museum.[102] In the Museum there are several specimens of the moa – the biggest bird in the world, now extinct. Perhaps it is as well – it must have been a somewhat terrifying animal.[103]

On Tuesday there was evidence again in the morning, and immediately it was over we were put into motor cars and shot off to the works of the Christ Church Meat Company. They lie about 7 miles outside Christ Church and are one of the largest meat freezing works in the whole country. The Company gave us a lunch (all of frozen lamb, turkey etc.) which was very good, and then the officials took us the round of the works, so that we could see the whole process from the slaughtering of the sheep to the emergence of the carcases and bye-products in the shape in which they are sent for sale. You may think it dull, and even horrible, to read about, but it was intensely interesting in fact. Practically every part of the sheep is used for something: everything is kept as clean and nice as can be, and outside (I suppose with the object of softening a somewhat brutalizing life by amenities) are flower beds.[104]

---

101. Witnesses in Christchurch as in Dunedin and later in Wellington explained their problem, and it was stressed by the Commission in its *Second Interim Report* on Australasia. In the *Final Report* the D.R.C. recommended that the dominions governments and the Women's Emigration Societies should increase their efforts to assist the migration of young women and their training for work as domestic servants. The difficulty of reconciling colonial with British needs was considerable: the employment of at least one (usually female) resident domestic servant virtually defined the British middle class.

102. Canterbury Museum was another design by Benjamin Mountfort, built in 1870. The basic collection was that of its first director, the Austrian geologist-explorer Sir Julius von Haast (1822–1887). The development of Hagley Park, containing the Botanic Gardens, began in 1859.

103. Also pretty stupid. One of New Zealand's famous flightless birds. The large species, standing up to three metres tall, were hunted to extinction by the Maori, probably by 1500. The smaller species may have survived until the early 19th century.

104. Haggard devotes several pages of his diary to a vivid account of the tour around the Islington Freezing Works, with its carcasses of 130,000 sheep, the 70 slaughtermen and their assistants disposing of 85 animals in an 8-hour day, the pitiful creatures standing 'dumb before their murderer', and the various processing departments, including that which produced each year enough sausage skins to stretch twice around the world.

Shipping Frozen Meat.

Postcard issued for the New Zealand
International Exhibition, 1907–08

Here I shall have to put down another 'impression' of New Zealand.
I had come out with the idea that their system of conciliation and
arbitration had settled strikes once and for all.[105] The truth is the exact
opposite. At the freezing works they had only settled a day or so before
a very serious strike amongst the slaughtermen, and on that very night
(on which we crossed from Lyttelton to Wellington) there was a threat
of a strike among the engineers of the Union Steamship Co. which
would have involved laying up the whole fleet, and as a result the
paralysis of most of the shipping trade of New Zealand.

Everyone who isn't 'labour' seems to be unanimous that the workers
have agreed to the arbitration system just as long as its awards have been

---

105. The Industrial Conciliaton and Arbitration Act of 1894 initiated a
distinctive system for dealing with industrial disputes. It initially earned
New Zealand an international reputation as a progressive society
supposedly free from the strikes endemic in other parts of the industrial
world. Harding may have been conscious of the subject because a record
number of working days were lost through strikes in Britain in 1910–13. In
fact, industrial relations in New Zealand were simultaneously going
through an unusually bitter period, including a nationwide strike of freezing
workers (affecting the export of meat) in 1912 and a virtual general strike
in 1913. 'Australasia', complained Haggard, '... is the land of strikes.'

S.S. Maori at Lyttelton.   *Postcard*

in their favour. As soon as the awards have gone a little in the other
direction, the men come out on strike.

I got a lot of information about the slaughtermen and their misdeeds
from one Campbell, the Secretary of the Meat Co., who sat next to me
at lunch. The slaughtermen, of course, had everything in their favour as
if they stop work all the other branches of the factory can't get their
materials and have to stop too. But, in this particular case, the Company
had managed to get in outside labour, and had made terms with the men
which they thought (i.e. the company) very satisfactory to themselves.

Now to return from a comment which I fear mayn't interest you, but
is I think worth making.

Christ Church ended with the usual rush of packing up, getting dinner
(I had about 10 minutes for mine) and going off to Lyttelton, which is
about 7 miles off in the train, to catch the Wellington steamer.[106]
We got the *Maori*, a turbine steamer, very comfortable and fast, and –
perhaps to make up for the *Warrimoo* – the Union Co. had given

---

106. The difficult road from Christchurch to Lyttelton over the Port Hills is
     about 20 kilometres (12 miles): the shorter railway and tunnel connection
     was opened in 1867.

Wellington.   *Postcard, issued by the New Zealand High Commission*
                              Emigration Department, received 13 October 1914

us the best berths in the ship.[107] So we had comfortable cabins and a very good night, while a lot of the passengers (the ship was crowded by reason of the fear of the engineers' strike) had to content themselves with berths in the dining room and music saloon and similar uncomfortable places.

The Lyttelton–Wellington service is like a long Cross-Channel service. We left at 9 and were in to Wellington by 7 in the morning.[108]

Here in Wellington most of us are quartered at the Wellington Club, which seems a haven of rest after two noisy hotels. It lies a little way up the hill (Wellington is practically all hills) and has a very good view over the harbour. It is very comfortable and perfectly quiet, and, as we are to be here 6 nights in all, I have had time to do some unpacking and even get out a trouser stretcher!

---

107. *Maori*, 3399 tons, 350 feet by 47 feet, 20 knots sea speed, was built by Denny on the Clyde and launched in 1907. She carried 423 first-class and 130 second-class passengers (plus a Bechstein grand piano) on the Union Company's daily each way service between Lyttelton and Wellington. She was laid up in 1931, but was bought by the United Corporation of China in 1946, operated out of Shanghai, and sank in a storm in 1951.

108. Wellington, one of several New Zealand towns named after prominent Victorian 'heroes', was the site of the first New Zealand Company settlement in 1840. It became the capital city, in place of Auckland, in 1865. It grew as a commercial and administrative centre and had a population of 70,729 by 1911.

Custom House Quay, Wellington, N.Z.

Wellington, Custom House Quay.   *Postcard*

All the same we have had a pretty strenuous time – what with the sittings of the Commission and other pursuits.

And for the first time in New Zealand, the Commission has really produced a 9 days wonder by getting from one witness – and that the President of the local Chamber of Commerce – a statement that New Zealand was on the verge of bankruptcy from over borrowing. The consequence has been that all the papers have had leading articles, and witnesses have turned up strenuously denying the unfortunate man's assertion (in which, I suspect, there is really a good deal of truth!). Anyhow, the interest in the proceedings has gone up very considerably.[109]

Sir Edgar Vincent says that Wellington reminds him very much of Constantinople and the Chatalja lines.[110] There are ridges of high hills, all round the city, and it lies in a beautifully sheltered and deep harbour

---

109. A. E. Mabin, President of the Wellington Chamber of Commerce, expressed his controversial views during the first of the five days which the Commissioners spent formally gathering evidence. They interrogated 28 witnesses between Wednesday March 5 and Tuesday March 11.

110. Chatalja or Catalca lies inland from the Sea of Marmara in Turkey, what was then the Ottoman Empire. It was here in October 1912 during the First Balkan War that the Turks successfully repulsed a Bulgarian attack upon their defensive lines.

with a narrow entrance some miles away. Another small and ill-constructed map will show you how it lies.

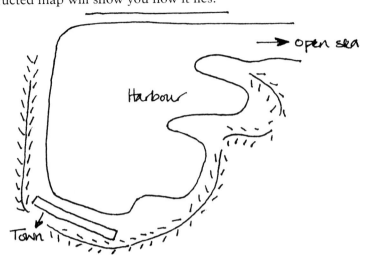

The level ground at the edge of the harbour is very small indeed, and consequently the city can only expand either by reclamation from the sea or by spreading over the hills. At present it is doing both. But as the hills are very steep on most sides, I can't quite conceive of Wellington expanding into a really big place. It has, I suppose, about 60 or 70 thousand people now. Still, it was chosen by a body of experts as the best site for the capital, and so far as position goes it is extraordinarily favoured.

As there has been more time for evidence here, things have been rather easier, and yesterday we had a 'whole holiday' and went out quite a long way into the country. I will leave that till the next letter and end this by saying that on Thursday there was a big dinner party at the Club given in honour of the Commission by the Minister of Internal Affairs. As a dinner party it was dull, though I got a good deal from my neighbour – one Duthie – as to the finances of New Zealand. He was one of the 'counter witnesses' to the President of the Chamber of Commerce, but was clearly doubtful in his own mind as to the financial strength of the Dominion.

What was interesting in the dinner was the fact that the Prime Minister (Massey) the Postmaster General (Rhodes) and the Acting Minister of Finance (Fraser) were there besides the Minister for Internal Affairs. Massey is a farmer by occupation – a solid looking man who looks dogged but not brilliant. He must be determined as he was in opposition for 15 years till last year. Rhodes is an Oxford (B.N.C.) man who was quite interesting so far as I could judge from the little I talked to him. Bell, the host, is a robust-looking person with an obvious sense of humour. Fraser seemed clever, but was rather old. The real Finance Minister is away in England, for the usual purpose of raising another loan.

I wish I could have spoken to Massey, but didn't get the chance. Anyhow, it seems funny enough to talk to most of the other Ministers of State at a dinner party. One's hair would be on end if it were England![111]

I have had to hurry over the last part of this, as I am due to go out to supper this evening. And I must apologize for its dullness – for the greater part, as you will have doubtless seen, has been the result of wanting to put down something of what one has been doing for my own subsequent benefit.

> Ever your affectionate brother
> E. J. Harding

DOMINIONS ROYAL COMMISSION
March 13th 1913
Central Hotel
Auckland

My dear Father,

Since I last wrote we have had a lot of travelling, but otherwise comparative peace, and I have no further 'preliminaries' in the way of troubles to record. So I will go straight back to the point where I left off – that was I think last Saturday when we had a 'day off' and went on a visit of inspection. It involved 3 hours travelling each way, and the object was to visit the experimental farm owned by the Government at a place called Levine some 60 miles up the west coast.[112] From this you can deduce that railway travelling in this country is not particularly fast.

---

111. William Ferguson Massey (1856–1925), 'Farmer Bill', was born in Co. Londonderry, Ireland, emigrated to New Zealand in 1870, was elected to Parliament in 1894, became Leader of the Opposition in 1903, renamed his party the Reform Party in 1909 and served as Prime Minister from 1912 until his death in 1925. Sir Francis Henry Dillon Bell (1851–1936) was leader of the Legislative Council, Massey's closest political colleague and briefly in 1925 his successor, the first New Zealand-born Prime Minister. R. Heaton Rhodes (1861–1956) was Postmaster-General and Minister for Public Health 1912–15. William Fraser (1840–1923) was first elected in 1893 and became Minister of Public Works in 1912.

112. Levin, the site of the Weraroa State Farm, was founded as a settlement in 1889 by the Wellington and Manawatu Railway Company and named after one of its directors, William Hort Levin (1845–93).

The journey was very interesting though – the North Island is much less settled than the South Island (for historical reasons chiefly, because the 'Maori Wars' kept it back till comparatively a short time ago)[113] and consequently one could see in action the process of clearing country for grazing or cultivation.

Originally there is bush, i.e. trees of various kinds and undergrowth: the latter is cleared first, and then the trees are burnt, so that only charred stumps remain: and these are left till a suitable opportunity arises to make use of the wood. The result is that the fields have a curious half and half appearance, and there is not of that air of tidiness that one expects from an English farm.

I might put in here, though it isn't very relevant to charred stumps, that the two most beautiful trees in New Zealand, to my mind, are the cabbage tree, which is rather like a palm tree on a small scale, and the tree fern which grows in gullies and woods. We have hanging ferns of course. These trees are like them, on an immense scale, and with an ordinary tree trunk.

But to go back to our expedition. There was the usual reception at the station when we got there – the Mayor (possibly the township had 1000 people!), the local member and a crowd of miscellaneous people that I couldn't sort out. Our party was pretty large too, as it was part Commission and part Wellington Chamber of Commerce, whom the Government had roped in as they substituted this expedition for another and less interesting one planned by the Chamber.

Anyhow, we escaped from the station with some difficulty and were taken off in motor cars to the farm, where there was a lunch, followed by speeches, and then an inspection of prize cows and other similar delights. The luncheon room had a large inscription, in letters made of ferns, 'Empire Peace and Plenty' – which induces the remark that the New Zealander, though very prosperous, is somewhat material in his ideas.

After the farm came a visit to a really charming lake (the name of which I have forgotten)[114] which was the scene of a great Maori Battle (similarly forgotten) and finally an inspection of the Government Reformatory School. A ten minutes' glance left the impression that it

---

113. The Maori or Land Wars raged mainly through central North Island from 1860 to 1881. Much Maori land was confiscated or purchased by the Pakeha (Europeans) during and after the wars.
114. This was Papaitonga (or Buller) Lake where Te Rauparaha (1768–1849), the 'Maori Napoleon', and his Ngati Toa people and their allies slaughtered the local Muaupoko in 1824.

was excellently run, but that the band needed much improvement. It welcomed the party in strains most abominably out of tune.

I spent most of the train journeys in working – they are, I find, as good opportunities as any for keeping things going – and one result was that it wasn't necessary to talk too much to the Chamber of Commerce people who were worthy, no doubt, but somewhat dull.

Sunday was pretty restful. We had a walk in the hills behind Wellington, going out to a place called Lower Hutt[115], and in the evening went out to supper with one of the shorthand writers attached to the Commission. He had a wife and a daughter just going off to a school in England.

Both of the shorthand writers are particularly good – the Government have put on two to the job – and they have varied interests besides shorthand writing and typing. One is the President of the Wellington Art Club and Secretary of the local Branch of the British Medical Association!

Monday and Tuesday were mostly 'evidence'[116] and packing up again – but on Monday evening I went to a Round Table group meeting (I think I mentioned these in an earlier letter) and listened to a paper on 'Labour questions in New Zealand'. The people there were very kind, but not so interesting as those at Dunedin. The idea of the paper was that there will soon be a real Labour party in the New Zealand Parliament, and quite possibly a Labour Government. At present, it seems, there are various grades of labour, just as there are in the party in England, and they haven't got enough cohesion to make themselves really effective.[117]

---

115. A good walk: Lower Hutt is about 15 kilometres from the centre of Wellington, on the alluvial plain at the mouth of the Hutt river, close to the first landfall of the 1840 settlers. It was named after Sir William Hutt (1801–82), a chairman of the New Zealand Company.

116. Harold Beauchamp (1858–1939) was one of Monday's witnesses. He was a director of the Bank of New Zealand for nearly 38 years and was knighted in 1923, but he is now perhaps mainly remembered as the father of Katherine Mansfield (1888–1923), one of New Zealand's most gifted writers. Their relationship became strained. He is portrayed rather sharply in some of her stories as 'Stanley Burnell'.

117. However, a Unity Conference of Labour representatives was held a few weeks later in July 1913 and created the Social Democratic Party. Some Labour men were elected in 1914. The party was broadened and refounded in July 1916 as the New Zealand Labour Party. But it only formed its first government in 1935.

'The South-Bound Express at Waiouru Railway Station   *Postcard*
showing Mt. Ruapehu and Ngauruhoe Volcano in Eruption
1 August 1909'.

The mail goes out tomorrow, so I will close this down and get it off. The next letter will be about our journey to Auckland and our experiences here.[118]

Ever your affectionate son

E. J. Harding

DOMINIONS ROYAL COMMISSION

Rotorua

March 17th 1913

My dear Father,

What with work and heat and mosquitoes, I didn't get a minute at Auckland to start another letter, so the 'work has to be brought up to date' now. We have just got here – for a week's rest I hope, which I shall be very glad of – and I am waiting for my luggage before changing. (I find that my despatch box just holds my cash box and things for the night – but it doesn't, of course, hold a dress suit!)

---

118. Meanwhile, a Committee of the Commission, consisting of Haggard, Lorimer, Garnett and Campbell, was despatched by rail to New Plymouth, where on Wednesday March 12 it took evidence from 7 witnesses and then sailed up the west coast of North Island to join the main party in Auckland.

I think I left off at the point where we left Wellington, that is last Tuesday night. The journey to Auckland is some 400 miles and takes 19 hours. We started at 9 in the evening, and arrived at 4 next day (Wednesday). But it wasn't particularly tiring. The trains are pretty slow, and not very exhausting therefore. Also I had a sleeping berth which was really comfortable and I got a very good night.[119]

We woke to find ourselves in the middle of the volcano country – Tongariro and Ruapehu – but unfortunately it was a cloudy morning (which turned to rain) and we saw very little except the lower snow slopes.[120] It was, therefore, more interesting further on where there is bush country and the line does curious gyrations rather like the St. Gothard. Further on still there was a lot of hilly country, mostly Maori, I think, and therefore largely undeveloped. And finally, there was ordinary English-looking country with a river or so and good pasture.[121] So much for our journey along what is called the 'main trunk' line.

At Auckland our quarters were at the Central Hotel, which is just off the main street: it was moderately quiet and quite comfortable, but the mosquitoes were certainly pestilential. They went for me, of course, at once, with the result that my face now looks like one of the half-cleared New Zealand fields about which I wrote last time. It is full of excrescences which, we will hope, Rotorua air and baths will cure.

March 17th 10 p.m.

I have just returned from my first bath (a bath soon after dinner sounds rather curious but this had a temperature of 98 and was most refreshing) and will continue the story a little.

The work of the Commission at Auckland wasn't very strenuous.[122] There were only sittings two days, last Thursday and Friday, and on Thursday afternoon we were taken in a launch round the harbour. But

---

119. The 680-kilometres North Island Main Trunk Railway from Wellington to Auckland took over 40 years to build and was only completed in 1908.
120. This area, given by the local Maori to the government in 1887, became the country's first National Park, only 15 years after the world's first at Yellowstone, U.S.A. The completion of the railway opened up the park to visitors. Tongariro is 1968 m. high, Ruapehu 2796 m. and Ngauruhoe 2290 m.
121. This was the Waikato district, heavily settled by Europeans after the Maori Wars.
122. Only 8 witnesses were called in two days, March 13 and 14.

Friday was a really hard day, and Saturday and Sunday were almost equally so with all the necessary packing arrangements and clearing up generally.

I found one small piece of amusement. The sittings were at the Town Hall, and they stored our numerous official boxes in one of the cellars beneath. Some humourist (perhaps from seeing them or from having heard our description of them – 'sarcophagi' and similar terms) wrote up 'The Morgue' on one of the walls.

Auckland is distinctly the least attractive of the four New Zealand cities.[123] The harbour is really beautiful, but the town itself seems to be mainly one long and very noisy street which runs down to the wharves and up to the suburbs. It isn't worth another even of my feeble maps.

What is really interesting about the site, as you will see from the map of New Zealand, is that the town is built on a very narrow strip which separates the East from the West coast. We went out to the west coast – there is a small port there called Onehunga – on Sunday afternoon,[124] and we also climbed one of the small ex-volcanoes which lie on the narrow strip – called 'One Tree Hill' – so as to get a view all round the country.[125] The air is quite good up there and the view magnificent – in fact it was the part of Auckland that I liked most.

I managed to find time to see both the Maldens, but wasn't immensely taken with either of them. The parson is the best of the two, and seemed pretty keen on his work. But the other, who is on the reporting staff of the *New Zealand Herald* – a very good paper by the

---

123. Auckland was chosen by Captain Hobson as the first administrative centre of the new British colony in 1840, and was named after the Earl of Auckland (1784–1849), his former commander and Governor-General of India. The land was purchased from the local Maori for £55 in gold and bundles of miscellaneous goods. Unlike New Zealand's other major cities, Auckland did not begin as a planned settlement for parties of organised immigrants. The city had lost its economic and political pre-eminence by the later 19th century but grew rapidly from the beginning of the 20th century. By 1911 with a population of 102,676 it had become the country's largest urban and industrial centre.

124. Onehunga, actually due south of Auckland's centre in Manukau Harbour, was in 1913 still a distinct settlement, but it was soon to be absorbed as a suburb of the rapidly sprawling city.

125. 183 m. high. It was made into a large Maori *pa* in the late 17th and 18th centuries and now supports a 21-metre obelisk above the grave of Sir John Logan Campbell (1817–1912), one of Auckland's first European residents, a successful businessman, landowner and public benefactor, who died shortly before Harding's visit.

Auckland, Wellesley Street
and Public Library.

*Postcard issued by the New Zealand
High Commission Emigration Department,
received 13 October 1914*

way – was just the ordinary reporter, neither more nor less, of whom I have had perforce to see rather too much the last month.[126]

On Friday evening we had the usual 'soup ticket' dinner at Government House.[127] Lord Liverpool, who is Governor, looks absolutely brainless, and Lady Liverpool distinctly ordinary, though by no means alarming. The general impression seems to be that neither of them is up to very much – and that Lord Islington, the last Governor, was very much better.[128]

I have got used now to the bowing and curtseying when 'The Excellencies' walk round the room to shake hands, and as there was

---

126. *The New Zealand Herald* began continuous publication in 1863.
127. The capital had become Wellington, but Auckland's economic importance, and probably the warmer climate, account for the maintenance there of a residence for the Crown's representative.
128. Lord Liverpool (1870–1941), formerly Comptroller of the Royal Household, had been appointed the 18th Governor of New Zealand in September 1912 and had taken up office shortly before Harding's arrival. His office was elevated to Governor-General in 1917, and he served until 1920. Lord Islington (1866–1936) was Governor from 1910 to 1912, and later became Under-Secretary of State for the Colonies (1914–15) and for India (1916–18).

nothing of much interest during dinner, and I was rather tired, I thought the whole affair rather dull.

But my neighbour at dinner – a certain Mr. Studholme – had, I found, just started a rubber plantation in Fiji, and he had stories, and views, as to Crown Colony Government which were amusing if not flattering to Colonial Office ideas.[129]

After the harbour and the view from 'One Tree Hill', the most interesting thing in Auckland is the Museum, where there are lots of Maori curiosities, including a canoe, sixty feet long I should think, elaborately carved, and made out of a single kauri tree (which is the most famous New Zealand tree, takes 6000 years or so to grow, and is now nearly extinct) and also a Maori hut similarly decorated with curious figures.[130]

On the whole, I am glad we are away from Auckland. It was too hot and too damp for my liking, and, as I said before, the mosquitoes were very vicious.

The Chairman indeed went off on Friday night by the *Moldavia*, a P. & O. boat, to Sydney where he will attend the famous Easter show and perhaps make preparations for Australia. We shall 'pick him up' when we get there.[131]

Speaking of ships reminds me that on Thursday afternoon, after we had completed going round the harbour, a few of the party inspected an emigrant ship – the *Hawke's Bay* belonging to the Teyser line – which had just arrived in Auckland on her first voyage. As she brings out

---

129. Tasman had been the European discoverer of Fiji in 1643. European sailors, planters and missionaries arrived in numbers during the 19th century, and the consequent social and political instability persuaded the British government to annex the islands as a British colony in 1874.

130. The museum was founded in 1869. The 25-metre canoe, Toki-a-Tapiri (Tapiri's battle-axe), was built about 1836 and the carved Maori meeting house, Hotunui, in 1878.

131. *Moldavia*, 9500 tons, 521 feet by 58 feet, built by Caird on the Clyde in 1903, was part of P. & O.'s substantial Australian fleet and carried 348 first-class passengers and 166 second-class: she was taken over by the Admiralty during the war and was torpedoed in the English Channel on 23 May 1918 with the loss of 64 troops.

132. G.D. Tyser and Co., an old established London firm, had been engaged in the frozen meat trade since 1886. *Hawkes Bay* 9600 tons, built by Workman, Clark and Co. in Belfast and launched in 1912, was designed to accommodate, after a fashion, up to 1000 emigrants in temporary quarters. The flows of immigration were determined not only by economic

emigrants and takes back frozen meat (and was preparing for the latter) one couldn't, of course, judge of the accommodation very well. But I fancy they must be rather cramped and uncomfortable.[132]

My pen is running dry and obviously I can't tell you about Rotorua till next letter.

> Best love
>> Ever your affectionate son
>>> E. J. Harding

Dominions Royal Commission
Grand Hotel
Rotorua
March 23rd 1913

My dear Eva,

This is the last of our days of rest, and very jolly they have been: tomorrow we start down for Auckland and get the boat to Sydney in the evening.[133] So I must try and get a letter up to date and tell you of all our doings here.

First of all as to Rotorua itself – you get to it from Auckland (it takes 8 hours or so) by a somewhat crawly railway that runs up over a range of hills, and through some fine bush country, and you emerge from the said range to find a large lake lying below, and at its edge an ordinary-looking town.[134] The town is quite a small one as is the hotel (though it is more comfortable than most we have struck), and the only strange thing to

---

circumstances in New Zealand and elsewhere but also by government policy. Assisted passages were resumed for selected migrants in 1903 after a lull of a dozen years. In the 12 months ending 31 March 1913 some 14,169 immigrants arrived from the United Kingdom, of whom 3928 had been granted cheap fares: £10 for third class.

133. This week of rest for the Commission followed the completion of their inquiries in New Zealand: 14 days formally gathering evidence from 76 witnesses plus several official visits. Vincent chose to go straight on to Sydney, cutting out the trip to Rotorua, which he described as 'a kind of New Zealand Harrogate with hot and cold springs and Maoris for tourist consumption'.

134. This area of intense Maori settlement only began to attract European visitors after the Maori Wars. The land upon which to build the town was acquired by the government from the Ngati Whakaue first by lease under the Thermal Springs Districts Act of 1881 and then by purchase in 1890 (for £8250). The railway arrived in 1894.

Rotorua, the Bath House.   *Postcard*

start with is that there is a 'spa' just down the road, and in it a somewhat oily bath with a temperature at blood heat. The thing to do (we did it the first evening we got here and have repeated it often since) is to walk down the street in pyjamas and a dressing gown, take the bath (you stay in it for 15 minutes about) and return to the hotel for bed.[135]

It hardly occurred to one to enquire why there should be a 'blood heat' bath – but the explanation was forced on us next morning. When you get a hundred yards or so outside the main streets, you find a sort of marsh, with tracks running through it, where are hot pools, tepid pools, mud pools and other horrible-looking things. The water seethes, and the mud spits, and everything feels as though the earth might gape the next minute and swallow one up altogether. The crust of the earth just here must be a few feet in most places, and in some there is no crust at all!

Just by the marsh aforesaid, and between it and the lake, which is quite cold, lies a Maori village. The Maoris have utilized the hot springs for their own purposes. There are washing pools, cooking holes, and bathing pools where the children (sad demoralization) dive in for pennies thrown to them by unthinking visitors. A Maori village generally has one or two old houses, which have the very curious Maori carvings on them (devils with their tongues out, and similar objects), and for the rest modern huts of tin or wood in various stages of neatness, or (more often) the reverse.

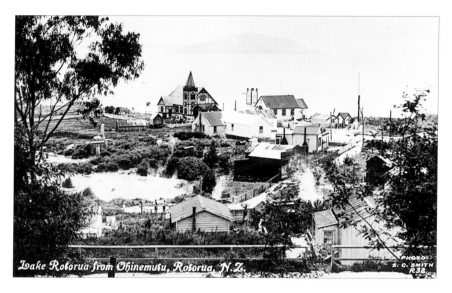

Lake Rotorua from Ohinemutu.   *Postcard*

However, the children look beautifully healthy – probably because they spend most of their time in the water, and they are also quite good-looking. When they get older, they get rather less attractive, and a lot of the older women are tattooed from the lips to the chin. Also they smoke pipes, and seem to enjoy it.

The particular village I have been talking about is called Ohenemutu. But there is another called Whaka lying a mile or so the other side of Rotorua which is even more remarkable.[136] It has the mud springs and all the rest of the 'thermal wonders' – also a high bridge from which the Maori children dive into the stream below for pennies to the great amusement of visitors[137] – but more than this, it has a geyser called 'Pohutu' which sends up a column of boiling water forty feet at least into the air. The geyser doesn't play always but it did the morning after our arrival and has again this afternoon – no doubt to welcome and speed so distinguished a party!

135. The government first built a bathhouse in 1882 and the present magnificent structure, the largest bathhouse in the Southern Hemisphere, in 1908.
136. Correctly, Ohinemutu and Whakarewarewa.
137. They still do. Haggard also concluded that this 'method of earning money was not enobling'. He also asserted that the 'Maori race is doomed' and would disappear in the next 50 or 100 years because of mixed marriages, unhealthy homes and the impact of white men's diseases and drink.

Close by the geyser is a model 'Pah' (that is the Maori name for a village) which was put up for the present King and Queen when they came here 10 years ago.[138] It has lots and lots of curious carvings and the whole is encircled with a wooden palisade by which in the old days – not so very old though, say up to 50 years ago – prospective head hunters used to be kept out.

Seeing these various sights occupied us all Tuesday, but after dinner we had the further experience of a Maori entertainment of singing and dancing. The singing was very good – the best I have heard since the Coldharbour Choral! – but the dancing was really splendid, particularly what are called 'Hakas' which are native dances to celebrate various things. I can't possibly describe them in a letter, but the effect is electrifying even in a small hall – and it must be terrific when 500 or 600 natives are going at once.[139]

The party was so much pleased that it went again on Thursday evening, and Mr. Foster, the Canadian member (who turned up a few days ago completing the Commission), made a speech in which he said he had come 15,000 miles just to see this particular performance!

I enclose programmes of both performances so that you can see what actually was done.

Wednesday was devoted to a very long excursion – the object being the boiling pools and the lakes round Mount Tarawhera, the big mountain that 'blew out' in 1886 and destroyed the whole countryside. I am afraid I have neither time nor pen to do justice to all the wonders but roughly the day was this. First a seventeen mile drive to a place called 'Frying Pan Flat', where there are more geysers and mud pools, and also a blow hole which emits clouds of steam with a noise like the largest of steam engines. Most of the ground is hot under foot here, and the soles of one's boots are liable to get burned!

Then a walk down a sort of ravine, really the remains of the cleft where the earth opened after the eruption, to Lake Rotomahanna – where were the famous pink and white terraces which the earthquake absolutely destroyed. We crossed the lake in a launch which landed us at

---

138. King George V and Queen Mary toured the Empire as the Duke and Duchess of York in 1901. For a detailed and illustrated contemporary account of their journey see Sir Donald Mackenzie Wallace, *The Web of Empire: A Diary of the Imperial Tour of Their Royal Highnesses the Duke and Duchess of Cornwall and York*, London, 1902.

139. Haggard, who found the entertainment 'novel and exciting', was moved to give a speech on the 'Virtues of Barbarism'.

the site where one of the terraces was. There is nothing now but hot stones which quite often are steaming, through the heat underneath. It is not a place to linger at. After the lake came another short walk, right under Mount Tarawhera itself which has a great 'gape' in its side where the volcano was. Then another launch across Lake Tarawhera and a look at a village (Wairoa) which was overwhelmed by the earthquake – practically everyone killed. And finally a 10 mile drive back in another coach through some beautiful bush country and past two lakes, the 'Green' and the 'Blue' lakes which by no means belie their names.

The man in charge of the launch which took us across the lakes – one Warbrick – was a halfcaste, but a most extraordinarily interesting person, and the one man alive probably who was near the mountain when it erupted and yet lives to tell the tale.

There was no warning – first flames from Mount Tarawhera, then an earthquake, and a splitting open of the ground for five or six miles. Then a shower of ashes from the mountain which lasted four hours and covered the ground for 20 miles round. Then next day inky blackness, when you expected daylight, and after that 3 days torrential rain. No wonder all the countryside thought that the end of the world had come, and no wonder most of the Maoris shun the place still. Lake Rotomahanna, which we crossed in the launch, was emptied by the earthquake – I suppose the ground opened underneath it and swallowed up the water – and it didn't get right for 6 years afterwards.[140]

There – now perhaps you will realize a little what sort of a day we had. Some day, perhaps, there will be another eruption and then you can fish this out. Certainly I should be very sorry to live round here permanently.

Thursday was mild by way of comparison, but nevertheless interesting. We had a launch across Lake Rotorua, and our first destination was a small stream running into the lake which has its source in a perfectly clear spring welling up with such a gush that, if you drop a penny down it, it will scarcely sink.

Having admired this sufficiently we went on to the outlet of Rotorua, a very swift and winding stream which the launch could just navigate,

---

140. Mount Tarawera above Lake Rotomahana exploded on 10 June 1886. The roar was heard as far away as Christchurch. Ash and debris were strewn over 16,000 square kilometres, at least 153 people were killed and the world-famous Pink and White Terraces disappeared. Te Wairoa was buried under 2.5 m. of debris. Two separate tourist parties reported seeing a mysterious, fully-dressed-and-manned Maori war canoe on the lake a few days before the explosion.

leading to another Lake – Rotuiti. Our destination there was *its* outlet where there are some fine falls, and a power station which supplies Rotorua with its electric light.[141]

We had a picnic lunch, after which some of the party did a little fishing, and returned by the launch in time for dinner. Lake Rotorua, on the way back, was quite rough – it must be about 7 miles long so that the wind has a fair chance. We rolled about a good deal, and some of the people looked near to sea sickness. But we got into smooth water fairly soon.

I ought to add that we did a little lake fishing on the outward journey, and I landed my one and only trout in New Zealand.[142]

Good Friday was an 'off' day, and I spent most of it in working, but in the evening some of us went down to the nearest Maori village – Ohenemutu – again, and crossed the river (quite warm) which runs into the lake beside it by borrowing a rickety Maori boat from some children playing near by. We got over without damage, and pursued our way along the lake for a little, returning finally to Rotorua by way of the swamp with the mud pools etc. – which proved to look no less vicious at a second sight of them.

Yesterday (Saturday) was another pretty long day. We had a motor drive, all along a chain of lakes of which Rotorua is the head, passing more boiling springs and lakes on the way (at a place called Tikiteri) which, if anything, were more horrible than any we have yet seen.[143]

But, for the rest, it was really a beauty drive – through some bush, practically untouched, and country full of Maori legends. One place we got to was a covered-in hole, where there was once a cave full of poisonous fumes. Some Maori out hunting was overpowered there and died, and since then it has been 'taboo'. Close by, the Maoris have put up one of their curious carved figures to represent a death's head – and, now it is there, they don't go near the place.

Today (Sunday) has been quiet again. We have been preparing to go off, and I have been settling accounts and doing various odd jobs. But we found time for a last visit to the other 'Maori village' – Whaka – and had a look at the boiling pools there, and the children diving from the bridge.

---

141. The outlet of Lake Rotoiti is the Okere Falls. The hydro-electric power station opened there in 1901 was the first government (as against private) supply in New Zealand.
142. Probably a rainbow trout, a native of California, first introduced to New Zealand by the Auckland Acclimatisation Society in 1877.
143. Tikitere is also appropriately known as Hell's Gate.

Whakarewarewa, Rotorua, Children Diving for Pennies.   *Postcard*

We have had a tame newspaper correspondent, and also a tame press photographer, with us most of the time. The efforts of the first I will send with this if I can get hold of them – those of the second we may see at Auckland tomorrow. But neither has been at all offensive, and as it is apparently the custom for visitors to Rotorua to get their photographs taken with 'thermal wonders' behind or in front, perhaps it hasn't been so bad to have had our own man.

Anyhow, I shan't very easily forget the wonders of this place, and as an 'interlude' it has been really splendid. We have had perfect weather – no rain and not excessive heat – and with this and the voyage to Sydney we ought to be well set up for the Australian tour.

       Ever your affectionate brother
       E. J. Harding

DOMINIONS ROYAL COMMISION
S.S. Maheno
March 27th 1913
(between Auckland and Sydney)

My dear Father,

This is a day after your own heart. It is blowing a gale, and we are 'moving' considerably. In fact we have been 'moving' more or less ever since leaving Auckland, and I must confess to not having felt first class.

In fact, once or twice I have been on the verge of succumbing to the enemy, but somehow I have escaped (I rather wish I hadn't) and I have been down to every meal, even if I haven't eaten much.

This boat has the taint of the *Warrimoo*.[144] She is bigger, and has better cabins, and has no permanent list. But there is the same old smell, which is accentuated by the fact that we have a cargo of copra on board, and the food is somewhat rough – and, I surmise, the cooking is none too cleanly.

In fact, our experience of the Union line hitherto (except the *Maori*, the 'ferry boat' between the South and North Islands) affords a strong inducement to brave the Red Sea in June and return by P. & O.[145]

I haven't really got very much to say, so far as experiences are concerned since I finished an account of our doings at Rotorua. We had a quite uneventful train journey back to Auckland, and came straight down to the ship, leaving at 8 p.m. I searched the recesses of the Auckland Post Office for letters, and found a few – but we shan't get any English mail till Brisbane, and we have 27 hours in the train before we get there!

So I think the thing to write is an impression or two more of New Zealand – and on looking back at our month there, I confess that the main regret I have is that I couldn't learn more about the country in general, because I had so much to do in my own particular line. Of course, I did learn a good deal, but I think that if one had had a month just to travel through 'on one's own', the total sum of knowledge would have been a good deal more.

As it is one's main recollection is of a wonderful climate, a country with great potentialities (I wish I could see New Zealand 500 years' hence), a people very kindly and extremely prosperous, self-confident and, to coin a word, self-contented.

Also the democratic spirit is very strongly developed – I don't expect much sympathy from your side here, but I confess that it appeals to me a good deal.

---

144. *Maheno*, 5282 tons, 400 feet by 50 feet, built by Denny on the Clyde, was launched in 1905 and became the first turbine steamer to cross the Pacific. She carried, rather slowly (sea speed 16 knots), up to 231 first-class, 120 second-class and 67 third-class passengers. When being towed away for scrap in 1935 she was wrecked off the coast of Queensland, to become a target for training the Australian Air Force during the Second World War.

145. The alternative implied was to travel by the Union Company's fortnightly service, probably on the *Maheno*, across the Pacific from Sydney to San Francisco or Vancouver.

There is also rather a remarkable belief in British institutions, and British power – particularly remarkable indeed because a large part of the cable news seems devoted to the German peril and the failure of the Territorial system![146]

Another rather striking point about the country is the excellence of its newspapers compared with its size. In each of the four big towns, there are two quite good morning newspapers and generally one good evening one. And I am told that in the smaller towns there are quite decent papers too.[147]

I don't know whether it is the effect of a 15,000 mile journey on the generation that makes it or its successor, but certainly another point about New Zealand is the number of people who travel about. Of course, on the main lines there are only one or two trains per day, but they seem always full, and the word 'trip' must be one of the ones in commonest use in a New Zealander's vocabulary.

(The zest for travel extends also to steamer travel: as the Union Co. have almost a monopoly of external transport, I can only regard the zest as misplaced!)

Perhaps this mobility of body is the cause of the mobility of mind which has made New Zealand the home of so many social experiments.[148]

The experiments, though, don't appear on the surface – and therefore there is outwardly a most surprising resemblance between England and New Zealand. In fact what really astonishes me is that there isn't a larger exodus to it, and I believe that if the country were rather more advertised at home, it would "mop up" any amount more emigrants.

Brisbane. March 31st 1913
Hotel Belle Vue 8 a.m.

I shall have a rush today, I know, and the mail leaves here tomorrow, so I will finish up about our voyage, and leave Australia for a further letter.

---

146. The naval arms race with Germany was much in the news in 1913. A Territorial Force had been established as a reserve army from 1907.
147. The first newspaper printed in New Zealand appeared on 18 April 1840. The greatest number of titles published at one time was 193, including 67 dailies, in 1910.
148. Many Europeans were impressed by the progressive labour regulations introduced in the 1890s, by the granting of votes to women in 1893, by the Industrial Conciliation and Arbitration Act of 1894 and by the old age pensions scheme introduced in 1898. Vincent nevertheless claimed that 'superficially at any rate, it's made no difference'.

It blew the whole of the time till we got to Sydney heads, and there was much discomfort among various members of the party. In fact Mr. Garnett only put in an appearance once during the four days voyage – and some of the others weren't much better. I got all right quite quickly, but all the same it was very unpleasant and quite impossible to write or do any work.

However, the entrance into Sydney harbour makes up for a good deal. There is a bold headland on the right as you come in, and a smaller one to the left. The entrance is quite narrow, and there is a sharp bend just after it. But, once in, there is a wonderful passage up the harbour for 5 miles or so, birth suburbs of Sydney on one side and wooded banks on the other. I don't know that in actual beauty the entrance is as fine as that to Hobart – but of the quality of the harbour, as a harbour, there can be no doubt whatever.

> Best Love
>   Ever your affectionate son
>   E. J. Harding

> DOMINIONS ROYAL COMMISSION
> Queensland Club
> Brisbane
> April 6th 1913

My dear Eva,

Since I finished my last letter on Monday, I really haven't had a minute to begin another one.[149] There have been really rather bad difficulties over the work of the Commission in Australia and it is only now that we are beginning to surmount them. As it is I feel very apprehensive as to how the Australian tour is going to work out.

Possibly we were overspoiled with the excellence of the arrangements in New Zealand, but anyhow on arrival in Sydney we found that the arrangements for housing and transport were bad and the arrangements for evidence practically non-existent! That was really the reason why I dashed up here from Sydney on Saturday March 29th instead of leaving with the rest of the party on March 30th.

Not that there was any particular inducement to stay in Sydney. We struck it at the tail end of the exhibition and race week – which is *the*

---

149. After one month in New Zealand, the Commission now faced over two months of investigation and travel in Australia. What lay ahead were 31 days formally interrogating 171 witnesses plus numerous official visits.

week of the year in Sydney. All the hotels were tremendously full, and I only got, with difficulty, half a room at the Hotel Australia – which anyhow is very large, noisy and crowded – so that I haven't the least desire to return to it.

But Sydney I must tell you about when we get there again, and I will go on straight to our journey up here, which I did in the company of Mr. Lorimer, who was also anxious to get to Brisbane early.

It is over 700 miles from Sydney to Brisbane, and there is a break of gauge and consequently of train half way at a place called Wallangarra.[150] There is the further disadvantage that there are no dining cars to speak of on the New South Wales and Queensland railways. We were reduced to baskets or refreshment rooms. However, we got a sleeping car which was quite comfortable, and on getting to the Queensland border we persuaded the stationmaster to give us free tickets and a separate compartment.

The country to the N.S.W. border is mostly hilly and full of bush – gradually being cleared – but soon after the Queensland border you get to the very famous Darling Downs. I had heard of them, but had never thought about them much, and had always pictured Queensland as a steamy hot, low-lying, rather tropical country, only suited for white immigration in the eyes of optimistic holders of the White Australia Theory.[151] Instead of that, one's introduction to Queensland is a slow climb up quite a high range of hills 3000 feet or so – to find on the top of them mile after mile of dry, aired, rolling country with a soil, as far as one could see, extremely rich, and quite well watered. It all reminded me of the Hampshire and Wiltshire downs,[152] and the possibilities of

---

150. Wallangarra lies in Queensland, close to the border with New South Wales. Queensland was occupied as a dependency of N.S.W., first by convicts from 1824 and then by free settlers from 1842. It became a separate colony and was granted responsible government in 1859. By 1913 the state had a population of 660,158. Each Australian colony developed its own railway system to its own specifications. Federation left the country with the problem of incompatible railway gauges. The first railway link of 1160 kilometres from Sydney to Brisbane was completed in 1889: in 1913 the scheduled service took 26¾ hours.

151. All the colonies of white settlement within the Empire restricted immigration largely to Europeans and especially to those of British stock. The White Australia policy was the unofficial name for one of the Federal government's first pieces of legislation, the Restrictive Immigration Act of 1901.

152. Agricultural counties of Southern England.

A Selector's Homestead, Queensland, Blackall Range, North Coast Line.
Photograph, Department of Agriculture and Stock, Brisbane, 1910

development looked immense. And I believe that the western parts of Queensland, which unfortunately we can't get to, are equally healthy and richer still, especially now that they have found it possible by boring to get artesian water.

Well, we spent five or six hours on Sunday in crossing this wonderful country and about six got to Toowoomba which is its capital, a town say of 20,000 people, which lies at the edge of the ridge dropping down to Brisbane and the coast country.[153] Here we had a hasty dinner and returned to the train to find a large party of politicians returning to Brisbane in a special carriage. We were invited to join them and did.

I, certainly, was getting rather weary by that time, as we had been travelling 24 hours on end, but I am glad we did go in as there were some very interesting people in the party – amongst them Groom who was in the Deakin Government (the Federal one) before the present Labour ministry came in and Tolmy who is the present Minister for

---

153. Toowoomba was first settled in 1852 and began to develop with the arrival of the railway from Brisbane in 1867. By 1911 its population was 13,119.

Lands in the Queensland (State) Government.[154] Groom is member for all the Darling Downs, and is now in the thick of a Federal campaign (the election is on May 31st). He was extremely interesting and obviously very able, but it must be a bit of a strain to have a constituency of some hundred square miles – and that, I imagine, is a small one.[155]

Arrived at Brisbane we had one night at a hotel – not a particularly good one – and moved on here next day, where I have been ever since. It is a most delightful Club, cool (so far as it can be cool here), very spacious, and most comfortable, in fact as a place to stay at I think it is the best we have yet struck.

On Monday our difficulties began. I started the morning by calling at the Chief Secretary's office – which resulted in discovery of the fact that there is very considerable friction, anyhow, between the State Government, which is Liberal, and the Commonwealth Labour Government, which reflected itself in the fact that the State Government weren't particularly interested in the Commission. This was accentuated by the procedure adopted by Knibbs, the Commonwealth Statistician who was selected to 'clear the way' for us – who, perhaps by instructions (I hope so for his sake) or else by mere stupidity, had flooded Australia from his own office with circulars asking for information, but hasn't apparently even begun to start getting things ready for us in a tangible form. The result, anyhow, is that the State Governments think that he has been trying to do work that they could have done themselves infinitely better and the mere mention of his name makes the State officials use lurid language.[156]

You can imagine (or rather I hope you can't) the result on the unfortunate me. I have to try and collect the necessary witnesses myself, and make all the arrangements for their coming at very short notice. And I have also to try to smooth things over as far as I can – no doubt with indifferent success.

---

154. Alfred Deakin (1856–1919) had been an enthusiastic advocate of federation. He was Prime Minister 1903–4, 1905–8 and 1909–10, losing office to Labor at the election. Littelton Groom (1867–1936) was M.H.R. for Darling Downs 1901–29 and 1931–6: he had been Minister of State for External Affairs 1909–10. James Tolmie (1862–1939) was Secretary for Public Lands in Queensland 1912–15.
155. Harding presumably means 'some hundreds of square miles'.
156. Evidently a black episode in the otherwise distinguished career of George Handley Knibbs (1858–1929): he was Commonwealth Statistician 1906–21, was knighted in 1923 and was heaped with honorary degrees. He was dutifully thanked by the Commission for his work as its local agent in the *Second Interim Report*.

Brisbane River.

*Above: Photograph, Department of Agriculture
and Stock, Brisbane, 1910; and right: Postcard*

Troubles are added to by the fact that I have to look also to travelling and luggage arrangements, all of which went like clockwork in New Zealand but are very hazy here, and by the intense desire of some of the members to upset such details of travelling as have already been fixed up!

Altogether I started the week with very considerable troubles. As they will, no doubt, have settled down long before you get this letter, (in fact they are already getting better), I may as well put them on record.

To go back, we did manage to get some evidence ready for Tuesday – by which time the other members of the Commission turned up – and we have been collecting it and hearing it at intervals ever since (at least a 'faithful few' who have stayed have heard it).[157] The rest of the party, having changed their ideas as to their route at least four times, have left on a tour as far as Rockhampton (some four hundred miles further

157. Six formal sittings of the Commission were held in Brisbane between Tuesday April 1 and Wednesday April 9, questioning 32 witnesses.

north)[158] and aren't expected back till Tuesday. Another party left on Friday night for Cairns by steamer – Cairns is right up in the north of Australia – and in the middle of the sugar country – and they won't rejoin the main party till half the tour in New South Wales is over.[159]

I have had such a lot to do in one way and another that my experience of Brisbane is mainly confined to the precincts of the Government Offices and to Parliament House where the Commission has been sitting.

But it is really a very beautiful city. There are splendid public gardens with subtropical trees and flowers, good public buildings, and a river which winds through the town just as the Thames does through London. Brisbane lies about 18 miles from the sea, and the tide comes up to it and well beyond.[160]

---

158. Gold rushes in the 1850s and the arrival of the railway in 1867 brought Rockhampton to life. The population in 1911 was 14,456. Foster, Lorimer and the Tatlows were in this party, arriving in Rockhampton on 4 April.

159. Cairns in northern Queensland developed from 1875 to serve the local gold and tin mines. It had a population of 5164 in 1911. Haggard, Campbell and Bowring, as a formal committee of the Commission, took evidence here from 13 witnesses over three days, April 10–12.

160. Brisbane, named after Sir Thomas Brisbane (1773–1860), Governor of N.S.W. from 1821 to 1825, was first established as an offshoot penal settlement in 1824 but was opened up to free settlers in 1842. It grew to become the capital of the colony (later the state) of Queensland and had a metropolitan district population in 1913 of 151,300. The major public buildings included the Parliament House (1868), city hall (1864), public library (1896) and university (founded 1909).

The river (which is called the Brisbane River) is getting quite familiar. We went down it in a launch for six miles or so on Thursday afternoon, in order to see the depth and the wharves etc., and today we have been right down to the mouth, and rather beyond, in one of the Government steamers, in order to see and inspect the Penal Settlement on an island, which has the familiar name St. Helena, lying outside.

The Penal Settlement sounds rather dull, but really today has been the most interesting day (except last Sunday with the sight of the Darling Downs) which I have had in Queensland. There was quite a large party on the steamer, including Mrs. Denham, the wife of the Premier (an aggressive and really dreadful woman), and several high Government Officials (heads of the Civil Service) and their wives. They all laid themselves out to be pleasant, and most of them were quite interesting. Moreover, it has been a beautiful though very 'steamy' day, and the river is delightful, as is the island where the Settlement is. The latter has beautiful gardens, with 'pawpaws' and other fascinating fruits of which one never heard before[161] and also a herd of prize Ayrshire cattle which were shown and described to me with great zeal and particularity by the head warder.

Which reminds me to say, if I haven't said it before, that I hope to return, if with nothing else, at least with a considerable knowledge of stock. I already know the difference quite well, between an Ayrshire and a Holstein cow .

You won't be interested in particulars of a convict settlement and I don't know that I have really very much else to write about except that yesterday we had a drenching day. It rained continuously for over 24 hours, and there was a gale which, as we heard, forced the steamer starting for Cairns with the Commissioners on board to anchor and wait for better things.

I seized the opportunity to get my hair cut, and to send off a telegram (at great expense!) wishing good luck to the Choral as I promised I would. I only hope the event will justify the good wishes.

There is some advantage, though, in giving up the excursions, and sitting in Brisbane working. The Queensland Club is apparently rather a hub of the state, and a lot of people turn up, who are very interesting to talk to. Quite apart from some of the Ministers and the heads of Departments, I have come across the leader of the Opposition – a barrister

---

161. The pawpaw – also known as the papaw, papaya or custard apple – had been introduced from the West Indies.

Mount Morgan Gold Mine, near Rockhampton, Queensland.
Photograph, Department of Agriculture and Stock, Brisbane, 1910

with Labour proclivities – and the Manager of the Mount Morgan mine, a very famous gold and copper mine in the north of Queensland, who was hauled in yesterday to give evidence before the Commission and also talked to me at breakfast one morning.[162]

So while I am pursuing Knibbs with unuttered imprecations up hill and down dale for preventing me from seeing the country (he himself is placidly accompanying the rest of the party in the north and doing no work whatever!), I am not sure that I am not really learning more about Queensland by staying here!

 Best love
  Ever you affectionate brother
   E. J. Harding

---

162. Mount Morgan developed especially from the 1880s, when gold was discovered, and from the early 1900s, when copper ores began to be mined. The workings were inspected by Foster's party of Commissioners on April 8 on their way back from Rockhampton.

Australian Club

Sydney

April 14th 1913

My dear Eva,

I can't get at our own stationery tonight, and anyhow I think our supplies are getting rather low, so I am reduced to another type of paper from that to which you have got accustomed. But I don't suppose you will mind much.

We have been 'racketing' about rather this last week, and I am quite glad to come to a halt again here. 'Here' is a comfortable club in Sydney, high up on the hill, overlooking the Botanic Gardens[163] and Harbour, quite quiet, and altogether very different from the Australia hotel where we were before.

Our last few days at Brisbane were pretty full up, but not enormously busy, as we had 'broken the back' of the work by the time I got off my last letter. The consequence was that on Monday night I went to the theatre, at the invitation of the Secretary of the Chamber of Commerce of Brisbane, an ex-sailor and a very good fellow, on Tuesday night we all attended a dinner given by the Queensland Club where we were staying, and on Wednesday night we had to drive miles or so (and it poured all the time) to a dinner at Government House. Add to that, that there was a luncheon given by the Queensland Government on the Wednesday afternoon, that the weather got appallingly close and very rainy on the Tuesday and Wednesday, and that we had to pack up and leave Brisbane by 7.50 a.m. on Thursday morning, and you will realize perhaps that I left the place feeling rather like a wet rag.

However, that was by no means the end of our doings for the week. Our stopping place for Thursday night was Toowoomba, which is about 4 hours away from Brisbane on the Sydney line, high up (about 2000 feet) and the capital of the Darling Downs. Here we found a most elaborate programme arranged for us – a civic reception at the Town

---

163. Botanic gardens were an important feature of many towns in the British colonies and dominions. Their value was not merely recreational but scientific and commercial: the cultivation of species and their distribution to other parts of the Empire were intended to unlock 'green treasure' by improving and increasing Empire production. Kew Gardens in London served as a clearing house and directed many operations. The appointment of the first superintendent in 1816 marks the formal creation of the Royal Botanic Gardens in Sydney. Other Australian botanic gardens were established at Melbourne, Brisbane, Adelaide and Hobart.

Toowoomba, Queensland, Street Scene.
Photograph, Department of Agriculture and Stock, Brisbane, 1910

Hall; motor cars in the afternoon to a foundry, a butter factory, and a malt works; a 'civic' banquet in the evening followed by innumerable speeches; and more motor cars on the following morning to see farms, the local cemetery (of which everyone seemed inordinately proud) and two schools. All of which you will find (or most of it) described in the *Toowoomba Chronicle* of which I am sending you a copy.

But really, for a very modern and 'country' town Toowoomba is really extraordinarily jolly. It has broad streets and green avenues, and the air was delightful – a great relief after Brisbane.

Unfortunately it was cloudy and wet all the time we were there, and we didn't do as much as had been intended. The original scheme was for a motor drive which would have taken us right over the Downs and landed us at Warwick, which is at the other end. But that had to be given up.

We got into the train at 12 on Thursday – and remained in it the rest of the day, and, after the usual break of gauge at the New South Wales border, through the night. But at 7 in the morning the process of being entertained began again. As many of the party as could be induced to stop, left the train at Newcastle, which is 100 miles or so north of Sydney, stayed there for the day, and came on in the evening.

You may imagine that few of the aged and aging Commissioners could be prevailed on to stop, so I was pressed into the service. Really though, I don't regret it, and I can't remember ever coming across so

Newcastle, New South Wales.   *Postcard*

hospitable a lot of people as those of Newcastle were. There was, of course, the usual Mayor (a very superior type this time), whose guests we were for the day. But, besides him, all the celebrities of the place seemed to turn up, and there was a tremendous gathering on the launch which took us round the harbour and at the 'civic lunch' which came after it. Between the two, by the way, was another reception at the Town Hall, at which, to my horror, I found myself in a seat of honour alongside the Commissioners, and forced to shake hands with all the people as their names were announced, one by one, by the Town Clerk! I was nearly in convulsions before five or six had gone past.

Newcastle, really, is a place with a future. It has a very good harbour, with unlimited wharfage, and there is coal at the very doors. In fact most of the coal, I believe, comes from about 2 miles out at sea. The place is really the Cardiff of Australia and therefore was very well worth a visit.[164]

---

164. Newcastle was first settled in 1801 as a camp for hardened criminals, but from the 1830s, like Cardiff and also its English namesake, it grew rich on coal. The 168-kilometre rail link to Sydney was completed in 1889. By 1911 the town had a population of 11,610, but it was to grow more rapidly from 1913 when the Broken Hill Proprietary Company began to build a major steel works there.

'Shipment of Sheep to China from Pinkenbah, Queensland'.
Photograph, Department of Agriculture and Stock, Brisbane, 1910

The remnant of our day, apart from the harbour and the lunch, was spent in more motor cars visiting more factories. It was a somewhat weary party that crept into the Sydney train just after 5, and went off to the accompaniment of a round of cheers!

I found myself talking a good deal to one Watkins, the member for Newcastle in the Federal Parliament, who turned out to be the Labour 'Whip' and, therefore I suppose the next Cabinet Minister, when a vacancy turns up. He certainly struck me as being very honest and extremely capable – and he started life as a pit boy![165]

The arrangements for the work of the Commission in Sydney are as chaotic as in Queensland, only the language of the local officials about 'our Mr. Knibbs' is somewhat more lurid. However, the State

---

165. David Watkins (1865–1935) was a miner and active trade unionist before being elected for Labor to the N.S.W. Legislative Assembly 1894–1901 and to the House of Representatives 1901–35. He was the Labor Whip 1909–14 and party secretary 1908–17, but in spite of his party loyalty, his unbroken parliamentary record and Harding's prediction he never achieved cabinet office.

Statistician, one Trivett, having blown off the steam in an interview which I had with him last night (and that between 9 and 10 after I had been on the go for 36 hours), has proved extremely kind, and has been helping me today in making the necessary arrangements.[166] So I hope things may go fairly smoothly; still life is by no means easy.

The small remnant of today I have spent in exploring the Sydney parks, and in getting glimpses of the harbour, both of which are extremely beautiful, especially towards sunset when everything is lighted up with the glow.

So far as Queensland is concerned, I leave it with a mixed impression. The high country looks as good as any country can be, and I can imagine the day when it will have an enormous population – I wonder of what race?[167] But if Brisbane has generally a climate such as it had the last days of our stay, and if the northern coast belt is anything like it, I can't think of a really strong people living there for any space of time. Even now, I think there is a certain want of vitality noticeable. It will be interesting to see what the members of the Commission who have been up in the north have to say when they return. So far as the vitality theory is concerned, the look and talk of the people one met seemed to confirm it. Certainly to my mind the 'back country' population is much more attractive than the average 'Brisbanian'.

However, this is akin to moralizing, and I haven't time enough for that, and will hastily stop.

> Ever your affectionate brother
> E. J. Harding

> DOMINIONS ROYAL COMMISSION
> Cronulla
> April 20th 1913

My dear Father,

No doubt you will not recognize the address – and I never heard of the place myself till this morning – but I am beginning this letter sitting by the wayside in a very 'mushroomsy' place on the shore of the Pacific waiting for a tram so I may as well give it fame by a headline.

---

166. John Burt Trivett (1859–1933), the State Statistician for N.S.W., also gave evidence before the Commission on Friday April 18.

167. Queensland's population had reached 2,743,765 by 1988. As elsewhere in Australia, it has become, since the Second World War, ethnically mixed.

Incidentally it will prove to you that I am not now so hard worked as not to be able to get out of Sydney.[168]

We have had rather a week of it though. There has been 'evidence' every day but last Monday and the whole of it has had to be arranged (except 1½ days) since I got to Sydney late on Saturday April 12th.[169] I therefore appeal again to Harry – as an expert in these matters by now – as to whether he would not have been rather appalled at the prospect, as I was when I wrote last Sunday. However, as it happens, everything has worked pretty smoothly, and I don't feel so apprehensive about Melbourne as I did.

Also the Commission has heard some rather interesting people – including the Administrator of the Northern Territory, who happened to be passing through on his way back to his post at Port Darwin, and the Commissioner of Railways in New South Wales, who apparently has hardly ever opened his mouth before in the 6 years he has been here.[170]

---

168. Sydney was the site of the penal colony established in 1788 and named after Viscount Sydney (1733–1800), the Home Secretary who had authorised the mission. The settlement grew into the colony of New South Wales in 1823, attracted free settlers from 1825 and prospered upon the profits of wool and later of gold and other minerals. It obtained responsible government in 1856. In 1913 the population of N.S.W. was 1,831,716 and of the metropolitan area of Sydney 725,400.

169. The Commission, meeting in the Parliament House, had so far gathered evidence in Sydney from 31 witnesses in five days from Tuesday April 15 to Saturday April 19, and there were to be two more sessions with 10 witnesses the following week on Tuesday April 22 and Wednesday April 23.

170. The Northern Territory had been claimed as a dependency by the colony of South Australia in 1863, but on 1 January 1911 it became formally the responsibility of the Federal government of the Commonwealth of Australia. Its white population in 1913 was a mere 3672. *H.M.S. Beagle* had explored the coast in 1839, and a tiny settlement had been established in 1862 which struggled to survive on the profits of local gold and pearl shell resources: it was renamed after Charles Darwin (1809–82) in 1911. The Administrator was John Anderson Gilruth (1871–1937). He took office in February 1912, after a distinguished career as a veterinary surgeon and professor in New Zealand and in Melbourne, but he experienced many disappointments, generated much hostility and was forced to resign in 1919. The taciturn Chief Commissioner for Railways in N.S.W. was Tom Richard Johnson (died 1935) who had joined the Great Northern Railway in 1872, served as Chief Commissioner 1907–14 and became a railway adviser to the Chinese government in 1919.

Sydney, New South Wales, the Botanical Gardens, Government House and Conservatorium.   *Postcard dated 12 January 1920*

Waiting for a launch
Place unknown

When I got to the end of the last page my tram came along, conveyed me a mile or so, and dropped me at a point whence I have walked about 2 miles to the shores of Botany Bay.[171] Here there is said to be a ferry across the Bay which one fetches by hoisting a white flag. I have hoisted the flag but see no visible results as yet. So I will go on writing.

Apart from the actual work, which has been pretty heavy as you will judge from the fact that I have been at it till 10 or 11 most evenings, we have had quite a quiet week.

The interludes have been a dinner given by the Chamber of Manufacturers on Wednesday, an excursion round Sydney harbour on Thursday afternoon, and yesterday (Saturday) afternoon and today when I have been exploring the suburbs of Sydney. But before I say anything about these, I ought to tell you that after the first night or so at the Australian Club they moved my room to one looking straight over the Botanical Gardens down to the Harbour – so that I must now have

---

171. So named by Sir Joseph Banks (1744–1820) who led a botanising expedition on its shores following the first European landing there in April 1770 during Captain Cook's first *Endeavour* expedition to the South Seas.

one of the best views in the whole of Sydney, and can take in the harbour and its surroundings while I am dressing in the morning.

The Chamber of Manufacturers' dinner was much more interesting than these functions generally are. There were no speeches, and after dinner there was only 'talk' – which I always find quite entertaining. Moreover, I found as my neighbour at dinner a man who had spent a long time in the northern part of Queensland and held very strong views as to its unsuitability for occupation by white people.[172]

The ferry is really coming – I must stop again!

The other side of the ferry –
place again unknown

This is really a most amusing peregrination. I have got across, and have now to wait half an hour for a tram. So I am getting some tea and incidentally will go on with this letter.

I was talking about the newspaper man at the Chamber of Manufacturers' dinner – he also interested me a good deal with stories of the manners, morals and home life of the average inhabitant of Sydney. Home life as we understand it hardly seems to exist here. The people spend most of their available spare time in the open air. If they want to entertain their friends they do it at a theatre or a picnic. They don't ask them to their own houses – chiefly I gathered because they generally can get no servants, and consequently have to do all the house work themselves.[173]

(That last remark, by the way, applies to hotels here, I think, but not to Clubs. At any rate at the Australian Club the service is very good – my only complaint against it is really the surliness of the Hall porters – perhaps they are secretly prominent supporters of the Labour party! The members of the Club as a whole certainly are not!)

---

172. Between 1863 and 1904 an estimated 57,000 Pacific Islanders (known as kanakas) had been brought into Queensland and northern N.S.W. mainly as cotton and sugar plantation workers, often under dubious contracts of employment. This practice had aroused humanitarian and White Australia opposition and had been banned in 1904: many planters resented the loss of a labour supply which was used to tropical conditions, and cheap.

173. In Australia as in New Zealand there were regular middle-class complaints about the shortage of domestic servants, generating proposals that special efforts should be made to recruit them, carefully, from among Great Britain's 'surplus women'. Haggard reckoned that one disadvantageous consequence of the White Australia policy was a shortage of domestic servants, causing difficulties in Australian home life and hence a lower birth rate.

Australian Club

Sydney

Just as I finished the last lines the tram turned up, and by it and train I have safely returned here. So I will go on again and try to get finished without further interruptions.

The Harbour sight seeing, of Thursday afternoon, was chiefly remarkable for the people on board. It was a Government party and the Premier – McGowen (who is just retiring) – and one or two other Ministers were there.

McGowen doesn't look a strong character, and the little talk I had with him wasn't of any very great interest.[174] I think that it was mostly a story on his part of convicts and rum in the old days.

But Edden, the Minister for Mines – commonly known as 'Alf' – was a fruitful source of entertainment. He started as an emigrant, then was a Miner and now is a Minister – and he has contrived to reach the latter position in spite of an obvious fondness, as shown by the tint of his nose, for the bottle in some of its forms. His language is – well, we will say primitive (anyhow it even exceeded the remarks of State Officers of which I have told you more than once when they talk of Knibbs) and his character is simple also. He told me with tears in his eyes, (and I know this is true because I saw them come) that he was a real patriot and would shed his last drop of blood for the old country. And just as I was going off the boat – I am sorry for the anticlimax – he turned to me and said 'would I mind when I got back letting people know that there was anyhow one patriot in Australia – of course I could see that it was put in the press all right'.[175]

After all this, it has no doubt become clear to you that New South Wales is ruled by a Labour Government. Some of their wives were on board, but in common with most other women in Australia, their accents were grating and unpleasant and I didn't find anyone worth talking to among them.

---

174. James McGowen (1855–1922) was Prime Minister of the Labor govenment of N.S.W. 1910–13: a modest and moderate man, he found it difficult to control his more able and energetic colleagues, and he lost touch with the party's rank and file.

175. Alfred Edden (1850–1930) was a coalminer who emigrated to N.S.W. about 1879 and settled near Newcastle. In 1891 he became one of the first Labor members of the Legislative Assembly and in 1910 Secretary for Mines. He was expelled from the party, with others, for supporting conscription during the war.

So much for the excursion – we cruised up and down the harbour, but didn't see anything of particular interest except Cockatoo Island where the Australian navy is beginning to be built.[176] There Mr. Lorimer was much delighted to find that most of the steel plates came from his own firm in Glasgow.

Manly, where I went yesterday afternoon, was a pleasant change from talking and being entertained. I was quite by myself and could just walk along the beach and watch the surf bathing.[177] I forgot to say (and this you will want to know, though Jack, if this letter goes to him, will know well enough already) that Manly is a seaside suburb of Sydney reached by ferryboat or tram where there is a splendid sandy beach and big breakers rolling in. I went by ferry, had tea there, and came back by tram. And really the last part of the tram ride might well have been through the main streets in Walworth or Peckham.[178] The only obvious difference is the arcading of the streets here, where the second rate shops are, to keep out the sun and the rain. The more I think of it the more absurd it seems that a country of the size of Australia should have a quarter of its total population collected in Sydney and Melbourne. My tour today – and the various remarks I have made in writing the previous bits of this letter will have shown you more or less what it was – really illustrates this absurdity rather well. I went out by train to the National Park, a big reserve about

---

176. Cockatoo Island had only ceased to be employed as a maximum security prison in 1908, and in 1913 its new use as a naval shipyard had just begun. The formation of an Australian navy was partly a response to British pressure from the turn of the century for some dominion contribution to the costs of imperial defence, partly an assertion of growing Australian nationalism, and partly a reaction to a perceived threat from emerging Japan. The decision was taken in 1909, the first ships of the Royal Australian Navy were built in Great Britain and launched in 1910, and the first to be built at Cockatoo Island (from imported parts) was the destroyer *Warrego*, completed in 1912. In 1913 three further vessels were under construction.

177. The suburb of Manly is 11 kilometres or 7 miles from the centre of Sydney and supposedly 'a thousand miles from care'. In 1911 it had a population of 10,465. It is reputedly the place where surfing began in Australia in defiance of the law in 1902: until then an Act of 1838 had effectively prohibited public bathing during the day. On 15 January 1915, not long after Harding's visit, Duke Kahanamoku (1890–1968) from Hawaii, who had won a swimming gold medal at the Stockholm Olympic games in 1912, demonstrated the art of long-board surfing to impressed locals on Manly beach: a photogaph of this magical moment in Australian culture appears in Nat Young's survey of *The History of Surfing*, 1983, p.47.

178. In London's dreary south-east inner suburbs.

Manly, New South Wales, the Ocean Beach.   *Postcard*

20 miles or so to the south of the city, and came back by launch, walking, ferry, tram and train as opportunity offered. Except just in the reserve itself (and hardly there), there was no feeling of being out in the open country. I should say that of the million and a half inhabitants of New South Wales, well over a million live within a 20 mile radius of Sydney.[179]

I don't see how the Australians can expect to keep a continent when this is going on. Of course the town life here isn't like London – there is more sun and fresh air and infinitely less crowding. Still the tendency must be to produce a parasitic population, and in a new country I don't believe that such a state of affairs can go on very long. This is more moralizing and I daresay I have said the same thing in previous letters, so I had better not go on.[180]

---

179. The National Park, the first in Australia and the second in the world, was dedicated in 1879. Harding's calculation on the distribution of population in N.S.W. is pretty accurate, and his point was already true of the country as a whole. Over 62% of Australia's population was classified as urban by 1921 (over 85% by 1986), even though the economy remained heavily dependent on primary production. By 1913 nearly 40% of Australia's population lived in the six major metropolitan centres.

180. The belief in the physical and moral virtues of the countryside and the corrupting influence of the town was a characteristic feature of early 20th-century British culture.

Therefore I will finish up this letter with two things – first that I hope to get a glimpse this week of some of the inside of New South Wales on the way to Melbourne. The Commissioner of Railways is taking a party of the Commission on a 'personally conducted tour' next Thursday morning, and I may with luck be able to go with them.

The second thing is that it looks now as though I should come back via the Pacific and across Canada – which all along I wanted to do. The Chairman is going that way, and as he meditates an 'interim' report on Australasia he wants me to go also. But I shall know more about that in a week or two.

> Best love
> Ever your affectionate son
> E. J. Harding

> DOMINIONS ROYAL COMMISSION
> Lockhart N.S.W.
> On a special train
> April 24th 1913

My dearest Mother,

As it is April 24th, I will send my letter to you this time, and take the opportunity of wishing you 'many happy returns' from somewhere underneath you. I fear they are rather belated!

I feel rather 'at the back of nowhere' as you will recognize perhaps from the address: the fact is that this is Friday,[181] and we have been travelling in this train since Wednesday evening ('we' is the Chairman and two other members of the Commission, Bridgman and I), the object being to see some of the 'back country' and the agricultural country of New South Wales, and very interesting it has been.

Nothing very particular happened during the first part of this week except that on Monday I went out to lunch with some of the pleasantest people I have struck yet in Australia – a man named Hay who is a big squatter, his wife and, I suppose, a daughter though I didn't catch her name. Anyhow, they had a big house close by the Australian Club, and I enjoyed my lunch very much – rather contrary to custom.

We started talking about a book called *Australia* by John Foster Fraser – a book which has a great if somewhat equivocal reputation in Australia because of its outspoken views. I hadn't read it, but had heard of it. Next

---

181. Curious: Friday was April 25, not 24.

day I found it waiting for me at the Club as a present from the said Mrs. Hay! Wasn't that kind? I have begun to read it on this train, and find it very stimulating, and, as far as I can judge, absolutely true. I would strongly advise you to get it from the Library.[182]

We closed up 'the evidence' on Wednesday morning, and were due to leave at 8.20 in the evening, so you can imagine that there was a fearful rush to get everything packed and ready to go off. However, we just managed it. Of course all the heavy luggage is going through to Melbourne. We expect to pick it up tomorrow night.

Now the tale of our wanderings on this train will be rather unintelligible without some kind of a map, so I will cut one out of a train timetable and send it along with this letter.

It is certainly a new experience. The Chief Commissioner of Railways is the 'cicerone' of the party: he has his own private car, and there is also a sleeping car, dining car and staff car, so we travel in comfort not to say luxury. Moreover, on occasion, we can stop to inspect a lucerne field or other attraction. Mr. Foster, the Canadian member, is particularly keen on such things. No doubt he draws contrasts with the maple leaf.

Our first destination was Condobolin which, as the map will show you, is well to the west of Sydney, and on a line which will presently connect with the mines at Broken Hill.[183] All the last part of the way is real 'back country' – that is to say the line is quite unfenced and runs for mile after mile through a perfectly flat country which is just used for sheep or grazing cattle and will, I suppose, presently grow wheat. Occasionally there are hills cropping up, covered with the everlasting gum trees (the general colour effect is not green as in England but blue), but usually there is just the plain.

We stopped at Condobolin for an hour and had a hurried walk round, including a visit to the school. It is just an ordinary township – tinroofed cottages, dusty roads, a shop or two, and some more or less pretentious public buildings – but the school was much as you might find at home – with a Presbyterian minister engaged in giving religious instruction to make the picture complete!

---

182. John Foster Fraser (1868–1936) was an extraordinary Scottish traveller, lecturer, journalist and prolific writer. One of his epic journeys began in 1896 when he set out to cycle around the world: it took him 744 days. His book *Australia: the Making of a Nation* was published in 1910.

183. The vast mineral riches – silver, lead and zinc – of Broken Hill had been revealed during the 1870s and 1880s. The Broken Hill Proprietary Company was founded in 1885 and went on to become Australia's wealthiest conglomerate.

For the rest of the day (that was yesterday) we travelled without a break. The great feature was the gradual change, as one got nearer towards Sydney, from grazing to cultivated country.

When the dark came on we were in orchard country: but we woke to find ourselves in 'back country' again, waiting at a station called Queanbeyan. The map will show you where that is.

The object in going there was to have a look at Canberra which is the name (and the site) of the future capital of Australia. The Commonwealth has taken over a strip of territory from New South Wales, in which the capital is to be, and a month or so ago (I daresay you saw it in the papers) they had an immense ceremony there and laid the foundation stone.[184] The actual stone lies about 9 miles from Queanbeyan station, and we drove there in motor cars, passing by the Federal Military College on the way, where the officers of the new Australian army go to be trained.[185] That was interesting too, but as we didn't stop, I won't describe it, and will go on to the site which is, as a matter of fact, the foundation stone, and, at present, nothing else but hills and the usual gum trees.

But they have really chosen an almost ideal place. On one side there is a plain extending for ten miles or so with a vista of blue hills beyond: in front there are hills close by, and on the other side there is another long stretching view while at the back there is a ridge of mountains about 5000 feet high.

As we saw it this morning – it was quite early and the atmosphere was perfectly clear – the site was really most beautiful, so beautiful in fact that the creation of a city there will certainly spoil it. One mistrusts any modern city, and I certainly shouldn't count an Australian one as an exception in spite of Melbourne and Adelaide.

---

184. The decision to establish the Federal capital on this virgin site and to create the Australian Capital Territory was confirmed by the Federal parliament in 1909, amid considerable controversy. An international competition to produce an appropriate design for the new town was won by a Chicago architect, Walter Burley Griffin, generating further division. Nevertheless, the foundation stone was laid on 12 March 1913 and building eventually began, only to be interrupted by war and post-war depression. The Federal Parliament first met there in 'temporary' quarters in 1927.

185. The separate Australian colonies had maintained their own modest defence forces, but following federation a Commonwealth army was created. From 1911 all males were liable to some form of compulsory military training, and a military college primarily for officers was opened at Duntroon in the Australian Capital Territory in June 1911.

However, Colonel Miller, the Administrator of the Territory, who came round and explained what the plan of the city is to be, is certainly a statesman – one could judge that from the extremely interesting description he gave us of his views of the future of Australian railways which I must tell you all about when I get back – so perhaps there is some hope yet.[186] At any rate there can be no doubt that the site is all that could be wished for.

We came back to Queanbeyan station along another road, across open country with occasional sheep to enliven it.

And having got on board our train again we have been travelling till half an hour ago when we halted for the night and I started this letter.

Just the last two hours of daylight were interesting – we came into a country which 'smiles' and is partially ploughed up. But for hour after hour before that it was really depressing. The country is 'yellow and blue' – that is to say the soil is yellow and the gum trees blue – instead of green and brown as one likes to see it in England. There are no rivers to speak of – if there are any they are muddy, if they are running, or more often a succession of pools. And as for the endless collection of gum trees, which seem generally withered or entirely leafless, I can't get out of my mind a comparison between them and the Dürer illustrations of the *Inferno*:[187] to travel through them for any length of time is like moving through a never ending army of withered ghosts.

You will think that my opinion of Australian country isn't very high. It isn't – except for patches. It looks to me as if it wanted something to correspond with a public house – a potential thirst quencher. If you could double the rain fall and halve the gum trees, New South Wales might be really a great country! As it is, I don't feel the least surprise that there is no great inclination to tackle cultivation on the land. For the man just out from England it must be a most depressing task.

Oriental Hotel
Melbourne
April 27th

This is Sunday, and we finished our travelling at 6.30 last night. That meant just 3 full days and nights in the train, so I am somewhat weary today. However, it was an experience I wouldn't have missed for a good deal.

We woke up on Saturday morning to find ourselves still at Lockhart, and as we weren't due away till 9.30 in the morning we had time for a walk round. It is a dismal place, though apparently very prosperous judging by the number of grain sacks stacked at the station waiting to be

Wheat Ready for Transport.   *Postcard franked 20 November 1912*

carried away; but, as for living there, well with a prospect of a fortune at the end of it one might stand it for a few years, certainly not otherwise.

So I left it without much regret, and the train made its way to the Victorian border, joining the main Sydney line at a place called The Rock, which name sufficiently describes the place. From there to Albury, which is the frontier town between New South Wales and Victoria, the line goes through the 'Riverina' Country which is fertile and flat. I could endure life there, I think, even if it weren't wildly exciting. At Albury there is the usual break of gauge (did I mention that before as a defect in Australia? There are at least 3 different gauges in the five mainland states), and therefore we left our special train and crossed the platform on to another, provided by the Victorian Railways.[188]

---

186. Colonel, later Brigadier-General, David Miller (1857–1934) raised the 1st Army Service Corps for the war in South Africa. He was Secretary for Home Affairs and Administrator of the Capital Territory 1902–17.

187. This must be a slip of the pen: Harding, who knew his art, meant to refer to the work not of Albrecht Dürer (1471–1528) but of Gustave Doré (1833–83). Doré's illustrations of *The Inferno* first appeared in 1861 and became well-known in Britain. They were reproduced in *The Vision of Hell*, the opening part of the *Divine Comedy* by Dante Alighieri (1265–1321), translated by the Rev. Henry Francis Cary and published in London in an opulent format by Cassell, Petter and Galpin in 1866.

188. The meeting at Albury in 1883 of the two incompatible halves of the Sydney to Melbourne railway had boosted the significance of this minor frontier town. It had gathered a population of 6309 by 1911.

Melbourne, Victoria, Flinders Street and Central Railway Station.
Postcard franked 20 November 1912

It wasn't so sumptuous though, there was just one car and the engine, and the chief point about it was the guard who had all the importance of the Commissioner of Railways and rather more besides. However, we got to Melbourne, as I said before, at half past six in the evening, whereas if we had waited till the ordinary train we shouldn't have arrived till eleven.

The country between the border and Melbourne is quite different to New South Wales.[189] Most of it is flat, though there is an occasional 'wold' and there are high hills in the distance. But it is, superficially anyhow, much less arid (though we happened to strike a day with very heavy rain showers) and it is also more settled and less untidy. There are trees after the English manner at most of the stations, and there isn't the same number of hungry-looking stumps of gum that one sees further north.

---

189. What was to become the state of Victoria started unhappily with abortive military and convict settlements beginning in 1803. Free settlers began to arrive from 1835, and the territory then grew spectacularly following the discovery of gold in the 1850s. The colony became independent of N.S.W. in 1851 and gained responsible government in 1855. By 1913 Victoria had become the most densely settled Australian state with a population of 1,412,119. The metropolitan area of Melbourne was by then a settlement of 651,000. The names of the state and its capital perpetuate their 19th-century British origins: a queen and her first prime minister.

If I were a prospective settler I should prefer to begin in Victoria rather than New South Wales, though I think I should choose the hill country of Queensland in preference to both.

We got to Melbourne to find the rest of the party safely arrived, luggage and all, and today has begun the usual struggle to get things in shape for the work of the week. It has been showery again (it has been also quite cold, by the way) so being indoors hasn't been much of a hardship.

Here I think I will stop: the mail doesn't go till the middle of this week, but I know I shan't have any time after this evening.

> Best love
> Ever your affectionate son
> E. J. Harding

> Dominions Royal Commission
> Federal Parliament Buildings
> Melbourne
> May 5th 1913

My dear Father,

If this letter is somewhat haphazard you must forgive me. I am beginning it while the sitting is going on, and I shall probably be interrupted every other minute. But I didn't have time to begin yesterday (today is Monday).

We have suddenly dropped from summer to winter. It is blowing and has been raining spasmodically for the last few days, and the temperature is rather like November at home.

I personally rather like it, but the Commission generally is rather 'sorry for itself'. The members have colds and lumbago, and other ailments of the kind. These (and the prospect of going home in a few weeks) have begun to react on their nerves. They are irritable at times, and begin to wrangle in a mild way as to who should go where, and who should be Deputy Chairman when Vincent is away.

The last question seems, to my mind, of infinitesimal importance, and I can't bring myself to take it seriously, which is perhaps as well. But these old men no doubt do. The great point is whether the Canadian member, who is a 'minister', does or does not take precedence over an English Knight and a K.C.M.G., that is Bateman. The two sit and glare at one another when the Chairman shows signs of wanting to go off!

We go to Tasmania on Friday – and it is likely to be cold. This accentuates the difficulty as the Chairman does not want to go. At present there are plots and counterplots and I don't know, in the least, how the crisis (for want of a less formidable word) will settle itself. I shall, no doubt, know when it comes to next week's letter.

All of which is very amusing, if one is able, as I still am, to appreciate the humour of the situation. But I think everyone will be rather glad when the next fortnight is over, and the Commission 'disbands' temporarily.

The question for settlement next will be by which route the 'Pacific gang' will return. There are two possibilities – the *Ventura*, an American boat, which goes to San Francisco, and the *Marama*, a boat of the Union Company, which has Vancouver as its destination. Oh I forgot: it is also possible to combine both – travel by the *Ventura* to Honolulu and from there to Vancouver by the *Marama*. At present we 'wait on' the Chairman who is hopelessly undecided and gets a different account of the two boats from everyone he meets.[190]

So we have reserved berths by both boats, and I still hang on to my cabin on the *Morea* by which the Suez Canal party are to travel.[191] Thus is one secured at present. Possibly I told you all this last week; if so, I must apologize for the repetition. But it is a topic which is rather uppermost just at present.

Meanwhile, we pursue our work at Melbourne – and evidence has been going on for nearly a week. Fortunately, it is now nearly through, and I don't suppose Tasmania and Adelaide will provide anything very exciting.[192]

Interspersed have been the usual functions – a lunch by one of the New Zealand Ministers who happened to be over here and another by the Chamber Commerce. The first was the most interesting, as the

190. The Union Steam Ship Company ran a monthly service to North America under the name Canadian–Australasian Royal Mail Line, with subsidies from the governments of New Zealand, Canada and Fiji (where its ships also called). *Marama*, 6450 tons, 420 feet by 53 feet, was built by Caird on the Clyde in 1907: she became a hospital ship during the war. The alternative, *Ventura*, 6253 tons, 400 feet by 50 feet, built by Cramp at Philadelphia, belonged to the Oceanic Steamship Company of San Francisco. The company ran a service every three weeks from Sydney to San Francisco: a first-class single ticket for the journey of 20 days, 10,760 kilometres, cost from £67 0s 2d to £71 11s 6d, second class £45 17s 2d, and third class £36 6s 4d.

191. *Morea*, a P. & O. boat, 10,900 tons, 540 feet by 61 feet, was built by Barclay Curle on the Clyde in 1908.

192. In the event the Commission worked hard in Melbourne, questioning 29 witnesses over 8 days, Tuesday April 29 to Saturday May 3 and Monday May 5 to Wednesday May 7.

Melbourne, Federal Parliament House.   *Postcard franked 20 Novenber 1912*

Governor General and Fisher, the Prime Minister, were both there.[193] It had also the novelty, and relief, of being cut short when about half way through. The G.G. and the Prime Minister, having come late, had to go early, and the speeches began before sweets and the coffee.

---

193. The Governor-General was Thomas, Third Baron Denman (1874–1954), who was shortly to depart, unhappily, from Australia. His career began as a soldier, but he became Liberal Chief Whip in the House of Lords in 1907. He was appointed Governor-General in 1911. He established good relations with the Labor government of Andrew Fisher, but worked less easily with the leader of the Liberal opposition, Sir Joseph Cook (1860–1947), who was soon to be Fisher's successor. He had also annoyed the Colonial Office by asserting Australia's right to control her own navy, rather than have it subordinated to the British Admiralty. He also suffered from chronic bronchitis, and the Australian wattle plant aggravated his asthma. On top of all this, his wife disliked the constraints and formalities of vice-regal life, and their marriage was strained. Lord Denman was allowed to end his term of office prematurely. He resumed his career as Liberal Chief Whip in the Lords 1919–24, while Lady Denman went on to chair the National Birth Control Association 1930–54 and directed the Women's Land Army during the Second World War. She died on 2 June 1954: he followed her on 24 June.

Melbourne, Inspecting Fruit.   *Postcard issued by Victoria Immigration and*
Intelligence Department, franked 14 July 1915

Tuesday May 6th

I am still writing at Parliament House, and Mr. Deakin is giving evidence – which is interesting.[194] So I may be more 'haphazard' than before.

The only 'interludes' in Melbourne up to now have been the Saturday afternoon and Sunday, most of which I spent in having a look at Melbourne and the 'surrounding'. Saturday afternoon provided a variety of entertainment.

It started with a football match at The Melbourne Cricket Club – the 'Lords' of Melbourne. We were received with open arms by Trumble, the Australian cricketer, who is secretary, and escorted to the Committee room which has a splendid view over the ground.[195] The Australian type of football is quite unlike ours – either Rugby or 'Soccer' – but as I don't understand the finer points of the game, and, if did, I don't suppose they

---

194. Parliament House, built 1856–92, where the Commission held its sessions, was the home of the Federal Parliament while Canberra was under construction.

195. Hugh Trumble (1867–1938) was a pretty useful batsman and medium-paced bowler: in his 31 test matches against England between 1894 and 1904 he took 141 wickets for 20.8 runs. Melbourne Cricket Club was founded in 1838.

would interest anyone at home very much, I won't pursue the subject, except to say that it is an open game, and quite good to watch.[196]

We left at half time, and went off first to the Botanical Gardens,[197] which are really splendid, and then to the remnant of a regatta on the River Yarra.

The Yarra, by the way, flows right through Melbourne, and ends at the port – which is a bad port. As a river it very much improves the city, and there are open spaces all along it.

On Sunday I couldn't resist the temptation to go out along a line which led to stations called Surrey Hills and Box Hill. I thought I should never hear the last of it if I came away from Victoria without seeing them. So we went out to Box Hill ('we' in this case is Bridgman and I) and had quite a long walk, 8 miles or so, over the hills ending at a place called Heidelburg whence we returned by another line to Melbourne. Our lunch place was called Doncaster – so you will see that the authorities have a fine catholicity in naming.[198]

As a matter of fact the country is more like Kentish than Surrey Hills. It is open and covered with orchards – apples, pears, plums, oranges and lemons. And the view is closed up some 15 miles away or so by ridges of hills which look blue and I suppose are covered with the usual gum trees. If so, at a distance, they lend enchantment. But I am told that the gum tree has a beauty of its own which grows on one. As you will have gathered from other letters I haven't learned to appreciate it yet.

Altogether Victoria strikes me as much more homelike than New South Wales – what the back country is like I can't of course say, as I shan't have much of an opportunity of seeing it.

To go back to Sunday. I had supper in the evening with the Allens – the people who, as I think I told you, were the best of our acquaintances

---

196. Australian Rules football combines elements of Gaelic football and English rugby football and is played on a cricket oval. It was devised as a purely Australian game by H. C. A. Harrison and T. W. Wills in 1858 and was sponsored by the Melbourne Cricket Club as a way of keeping its members fit in the winter season. The rules evolved over the next half century. The first inter-state Australian championship under the auspices of the recently formed Australian Football Council was played in Melbourne in 1908: Victoria won.

197. Melbourne's Royal Botanic Gardens were formed in 1846.

198. Surrey Hills, Box Hill, Heidelberg and Doncaster were suburbs to the east of Melbourne. The English Box Hill in Surrey is near Coldharbour where Eva lived.

on the *Medina* – a Professor, his wife, and three daughters. They have rather a jolly house up at the University, and I enjoyed seeing them again. The only drawback was that the daughters insisted on showing me volumes of picture post cards of England! I think I have come to the end of my budget of news, so I will close down for the week.

But since I started to write yesterday the scales have fallen on the side of the *Ventura*, and it looks almost certain that we shall take her to Honolulu at least. That may mean an overland journey from San Francisco to New York, with a possible detour to Ottawa. If possible I should like to see some of the Canadian authorities and try and rescue the Commission from some of the many pitfalls into which it has fallen in Australia!

> Best love
> Ever your affectionate son
> E. J. Harding

DOMINIONS ROYAL COMMISSION
Tasmanian Club
Hobart
May 11th 1913

My dear Eva,

I think it is your turn for a letter though I can't be sure, but anyway it doesn't matter much, I suppose. My letter has, of course, the usual change of address. We are 'picnicking' in Tasmania for a few days – that is, it is more like a picnic than anything we have had lately. I have only five members to look after instead of the usual ten, I have only five pieces of luggage instead of the usual eight, and the Commission has only one 'sarcophagus' of papers (and that the smallest) instead of the usual five.

The question of the Chairmanship in Tasmania settled itself by all the 'belted Knights' of the party refusing to come, so Foster is left in undisputed possession.

I think I finished my last letter last Tuesday night. I had an 'evening off' then, and went out to dinner in a suburb called Toorak with Atlee Hunt who is Secretary for External Affairs to the Federal Government.[199]

---

199. Atlee Arthur Hunt (1864–1935), a lawyer by training and an enthusiast for federation, became a civil servant and served as Secretary at the Department of External Affairs 1901–17. He had a major impact on immigration policies and on the administration of Papua, upon which he had reported in 1905 after an official visit. He had given evidence before the Commission on Thursday May 1.

He has been over several times to Conferences, and obviously prides himself rather on his knowledge of the C.O. and its officials. He has a wife who similarly prides herself on her acquaintances with the English peerage. With the obvious limitations caused by these predilections, both are quite nice, and he, moreover, has a very good collection of curiosities from Papua.[200] So I enjoyed my evening, and played bridge with such zest (I hadn't had a game since the outward voyage to New Zealand) that I barely caught the last train back to Melbourne.

Wednesday, Thursday and Friday were a bad contrast. Everyone was hopelessly undecided till the last whether they would come to Tasmania or not. They changed their minds, I should say, at least six times. Finally they split into four lots. One has gone to South Australia already. (At least I hope it has got there.) One goes down from Melbourne tomorrow. One has gone to Burnie on the west coast of Tasmania.[201] One has come down here.

All the various members had to be fixed up with (a) railway tickets (b) sleeping cars (c) steamer tickets (d) conveyances for luggage (e) cabs (f) hotel accommodation – and in addition we had to keep the South Australian and Tasmanian Governments posted up. So you can perhaps imagine that by the time I got on board the Tasmanian boat I was pretty well tired out. Of course besides all these arrangements we had to 'clear up' after the Melbourne sittings, a process which proved more difficult than usual.

My only consolation was that I got out of the speeches at a Lord Mayor's lunch, on the plea that I had too much to do.

Of our sea experiences up to now our voyage to Tasmania was decidedly the worst. We struck a boat called the *Rotomahanha* – commonly known, I understand, as the 'Rotten Banana'. She is very

---

200. Possession of the island was disputed by Europeans from their first discovery of it in the early 16th century. The western part was eventually taken by the Dutch in 1828 and the eastern half was finally partitioned between Great Britain and Germany in 1884. The British protectorate of Papua was administered by Australia from 1906, in a significant gesture indicative of Australian imperial aspirations in the Pacific. The Australians captured the German portion, New Guinea, on the outbreak of the First World War and retained possession as a League of Nations mandated territory in the share-out of the German Colonial Empire among the victors.

201. Burnie is actually on the north coast, facing Bass Strait. This party was deputed to visit the mines at Mount Lyell and the Zeehan district of Tasmania, while the groups going to South Australia were to inspect Iron Knob.

small, under 1000 tons, and very old – in fact a generation old, I believe, and I am told that she was the first screw steel ship to come south of the line. She has at least a smell for each year of her age, and an indescribable stuffiness. The engines went wrong on the way over and we were held up for an hour or so while they were being patched up.[202] Also the sea was more than a little rough, and the boat moved about a great deal and very quickly. All which details may perhaps explain the fact that I, for the first time, definitely succumbed to the enemy and had a most miserable night. But indeed most of the party, if they breakfasted at all, did so, like myself, on soda water and an apple.

However, the straits once passed, our visit has had its compensations. We came up the River Tamar to Launceston.[203] The town is 40 miles from the mouth, and the river has either wooded hills or homesteads with apple orchards all the way up. At Launceston we were so late in arriving that we missed a Mayoral reception and barely caught the train to Hobart (I had better explain by the way that Launceston is in the north and Hobart the south of Tasmania). And we have had today an expedition which I shall count as quite one of the finest in Australia – right into the heart of the bush country.

But, before I tell you about today, I will go back a little to our journey through Tasmania from Launceston. The Premier sent his Secretary – one Addison – and the Government car[204] to meet us at Launceston, and we had 3 hours daylight to see something of the interior. (We left Launceston at 3 and got to Hobart just before 9.) To my mind Tasmania is *initially* more attractive than any other of the Australian states. Possibly this is because the distances aren't so large, and the island has consequently the appearance of being more closely settled. Possibly it is that the country has been *longer* settled, and so has a more English appearance. Anyhow, the houses are more in the English style,

---

202. Shipping enthusiasts might claim that Harding was privileged to sail on such a historic vessel as the *Rotomahanha*: 1727 tons, 298 feet by 35 feet, built by Denny at Dunbarton on the Clyde in 1879. She was the world's first steel ocean steamship, she recorded the fastest passage of her time in her maiden voyage to New Zealand, and her rakish lines and steam yacht appearance have been lyrically described. She ended her career on the Melbourne to Launceston run from 1908 to 1921, and was broken up for scrap in 1925.

203. Launceston, up river from the north coast, was first settled in 1805. It was named after the birthplace in Devon, England, of Philip King (1758–1808), the third Governor of N.S.W. Its population in 1911 was 20,754.

204. That is, railway car. The railway to Hobart, 200 kilometres of 3ft. 6ins. gauge, was completed in 1876.

and one might almost call the 'townships' villages. They are essentially the same, though rather more ragged. Or there is a third reason which occurs to me – that one is used to sheep and apple orchards, and is not used to vast areas of gum. It all comes back to the fact that Tasmania is more like the home country, a quality which I, for one, shall insist on counting as a virtue.

The people, too, have been extremely kind. The Premier came down to the station at Hobart to meet us. The ex-Premier put us all down as members of the Tasmanian Club and gave us a little supper when we got in (which was particularly grateful after the soda water and the apples). And today quite a lot of people lent us motor cars, so that we could see something of the country, and came themselves to show it to us. In fact almost half the witnesses who are going to be heard tomorrow were collected in the course of the day. (As usual nothing in the way of evidence was ready beforehand.)

I suppose that today we must have travelled 70 miles or so by motor car. We went up over the slopes of Mount Wellington (the mountain which lies at the back of Hobart), and after crossing another ridge or so, came down to a country full of orchards and a river called the Huon which flows into the sea, I think, in the south west corner of Tasmania. Our destination was a saw mill belonging to the Huon Timber Company, and after we had been shown the timber on the wharf we were taken up the hills on a most curious light railway so that we might see the big trees and the real Tasmanian bush.

The train consisted of a woodburning engine and two trucks entirely without springs in which we travelled, I suppose, 10 miles or so each way. There was a fearful rattle, but the experience was worth every bit of it. They have built this railway through bush which is so thick that if you try to walk through it, 3 miles a day is a very good average. There are most beautiful mosses, ferns and tree ferns. And finally there are immense trees (all of the gum variety, I am sorry to say, but really I am beginning to have a respect for the gum!) which run up to 200 feet or so high. One was felled for our special benefit. It came down with a terrific thud, and crushed all the lower bush so that there was immediately a strong scent of eucalyptus. The men measured it roughly and found that it was 13 feet round and about 180 feet long.[205]

---

205. Foster reports: 'After having been photoed standing in line on the prostrate form of this venerable personality, we filed silently out from the prone presence that had graced ten centuries of constant growth.'

Even the run back in the cars added something to the interest of the day. It was bright moonlight, and the road winds through the mountains with every variety of curve.

You must think, after reading through all this, if you get as far, that Tasmania has fascinated me. And indeed what I have seen of it certainly has. I hear that you can make anything from £30 to £100 an acre by planting it with apple trees. That certainly seems a vocation which is well worth considering.

Well, I have said my say, and as we shall have a hard day tomorrow I had better close up and go to bed.

The die is cast, I think, for the *Ventura* for our voyage back across the Pacific. But the accounts we hear of her are none too good, so there is always the possibility of the Chairman changing his mind at the last moment. Meanwhile, he has gone so far as to engage a cabin costing £145 on the Hamburg–America *Imperator* across the Atlantic.[206] I trust he won't expect me to come with him and pay a similar sum!

> Best love
>> Ever your affectionate brother
>>> E. J. Harding

DOMINIONS ROYAL COMMISSION
Grand Central Hotel
Adelaide
May 18th 1913

My dearest Mother,

It seems funny to think that this letter will travel most of the way home with two of the members of the Commission. Haggard and Garnett leave this week by the *Mooltan*, and by the same boat travel the members who are going to Western Australia.[207] So I am in the happy position of feeling that by the end of this week I shall have got rid of the

---

206. The Hamburg–Amerika Line had become one of the world's premier carriers since beginning in 1847 an emigration service from Germany to the U.S.A. and later to South America and the Far East: the company had a fleet of 168 vessels in 1910. *Imperator*, 52,250 tons, 883 feet by 98 feet, was one of three enormous liners built in Hamburg for its prestige transatlantic service. She was launched in 1913 and had recently made her maiden crossing. This was one of the vessels confiscated by the British as reparations from Germany after the First World War. She was purchased by Cunard in 1921, renamed *Berengaria* and operated until 1938.

majority of them. Then we shall have just over a week to 'clear up' in and get to Sydney. We expect to sail by the *Ventura* on May 31st – how far we go in her, and whether we get to San Francisco or Vancouver, is still delightfully vague.

From my point of view – now that we have safely got through Sydney and Melbourne – the work isn't so hard. But it is certainly quite time that the Commission disbanded for a time. The Commissioners have all got safely to Adelaide (that is except Garnett who is staying at Melbourne because he has so many relations to see – it is quite a 'hornet's nest' to him for his daughter married the Editor of the Melbourne *Age*, the chief paper). But that is about all I can say of them. At least five, including the Chairman, are sorry for themselves on account of chills and similar ailments. I hope the Australian Bight will do them good!

After all this preliminary I will return to Hobart. I think I got, in my last letter, as far as the Sunday we had there. Monday was spent in taking evidence – a process which became almost farcical on account of the number of witnesses who were 'polished off' in the day. I think there were twelve in all – they were mostly collected by telephone in the course of the day – and a good many were those who had lent us motor cars on the previous day. (As usual nothing had been arranged beforehand.)[208]

It was all over by 5 p.m., and the result was that most of the party were able to devote Tuesday to sightseeing (or 'seeing selected districts' to use the proper official phrase) on their way back to Launceston.

We had arranged to return by the 'night express'. When we got to Tasmania we found that it consisted of a 'mixed train' which took 12 hours to cover 120 miles, and shunted at most stations. So we persuaded the Government to provide us with a special which took us up in the riotously fast time of 5½ hours. As there was some 'clearing up' to do, I couldn't get away to the sightseeing on Tuesday, but as a matter of fact I was able to see most of the country immediately north of Hobart from the special train. It only confirmed the previous good impression, which I think I told you of last week. But I must just add that Tasmania is a hop

---

207. *Mooltan* was another ship in P. & O.'s Australian fleet, 9600 tons, 520 feet by 58 feet, built by Caird on the Clyde, launched in 1905 and sunk by a submarine in the Mediterranean, south of Sardinia, on 26 July 1917.

208. Thus demonstrating the convenience of the telephone, first patented by Bell in 1876 and well-established worldwide by the 1880s. The session on Monday May 12 was held in the House of Assembly in Hobart. Foster went on in the evening to give a speech of an hour and a quarter to the townspeople in the Town Hall: they 'seemed very appreciative'.

country as well as an apple country. We saw lots of poles and even an Ost house (is that spelt right?). But the hops themselves had been cleared.

They tell a good story of the Tasmanian night express. An Englishman travelling by it got very restless after an hour or so, and began to walk up and down the car to the annoyance of his fellow passengers. One of them said at last 'Why the something or other don't you get out and walk?' 'Well', he said, 'I would, only they don't expect me till the train arrives.'

We completed our picnic at Launceston. Evidence at Town Hall 9 a.m. Three witnesses examined as speedily as could be managed. 11 a.m. to 1 p.m. motor drive round Launceston accompanied by the Mayor, the Town Clerk and other notabilities. 1 p.m. lunch. 2 p.m. leave by steamer for Melbourne. A good morning's work, as I think you will agree.

As a matter of fact, I was sorry that we had so little time at Launceston. There is a beautiful gorge just outside it, which is the pride of the place and has in it a pool that has no bottom! There is also a Power House reached by a road on which, some hundreds of yards before the House itself is reached, is seen a notice saying 'Drivers proceeding beyond this point do so at their own risk'. Our drivers took the risk. But you will see that the country isn't exactly flat.

The voyage back to Melbourne was about as smooth as any voyage could be. In fact, it was so smooth that I could see the reflections of the stars in the water. Perhaps it was as well as the *Loongana* by which we travelled, though less smelly than the *Rotomahanha*, has the reputation of being a very bad roller.[209] And, even in the weather we had, I couldn't really fancy the food.

We got into Melbourne on Thursday morning, and weren't due to leave for Adelaide till Friday afternoon. But there was a good deal to do in the interval. Letters had accumulated, and I had to fix up the arrangements for sleeping berths etc. which proved none too easy. Apparently we struck the breaking up time in Australia. Every place seemed full of boys and girls going home from school.

However, we got settled eventually quite comfortably, and the only incident of the journey to Adelaide was that most of the party got no breakfast till they arrived. You get turned out for breakfast at 6.30 a.m. If you refuse to get up then, you can, if you like, order some breakfast to

---

209. *Loongana*, 2448 tons, 300 feet by 43 feet, built by Denny on the Clyde for the Union Company and launched in 1904, was the world's first ocean-going mercantile turbine and was designed specifically for this route. She carried 246 passengers first class and 136 second class. Her name was a Tasmanian word for 'swift': she could reach 20 knots.

Launceston, Tasmania,
Electric Power Station.
Postcard dated
13 August 1912

be brought to you in your berth. But if you don't do that, or if you do and the conductor forgets (and we suffered in both these ways), there is nothing to do but to wait till you get to Adelaide at 10.

I forgot to add, before leaving the subject of Melbourne, that Bridgman and I managed to snatch a few hours on Thursday afternoon and went down to Brighton which is a tiny watering place down the coast. It isn't as pretentious as our one, and is, in fact, just an outlying suburb of Melbourne so it isn't worth more ink.

I am writing on Sunday night, and our experience of Adelaide up to now has been mostly rain. But, as I expect I told you when I was writing of our flying visit here in February, it is a really beautiful city, very well laid out (it has parklands completely encircling the city) and with quite good public buildings.

This afternoon we have been taken out again in motor cars, and in them despite the rain we must have been some 50 miles. Our route lay up the Mount Loftie ranges[210] (where we went when we were here before) and along the hills and valleys inside the ridge which runs parallel to Adelaide. The illustration at the side may give a faint indication of what I mean.

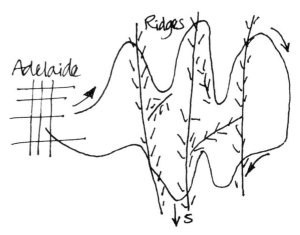

Anyhow, we went first to the Governor's country house in the hills, which I believe have a splendid view, only we couldn't see it for clouds and rain, and then on to the house of Dr. Sterling, a Professor at Adelaide University I think, who gave us tea.[211] His garden would have fascinated you. It was full of rare trees, shrubs and flowers (including gentian), so laid out as to give a colour effect from almost any point. I can't attempt a list of them – but I must just mention the maidenhair fern tree which, so the Professor told us, was a relic of the secondary period, when it was browsed upon by the iguanadon and the ichthyosaurus. Can't you imagine them doing it?

Altogether I take away, despite the rain, a very good impression of the country we went through. There are 'pockets' of good soil between the hills where anything will grow. The tints of the apple trees and the cherry trees were astonishingly vivid. (It is, of course, getting late autumn here.)

---

210. Mount Lofty, rising to 710 m., was so named in 1802 by Captain Matthew Flinders (1774–1814).

211. Professor (later Sir) Edward Charles Stirling (1848–1919) became the first professor of physiology at Adelaide University in 1900 and helped develop the medical school. He was also a noted anthropologist, who studied Australia's aborigine peoples, and a palaeontologist, who in 1893 found a remarkable collection of fossil bones of enormous marsupials and wombats. He was a campaigner for the prevention of cruelty to animals, for the welfare of children and for the political rights of women: he was elected to the South Australian parliament in 1884 where he introduced unsuccessfully the first women's enfranchisement bill. And he was an enthusiastic gardener.

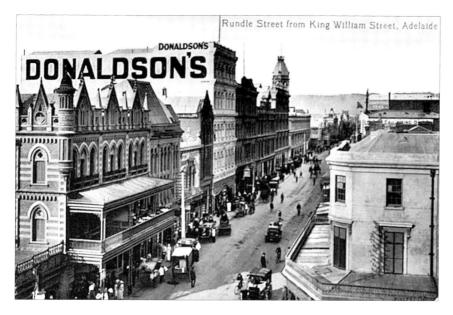

Adelaide, South Australia, Rundle Street from King William Street.
Postcard dated 27 July 1913

And there are scattered about country houses and villages – beg their pardon, they are called townships – which take away any feeling of emptiness.

One of the townships, we were told, is called Piccadilly (so called originally because the first inhabitant hadn't a neighbour for several miles.)

I think that is about all for this week, but I will say again, in case I didn't say it in my last letter, that the people of Tasmania were really astonishingly friendly. It was like going back to New Zealand again.

The Premier – one Solomon – came up with us from Hobart to Launceston. He is an unhealthy-looking man[212] (possibly because his party has a majority of, I think, one) and he certainly doesn't shave every morning. But, for unassuming friendliness (if 'unassuming' is a proper word to use of a Premier), we haven't seen anyone in the political line approaching him.

> Ever your affectionate son
> E. J. Harding

---

212. As noted earlier, Solomon died the following year.

DOMINIONS ROYAL COMMISSION
Oriental Hotel
Melbourne
May 27th 1913

My dearest Mother,

I was going to start this letter by saying that after you got it you wouldn't hear anything of me for six weeks. Then I remembered that I expect to get home nearly as soon as it does, and that other letters, lots of them, are on the high seas which you will be getting week by week. However, if the *Ventura* doesn't sink (and, since you can't get this letter till we are off her, I may as well say that we have heard strange stories concerning her) and if I have time, I will go on writing so that there may be a record of our journey home.

It will be pretty strenuous anyhow, I expect. To say nothing of the vagaries of the Chairman as to his route, we propose to tackle the question of an interim report, which will need some doing.

However, for the moment, we have a few days comparative peace. Last Thursday saw the majority of the party go off from Adelaide by the *Mooltan* for Perth.[213] The sittings of the Commission, so far as I am concerned, are suspended for quite a long time – 5 months or so. And the remainder of the party has been returning in detachments to Melbourne.[214] I got back on Sunday morning, and have been 'clearing up' in various ways since. We leave tomorrow (which is Wednesday) for Sydney and sail on Saturday.

Now to go back to Adelaide. It is really a very jolly town – in my opinion nicer than Melbourne which in its turn quite outdoes Sydney. The streets (here I go back to Adelaide) are well laid out, the public buildings, though on a small scale, exceptionally good, there is a very good museum and art gallery, and finally there are parklands all round the city as well as gardens and squares.

213. The Commission, meeting in the Legislative Council Chamber in Adelaide, had collected evidence from 13 witnesses, Monday May 19 to Wednesday May 21. Two Commissioners from the Perth party which left on May 22, Haggard and Garnett, were sailing for home, but Lorimer, Tatlow, Bateman and Campbell stopped to gather testimony from a further 28 witnesses from Western Australia in five days, between Tuesday May 27 and Friday May 30 and, following a visit inland to the Kalgoorlie mines, at a final session on Saturday June 7.

214. Sinclair was about to return to New Zealand, and Foster would eventually embark on a personal tour of the Far East. That left Harding, with Bridgman, to shepherd home just two remaining Commissioners, Vincent and Bowring.

We went, the last afternoon, to the 'Zoo' which took my fancy a great deal.[215] Most attractive of all were the flamingoes – curious creatures reminiscent of *Alice in Wonderland* (or is it *Through the Looking Glass?*).[216] They have legs like pink bamboo poles – very slender, and bending backwards (⟨I mean) instead of forwards. They have also delightful pink and white plumage.

I don't know what Adelaide is like in summer – pretty hot, I expect. But in May it has a superlative climate, blue Italian-like skies, and a crisp atmosphere. I was very sorry to leave it. (But I ought to add that there were mosquitoes even in May.) We had a pretty strenuous time there, all the same. Three days evidence, Monday to Wednesday, and, sandwiched in, two lunches and a Mayoral reception. I am sending home an Adelaide newspaper with a picture of the latter, from which you will perhaps be able to gauge the precise value of the function! Thursday was devoted chiefly to seeing the Perth party off and Friday to packing up. On Saturday we started back for Melbourne. The journey is 17 hours or so. This, I may add, by now seems quite a trifle!

There was one incident in Adelaide which deserves a word or two. I think I told you before that there is some 'feeling' over the question who should take the chair when Vincent is away. Up to Adelaide it hadn't risen acutely as Vincent had always been there, except in Tasmania, to which neither he nor Bateman went. Foster, therefore, so far as Tasmania was concerned, was left in undisputed possession. But Vincent, during the Tasmanian interlude, had spent his time in making a journey to Oodnadatta. This, as the map will show you, is right up towards the centre of Australia and the beginning of one of the possible routes of the Transcontinental Railway.[217] It was a long and rather tiring

---

215. Zoos were characteristic 19th-century creations in several colonial cities. Adelaide zoo was established in 1883, that in Sydney in 1880, and one in Melbourne as early as 1862.

216. The former: flamingoes are used as mallets on the croquet-ground of the Queen of Hearts in Lewis Carroll's *Alice's Adventures in Wonderland* (1865).

217. The railway from Port Augusta on the coast of South Australia to Oodnadatta in the far north was purchased by the Federal government at the time of federation. The intention was to continue the line up to Port Darwin. The connection was never completed: railway lines end at Alice Springs going north and Birdum going south, and the transcontinental route was only completed as a road. Vincent declared Oodnadatta as 'the Ultima Thule of the railways of the world'. Haggard described it as 'just a collection of straggling tin-roofed houses set down in the midst of an endless sandy plain', on whose edge was 'a sea of rusty tins and broken beer bottles – great marks of the white man's progress in all lands'.

journey, narrow gauge railway, lots of flies, and other disadvantages. Anyhow, the result on the Chairman was that he developed a rather bad sore throat, could hardly speak on the Monday morning, and couldn't possibly come out. He, therefore, sent a note to Foster asking him not only to take the chair, but to represent him at the functions. It so happened that the Mayor's reception and the Government lunch were timed for that morning.

This was too much for Bateman. To 'sit under' Canada at a meeting of the Commission was just possible. But that Canada should 'oust' the Mother country at a public function was intolerable. He made a bad imitation of Achilles. In other words he sulked the whole day and refused to attend both sitting and functions on the ground of 'indisposition'. No efforts could move him! Next day, Vincent being still in bed he relented so far as to come to the sittings – though he continued to glare somewhat till the end of the proceedings.

It sounds funny enough now, and in fact most of the members were hugely amused. But, as you may imagine, it was somewhat disconcerting at the time particularly for me who had to try and persuade him to come. And I am not so sure that we have heard the end of it yet. He will probably want, when he gets back, to get a ruling on the question of precedence, and then there may be trouble.

I said the incident was worth a word or two. I fear I have given it a good many.

A somewhat similar episode is the complaint that Sinclair, the New Zealand member, made to me that the Governors of Victoria and South Australia 'slighted' the Commission because they only entertained 'selected' members, particularly the 'belted knights', and not the members as a whole. As he admits that he dislikes functions of the kind, I don't quite see where the point comes in. I delicately suggested that the remedy might be for all the members to be made knights. This seemed quite to cheer him up! This letter is mainly 'episodical', I fear. However, I suppose it is all in the game. Many are the afflictions, or inflictions, of a secretary!

Since we have got back to Melbourne I have actually had time, in the intervals of clearing up, to look round a little. On Sunday afternoon we had a look at the picture gallery and museum – the former bad, compared with Adelaide, though there is a delightful Raeburn – the latter very interesting, with a lot of South Sea Island curios.[218] Today, incited by the memory of the Adelaide flamingoes, we set out to look for the Melbourne Zoo. We didn't find it, but saw instead the north part of the city which has a lot of very excellent parks. For its size Melbourne must have a lot more open spaces than London.

One more thing, and I must stop. I had to go up to Government House this evening to see Vincent who is staying there and I found him with a most interesting personality, one Sidney Kidman who is known as the 'Cattle King'. He knows, probably, more of the interior of Australia than anyone else, so it was more than worthwhile to talk to him. Amongst other episodes in his life, he bought a fourteenth share in the Broken Hill mine (one of the most famous silver and lead mines in the world) for 10 bullocks. He sold it, a few years later, for £450,000![219]

Ever your affectionate son
   E. J. Harding

DOMINIONS ROYAL COMMISSION
S.S. Ventura
June 5th (B) 1913
Nearing Pago Pago

My dear Eva,

I must really begin a letter this evening, even if I don't get very far with it, as it is probably the only time in my life when I shall be spending two Thursdays in one week. This fact, you will see, is duly marked on the heading of this letter. We have crossed the 180th meridian (I think that is the proper term), which means that we are half way round the world. Consequently we have gained 12 hours, and we shall have gained another 12 before we get home. Today, therefore, is 'thrown in'. I foresee interesting controversies with the Treasury, who count one's allowance by nights, when I send in a claim for 31 nights in June!

Having got so far, I fear I must stop. We are due at Pago Pago, the American part of Samoa, early tomorrow morning. I must get out a camera, and a sunhat in view of emergencies, and then go off to bed.

---

218. A Museum of Art was first opened in Melbourne in 1861 in a section of the public library: it became the National Gallery of Victoria in 1875. The picture by Sir Henry Raeburn (1756–1823) was a portrait of *Admiral Robert Deans*, purchased in 1910–11 with money left to the gallery by Alfred Felton (1831–1904): his endowment enabled the gallery to transform the quality of its collection by the acquisition of many works by distinguished masters.

219. Sir Sidney Kidman (1857–1935) also built up his fortune through stock-grazing and land purchase: eventually he owned or controlled an area greater in size than England.

June 6th 6 p.m.

We have just left Pago Pago, and are getting out to sea. I have half an hour before dinner, and will go on with this letter if the rolling of the boat, which is getting considerable, will permit me! I haven't got much to say of our last three days in Australia. We left Melbourne on Wednesday of last week, and got to Sydney on Thursday morning. There was nothing exciting over the journey (which of course was mostly 'familiar ground' and was also mostly done by night) except that we arrived two hours late and that it was bitterly cold during the night. Which induces the reflexion that on the whole, the weather we had in Australia was really very much colder than I had at all expected. Of course, we hit autumn and the beginning of winter, but really with the exception of Brisbane and a small part of Sydney, the weather we had was distinctly cool, and Melbourne at any rate was quite reminiscent of London in November. There was also a good deal more rain in Australia than I had expected, and at least twice we read of quite serious floods. I dare say that condition of affairs is rather exceptional, but I don't think the climatic conditions could have been.

The two days we had in Sydney – we sailed last Saturday – were, like those in Melbourne mainly 'clearing up' – which meant for the most part, fixing up ticket arrangements and telling the Union Co. (the Vancouver route people) that we didn't propose to travel by them.

But to my great pleasure I ran across an 'old friend', one Dean, who was at Hertford with me (just a year senior) and has since been living in Australia (about which he has written some books – notably one called *On the Wool Track* which we had on the *Medina*) and also in London as correspondent of the *Sydney Morning Herald*. I foregathered with him both evenings, and enjoyed talking to him a great deal.[220]

Which induces another reflexion – that one of the chief disadvantages, to my mind, of touring round the world in this way, apart from being away from home, is the absence of all one's friends and contemporaries with whom to talk over things. That is one of the pleasures I am most looking forward to when I get back. At present, one has first the

---

220. Harding's Oxford colleague, Charles Edwin Woodrow Bean (1879–1968), was a distinguished journalist, writer and historian. *On the Wool Track* was published in 1910. He was later the editor and part-author of the massive *Official History of Australia in the War 1914–18* which, together with his many other books about the war, did much to excite Australian national pride and fuel the ANZAC legend.

company of a somewhat older generation, and secondly the necessity of being pretty careful about what one says to any of them!

This by the way – the only other things I need to say about Sydney are these, first that I had quite a shave of being left behind in hospital (owing to the disgusting state in which the Sydney roads are kept, I slipped in boarding a moving tram and had a fall on the road – fortunately I got off with a bruise) and secondly that I spent the whole of my last morning up at Government House. Sir Gerald Strickland, who has only recently come, thought, I suppose, that the presence of a C.O. official was an opportunity for him to air his grievances. He has been a Crown Colony Governor which may have something to do with so misguided a taste.[221] I won't go into the details of what he told me, as they are, I suppose, for the C.O. only. But I may, at least, say that his conversation was another instance to show that the Federal-State friction in Australia doesn't affect Governments only but Governors as well!

The chief effect of having so long a talk with him, so far as I was concerned, was this – that I missed the opportunity of seeing anything of the polling for the Federal Elections which took place that day (incidentally that I was late in arriving because he lives four miles out and all the taxis had been engaged for the day!). I am rather sorry to have seen nothing though there was no apparent excitement. As a matter of fact, all the excitement seems just about beginning because we hear (I don't know if it is true – as our 'wireless' isn't too reliable) that the result has been pretty nearly a tie between Liberal and Labour.[222]

---

221. Sir Gerald Strickland (1861–1940) began his remarkable political career in the British colony of Malta (ceded to Britain by France in 1814) where he was born. He served as Chief Secretary 1889–1902. He was subsequently Governor of the Leeward Islands from 1902, of the Transvaal from 1904, of Western Australia from 1909 and of N.S.W. from 1913 to 1917. He then retired from the colonial service, but remained involved in both Maltese and British politics. He helped draft a new constitution for Malta in 1921. He became a member of the island's legislative assembly from 1921 and a party leader. However, he was also elected Conservative M.P. for Lancaster Division in 1924 and thus became simultaneously a member of the British Parliament. In 1927 he became Prime Minister of Malta, was created Baron Strickland in 1928, resigned his Lancaster seat, and concentrated upon the controversial politics of Malta, where he remained premier until 1932, narrowly escaping assassination.

222. In fact Labor was narrowly defeated and the Liberals under Sir Joseph Cook formed a government with a majority of one seat. It lasted only until new elections were held in September 1914 when Labor returned with substantial gains.

Sydney, New South Wales, Government House. *Postcard*

Oh – I forgot to mention one more incident at Sydney – that is the visit I paid to a Library just opposite the Australian Club where we stayed for the second time. I have forgotten its name – but it doesn't greatly matter, the point is that it is a Library practically devoted to books and manuscripts on Australia and the South Sea Islands and is quite the best of its kind that I have ever seen. Presently it will become a most valuable national possession.[223]

Now for the voyage back. I think I told you in one of my last letters that we had heard all sorts of rumours about the *Ventura*. So far at any rate they haven't at all been justified. Bowring, the Newfoundland member of the Commission, who is the only other member besides the Chairman returning this way, went on to Sydney a day or so before we did, so that he could have a look at her. His verdict was '*Ventura* second class – think quite safe' – and I think that sums her up pretty well. Apart from my wish to see Fiji (and after all one wouldn't have seen an immense amount) I confess that I hadn't the least desire to cross the Pacific by the Union line, as our experiences before hadn't been of the best. This you will have gathered from previous letters, so I needn't dilate on a painful topic!

---

223. This was the Mitchell Library, built around the unique collection of 61,000 volumes and other items amassed by the obsessive bibliophile David Scott Mitchell (1836–1907), one of the first graduates in 1856 of the new University of Sydney. His wealth derived from land on the Hunter river, rich in coal.

The *Ventura* is American, which, by way of a change, is rather refreshing (though it has caused the scoffers, of course, to make much of the fact that Empire Trade Commissioners are travelling by a foreign line). We have curious American foods, such as 'squabs on toast', and amongst other tastes I have acquired that of beginning every meal with grapefruit. The Captain and officers, the stewards, and a good proportion of the passengers (there aren't very many) are American too. I must say that they (I mean the Officers, stewards etc. – the passengers are dull) are all extremely nice. Here again the contrast with the Union line is somewhat marked.

As to the voyage, it hasn't been rich in incident so far. Between Sydney and Pago we sighted two sailing vessels, one island (the extreme south of the Fiji group called Turtle Island) and nothing else whatever. The only things therefore we have had to do are to work, a good deal of that, to struggle against sea sickness (we started with a 'fresh gale' behind us the first day out, and since then the Trade Winds have been blowing pretty strong from the north east), and finally to practise 'Deck Golf', which the Chairman has carted round the world, and which comes in very useful now.

I am beginning to vary this now by being taught cribbage by the Captain in the evening. The other four members of the party (that is the Chairman, Bowring, Green, his cousin, and Bridgman) are all rather expert cribbage players and have played a good deal already in the evenings.

This letter is getting so long that I must have a rest. I will leave over till the next instalment a description of Pago Pago and our day there.

Sunday, June 8th

We are now nearing the Equator, we expect to cross tomorrow morning, and so I must really begin by saying that, up to now, we have nothing to complain of as to heat. In fact I only left off a blanket last night, and that was only because the wind had at last died down.

But the Equator sea today is quite up to expectations. We have had it almost calm (just a little swell), blue sky with just a few clouds, and a splendid sunset to finish up with. The only thing needed to complete the picture has been 'a painted ship upon a painted ocean' – in other words a becalmed ship.[224] But that we haven't had. One more natural

---

224. 'As idle as a painted ship / Upon a painted ocean....', Samuel Taylor
      Coleridge (1772–1834), *The Rime of the Ancient Mariner*, lines 117–8.

phenomenon to describe. The new moon in the Southern Hemisphere rises like this ⟮ . In the northern Hemisphere it rises, as you know, like that ⟯ . But here between the two it is like this ⌣ . I know that because we have been fortunate enough to watch it both last night and this evening.

Now to go back to Pago Pago. As I said before, it is in the American part of Samoa (the rest is German).[225] The island itself is Tutuila – Pago is the harbour, and a very fine one it is. There is a small American Naval Station there – just a bungalow or two, and a gunboat.

Apart from the station, the island is most primitive, just high densely wooded hills with coconut groves all along the shore and native huts among the trees. The people are primitive too but very friendly. They are Polynesians – brown skinned, dark haired, brown eyed, quite good-looking for the most part, and with a splendid carriage. Costume very scanty. The men wear a loin cloth, the women a 'Mother Hubbard' costume (I believe it is called). The children from nothing upwards.

We walked round the bay and looked into quite a lot of the huts. I suppose the main occupation is to wait till the coconuts drop off. But some were engaged in weaving native mats. And all sorts of people turned up at the quay with various things to sell, ranging from a fan made of fibre to a native 'mace'.

They are quite ready to buy too as well as to sell. One of the natives fingered my grey flannel coat, and wanted to know how much it was. And the Chairman, to his great satisfaction, actually sold an umbrella to a native for the huge sum of 10/–!

The great event of the day was a native dance, specially arranged for our benefit by the naval officer in charge. There is one special 'dancing

---

225. Control of the Samoan islands had been disputed by Britain, Germany and the U.S.A. in the later 19th century. In November 1899 Great Britain renounced her interests, and the islands were formally shared out and annexed by the other two. Perhaps it was a kindness that R.L. Stevenson (1850–94), a trenchant critic of imperialism who had settled in Apia, had already died there in 1894, before this happened. The partition marked another episode in the acquisition of a colonial empire by the U.S.A. who in the previous year had annexed the Hawaiian islands and, after the Spanish-American war, the islands of the Philippines and Puerto Rico. American Samoa is still under U.S. control, administered, curiously, from the Department of the Interior. New Zealand troops occupied German (or Western) Samoa on the outbreak of the First World War and retained possession of these islands as mandated territories, thus satisfying some of her own long-standing imperial ambitions.

Samoa, Kava-Making.   *Photograph*

girl', apparently, kept in each village. As it happened, another of these girls was in Pago for the day. So these two, with a troupe of about 20 lesser lights came down in procession to the main open space of the village, and started their performance.

It was really most entertaining. A good deal is arm motion (very like what we saw from the Maoris in Rotorua) to the accompaniment of singing and the beating of a drum. Afterwards there was a certain amount of dancing.

But the really interesting part of the performance was the extraordinarily good rhythm – and also the presentation of a native drink called 'kava' by the principal girl to the principal visitors. The drink was solemnly presented in a cup to each person in turn. He had to drink it and make a sort of circular bow to the performers, using a phrase which I can't remember, but which means, I believe, 'Here's luck'.

Our last hour in Pago was also interesting. The dancing girls and the naval band (also natives) were invited, as a special honour, on board the *Ventura*. The Chairman presented the two leading dancers each with a sun umbrella. The band played varioùs tunes (really very well considering that it had only existed for a month) and ended up with 'Home Sweet Home' because it couldn't play 'God save the King' without its notes!

There was a small steamboat in the harbour to which we transferred a good deal of stuff. Her name is the *Dawn*, and she trades among the islands – to the Gilberts, I believe, a good deal.[226] I thought it would be worthwhile to board her and did. All I can say is that I should be very sorry to travel in her for very long.

Sunday, June 15th 1913
Between Honolulu and San Francisco

There is nothing really to say about the voyage from the time when I left off to the day we got to Honolulu. The only variation on previous days was that they rigged up a swimming tank in the bows. It was a refreshing interlude to be able to swim, if only for a stroke or two. But, with the exception of two days, we really had no heat in the tropics. I only had the blankets off my bed for two nights.

So I can go straight on to Honolulu. We got there last Friday about 7 a.m., and left at 5 in the evening. And in the interval we had a day which I can only describe as 'gee whiz wonderful'.

The Chairman had a friend or at any rate an acquaintance there. I think he had met her once in England. Anyhow she and her husband met us at the wharf with a motor car, showed us all the sights, gave a luncheon party in honour of the occasion, and finally deposited us on the wharf so near to 5 that I only got up the gangway just as they were preparing to lower it! Honolulu is the town – the name of the island it is on I don't know, but it is, of course, one of the Sandwich Islands.[227]

---

226. The Gilbert Islands (now known as Kiribati), 2500 kilometres to the north west of Samoa, were annexed by Great Britain in 1886. Sir Arthur Grimble's cheerful and highly selective recollections of British rule there while he was a young colonial service officer from 1914 were published as *A Pattern of Islands* in 1952.

227. Honolulu is the principal town of Oahu. Captain Cook was astonished to stumble upon these well-populated Polynesian islands in 1778, and probably more astonished to be killed there by the islanders in 1779. He had named the group the Sandwich Islands after his patron, the Earl of Sandwich (1718–92), First Lord of the Admiralty, but they became better known particularly outside Great Britain as the Hawaiian Islands. American vessels began to call before the end of the 18th century, and American traders, settlers and missionaries were largely responsible for eroding the independence and stability of the islands before formal annexation was effected in 1898. Hawaii became the 50th state of the Union in 1959.

And it is interesting for many reasons. First, there is an immense Japanese colony, with all the women in Japanese dress.[228] Secondly, there is the native population, Polynesian, but rather unduly civilized now, and not nearly so attractive as the Samoan islanders. Thirdly, it grows all sorts of tropical products – such as rice, sugar cane and pineapples which I hadn't seen before, even in Queensland. And, last of all, there is the American population, very up to date, with lots of motor cars.

Rice, by the way, looks very much like oats, and it rustles in the wind just as they do. And pineapples, seen from a long way off, have a curious bluey green colour which I don't remember seeing before. They don't grow on a large tree, as perhaps you might expect, but on little stumpy shrubs.[229]

All this sounds rather material. The real beauty of Honolulu lies certainly in none of these things, but in the extraordinarily beautiful flowers and trees. To my mind it certainly excels Ceylon in that way. And it also boasts a most astonishing collection of rock fishes, specimens of which are to be seen in the Aquarium, to which we went. They are of every shape and colour and with extraordinary markings – so clearly cut that they look as if they must be hand painted.

With the aid of the motor car aforesaid, we saw quite a lot of the island – first the 'Pali', a ravine at the back of the town which ends in a gap in the mountains from which, in the old days, there used to be a sheer drop of 1500 feet or so. Then the 'Country Club', a golf club overlooking the town, where I had my first experience of an American cocktail, then some sugar and rice country, and the Museum, which has some very good South Sea Island curiosities.[230] And finally after lunch, the collection of fishes which I have told you about already.

Interspersed with these, were visits to various people's houses, to see either them or the views from their gardens. In Honolulu there are no

---

228. Native Hawaiians were rapidly swamped by immigrants in the late 19th century. By 1900 there were 29,799 Hawaiians but 26,819 Caucasians, 25,767 Chinese and an astonishing 61,000 Japanese. It is not surprising that Harding was conscious of this community. They had been brought in initially as contract labour largely to work on sugar and fruit plantations.
229. The commercial growing of pineapples in Hawaii had expanded rapidly following the launch by James D. Dole (1877–1958) of the Hawaiian Pineapple Company in 1901 and the building of a cannery in 1903.
230. By 1913 the Bishop Museum already had a distinguished international reputation as a centre for Pacific and Polynesian studies. It had been established in 1889 by the banker Charles Reed Bishop (1822–1915) as a memorial to his wife Bernice, the last princess of the Kamehameha dynasty.

Hawaii, Duke Kahanamoku.   *Tourist brochure, 1918*

garden fences, and no entrance gates. You just drive up or walk up, and apparently go straight in!

I have forgotten, I now remember, the most extraordinary sight of all. The wind blows very strong down the ravine which I described, so strong that it blows back (or at any rate does sometimes) the water which tries to come down from the mountains on each side. So one sees water running uphill. That is an absolute fact.

There are disadvantages in being 'shepherded' all through the day. One was that we had no time to look at the shops – though I should have liked to, particularly at the Japanese ones – and another that there was no opportunity of getting trophies to bring away. In fact it was with the greatest difficulty and at imminent risk of losing the boat that I got a photograph or two. We must hope to find Japanese shops at San Francisco.

Still the advantages are considerable. We saw much more in the limited time than we could have otherwise and I shall remember for a long time the kindness of the American 'acquaintances'.

When a boat leaves Honolulu the custom is for all the passengers to be garlanded with flowers by their friends. It is a very pretty, and quite unique, sight, I should think. We only got one wreath, and barely that for want of time. But some of the people were almost smothered in them.

If I don't stop this letter now, it will get so thick that no envelope will take it. So I will end up by saying that the next thing we have to think about is the route across America. We, of course, are in the Chairman's hands and he is, as usual, undecided. At present he leans to a railway called the Atchison, Topeka and Santa Fe and to stop for a night (the Americans say 'stop over') to see the Grand Canyon of Arizona.

Ever your affectionate brother
E. J. Harding

P. S. I enclose a passenger list of the *Ventura* which has a picture of her. She isn't really half so imposing.

DOMINIONS ROYAL COMMISSION
Hotel Belmont
New York
June 28th 1913

My dearest Mother,

It seems years since I last wrote a letter – really I suppose it is just 10 days ago – and this one will, I believe, get taken across in the *Mauretania,* so it will perhaps reach you later than I do myself. Still, if only for the purpose of 'completing the record' I must write something of our experiences coming across America.

I think I ended up last a day or so after we left Honolulu. There isn't much to say of the rest of the voyage – except that it was quite calm, that the passengers from Honolulu were a 'lively lot' and organized all sorts of entertainments, and that I won a prize for a hopping race, which brought me a rather interesting pack of cards with California views on them.

Certainly I shall have pleasant reminiscences of the Pacific and the *Ventura.* I couldn't have imagined the tropics could have been so cool, nor could I have wanted a more comfortable boat. And our experiences at Pago and Honolulu make me want to see some more of the South Sea islands – a wish, I imagine, unlikely to be fulfilled just yet!

We sighted the American coast early on Thursday morning the 19th – it is high and almost mountainous. But the 'Golden Gate' into San Francisco harbour is nothing very exciting.[231] The entrance is wider than that into Sydney, and the cliffs not so steep. Once in, the balance turns, I think in favour of San Francisco, as the hills surrounding the harbour are higher and more broken. Not that it matters very much. They are both very fine, and there's an end of it!

We got inside by 11 a.m., but didn't land till after 1 p.m. If possible, the landing formalities are worse than they are in Australia. The doctor, the immigration officer and the customs authorities all have a look – or several looks – in, particularly the latter. However, by having a customs man specially 'attached' for our benefit we got off very well. There only remained the inevitable photographer and interviewer whose handiwork I sent you in a paper next day. And even that wasn't very appalling.

Visitors to San Francisco never hear the earthquake mentioned. It is always the 'fire' of 1906. Really, of course, the fire only completed the destruction caused by the earthquake. Anyhow, the whole city was in ruins and had to be rebuilt, and though a great deal has been done, and there are some wonderfully fine buildings, the whole has a curiously patchy appearance – one sees next to the newest skyscraper the charred ruins of one of the old houses.[232]

That is the first thing that strikes one: the second is the extraordinary steepness of some of the roads. Really they are so steep that one almost slips sometimes coming down, and the bus that took us to the hotel – the Fairmont – had to make a 'circumbendibus' to get there at all. If Francisco ever had snow, but I suppose it hasn't, its streets would be ideal for 'skiing'.

---

231. California, including the territories later forming the states of Utah, Nevada and large sections of Arizona and New Mexico, had been part of the Spanish Empire and subsequently a province of Mexico before being ceded to the U.S.A. by the Treaty of Guadalupe Hidalgo which concluded the American war with Mexico of 1846–48. A major attraction of California was the port of San Francisco, a rare safe haven on the long Pacific Coast of the Americas, and a gateway to the Far East. The population of barely 500 in 1848 was boosted by the gold rush of 1849 and had reached 416,912 by 1910. The famous Golden Gate bridge was not constructed until 1937.

232. The earthquake struck in the early morning of 18 April 1906 and fire swept the city for three days. Four-fifths of the buildings were destroyed, over half of the population of 400,000 were left homeless, 315 people died and 352 were reported missing.

San Francisco, the Fairmont Hotel and James Flood Mansion on Nob Hill, following the Fire of 1906.   *From a photograph*

The other striking points about the city are its wonderful atmosphere, its sky signs and Chinatown. The first is quite Italian – at least as I imagine Italian atmosphere to be, very bright, crisp, dry – not enormously hot. The second I suppose San Francisco shares with most other American cities – at any rate they have invented a word 'rubbernecking' for looking at them. But to the newcomer the sky signs are amusing, and bewildering. The main street of San Francisco at night time is like a continuous kaleidoscope. As to Chinatown it has had to be rebuilt like the rest of San Francisco, so I suppose it isn't what it was. But I found it interesting enough. Some of the houses, but only a few, are Pagoda style. The rest make up for lack of a distinctive style by their variety of Chinese wares.[233]

We left for the east on Friday evening, having in the interval done a little work for the Commission by making enquiries about cotton growing, as well as sight seeing.[234] I called on the acting Consul General,

---

233. Chinatown was a by-product of the gold rush, the building of the transcontinental railroads and the demand for cheap immigrant coolie labour (from the Hindi word *kuli*, related to the word meaning hireling). The Baedeker guidebook of 1904 urges tourists who visit Chinatown after dark to go accompanied by a regular guide, 'who are generally detectives'.
234. In their *Final Report* the D.R.C. recommended measures to increase Empire production of cotton.

a somewhat 'blasé' official of the 'Algy' type (Harry will know what I mean), and was by him sent on to an institution called the California Development Board which gave me quite a lot of information.

Apparently most American cities pride themselves on having the main exit by ferry. San Francisco certainly does, and so does New York. There is only one railway, I believe, that runs right into San Francisco. The others go from Oakland, the other side of the harbour. The plan has the advantage, if you start by night as we did, of allowing you to see the lights of the city across the water and to get a cool start. As a matter of fact the start was about the only cool thing about our journey. To get from the California side to the East, whatever route you take, means crossing a desert. We took, finally, the Santa Fe route which is very good, but doesn't escape the evil. We reached the desert at 10 on Saturday morning, and left it about 10 at night. The thermometer in the dining car got up as far as 110 and stopped there because it wasn't constructed to go any higher! And at Needles which we reached about 8 in the evening it must have been at least as high.[235]

To add to the situation a brass band had assembled at the last named station and commenced to play as hard as it could. The players, I think, were Mexican Indians. I can't imagine any white people, not even the Longmans, having the energy to discourse sweet music at that temperature.

If it hadn't been for the heat, the desert would have been quite interesting. There were mountains and mirages and salt scrub, and all the rest of whatever goes to make up the real thing. Even the names of the stations were sometimes amusing. One I remember was 'Baghdad Cal.'!

One of the chief reasons for choosing the Santa Fe route was because it provided what the Americans call a 'stop-off'. Having started on Friday night we found ourselves on Sunday morning at the 'Grand Canyon of Arizona' – and there we stopped, much to our relief, till Monday evening.

The Grand Canyon is certainly one of the 'wonders of the world'. The Colorado river has gradually cut a way through sandstone cliffs till it now runs through a gorge seven miles across and at least 4000 feet deep.

---

235. Needles, named after the nearby granite pinnacles, lies close to the border between the states of California, Nevada and Arizona. This rail route across the continent, following the old Sante Fe pioneering trail, was begun in 1863 and completed in 1883. The first rail connection between east and west had been secured by the Central Pacific and Union Pacific railroads in 1869.

All its tributaries have done likewise and contribute to the effect. The result is (but it is really impossible to describe it in words – you must see either it or a photograph to appreciate it at all) an immense chasm which from above looks rather like a honeycomb. The various cliffs inside the main gorge are of all colours from purple to orange. The effect, especially when the sun is setting, is truly magnificent. The cliffs are also fretted so that they have formed amphitheatres, pyramids, and shapes of all kinds. The whole setting is Babylonian. One rather expects to see an Eastern monarch sitting on a throne in the middle of all these splendours.

We were quite content to sit on the edge and admire, and didn't attempt to go down into the chasm, though that is possible, and a lot of people do it by way of an excursion. We thought all our energy would be needed to stand the rest of the journey, and that as a matter of fact proved only too true. It takes three nights and two days to get from the Grand Canyon to Chicago – and the temperature hung round 90 on the first and 100 the second day. So you can imagine that we weren't sorry to get to the end and have another rest. Fortunately the heat was dry and therefore just bearable.

The country through which we went the first day is described as 'cattle country'. That is another way of saying, euphemistically, that it is a shade better than the desert. It would pasture, perhaps, one cow to 20 acres.

By the second day we had got over the high country and down into the Mississippi valley. There was a lot of irrigation and quite a 'settled' look. The main crop, so far as I could see, was maize.

Not that there was anything of particular interest. In fact the most attractive things on the journey were the Indians and the Station Hotels. I had no idea that there were so many native tribes left in America. One thought of it as a country principally of Poles and Irish. As a matter of fact the Indians were very much in evidence (though no doubt we came through the region where they are thickest).[236] As to the hotels the Santa

---

236. What remained of the indigenous Indian population was estimated at 220,000 in 1910: the total population of the U.S.A. was 92,407,000. Irish immigration had been on a large scale since the mid 19th century (3.3 million 1846–95), but Poles and other immigrants from Tsarist Russia arrived in huge numbers from the end of the century (2.75 million 1896–1915): many Americans found this much more disturbing. '...Give me your tired, your poor, / Your huddled masses yearning to breathe free/ The wretched refuse of your teeming shore....' by Emma Lazarus (1849–87), *The New Colossus*, published in 1883, was carved into the base of the Statue of Liberty erected in 1886. Tight United States immigration controls were introduced after the First World War.

Mauretania Docking.   *Postcard franked 11 July 1908*

Fe Railway seems to have produced a genius called Fred Harvey, who brought the restaurant car service to perfection and also constructed hotels to suit the traditions of the country where they were put. For instance most of those in the far west were in the old Spanish style, and they looked ideal.[237]

As to Chicago (we got there on Thursday morning), it is best to draw a veil as far as possible. We found an admirable hotel (the Blackstone). We also found a big park, with an open air restaurant, on the shore of Lake Michigan. But those were the two redeeming features. The streets were stuffy and crowded. There is a villainous overhead railway that goes along the main streets, and makes an appalling noise. There wasn't a breath of air, and there was a hot yellow fog all along the shores of Lake Michigan.[238]

---

237. Frederick Henry Harvey (died 1901) had revolutionised from the 1870s the quality of catering and accommodation on the Santa Fe Railroad. Customers in his hotels and restaurants were served by Harvey Girls, 'young women of good character, attractive and intelligent'.

238. By 1910 Chicago had a population of 2,185,283. It was the world's largest market for grain, meat and lumber. It was also a major manufacturing centre and port. The Lake Park, fronting Lake Michigan, had been recently extended. The South Side Elevated Railroad had been constructed in 1892 and the Loop in downtown Chicago in 1897.

I never want to see Chicago again. Nor do I want particularly to repeat the journey from Chicago to New York. The temperature in the car got up to 103 soon after we started, and though it went down a little after that you can imagine that it was trying. On the whole we 'stuck it out' pretty well, though the Chairman, who laughs at heat as a rule, was somewhat laid out. Certainly my recollections of America will include that of its temperature. As to the journey itself, there isn't much to say of it. It is exactly like travelling through the English Midlands. Fields, hills rivers, rivers hills fields – occasionally a big manufacturing town.

R.M.S. *Mauretania*
July 6th 1913

This is Sunday – indecision sticks to us to the end as the question arises whether to get off at Fishguard, and get to London at midnight tomorrow, or to go on to Liverpool, and come down on Tuesday morning. At present I sit on the fence, but have a slight bias in favour of Fishguard.[239]

One thing is quite clear – if I don't finish this letter tonight, I shan't finish it at all – so I will start away and tell you something about New York.

It is really rather impressive – much more so than San Francisco, and certainly miles better than Chicago. The Hotel Belmont where we stayed is a skyscraper of the second quality – that is, it has about 34 stories – some of the biggest are nearly 800 feet high and have 60! It calls itself in the centre of New York, i.e. it is in the region of what Charing Cross is to London, and certainly it is very convenient for getting about the city.[240]

New York, as you probably *don't* know, is built on a peninsula. The fashionable centre is Fifth Avenue, which might be called the backbone. The Hotel Belmont is close to it, and about half way down the peninsula.

I think the most striking thing in New York is the absence of the two things one most expects – hustle and the average Yankee. Really the 'go'

---

239. Fishguard was the first port of call, a modest town of just 2002 people in 1901 but the terminus of the South Wales system of the Great Western Railway. Liverpool, in contrast, was the premier port for the Atlantic trade, a major commercial and manufacturing centre and a city of 753,353 people by 1911.

240. New York and its suburbs had grown to a vast size by 1913. With a population of 4,766,883 in 1910, it had become the second largest city in the world, after London. It was already famous for its peculiar architecture. The Metropolitan Life Insurance Building with 52 stories was completed in 1910. The Woolworth Building, 60 stories, finished in 1913, remained the tallest building in the world until the Empire State Building of 1931.

New York,
Metropolitan Life
Insurance Building.
Postcard issued 1912

isn't any greater than it is in London, and as far as the population goes, 3 days' experience leads me to think that it is mostly Jews and Southern Europeans. Perhaps most of the true Americans were away for summer holidays – it certainly was pretty hot.

We spent our three days alternating between business and pleasure. Business was seeing the Consul General, the Harbour authorities, the inventor of a cotton picking machine, and various other people. We got a lot of information which should come in very useful. Pleasure was in looking about New York as much as we could. We went to the Central Park and the Metropolitan Museum (a really splendid art gallery), to Coney Island on Sunday (it is away towards the open sea and consists of about 12 second rate Shepherd's Bush exhibitions – I mean the purely amusement part of them – scattered along the beach, each with all sorts of facilities for eating and bathing) and to a roof garden theatre on one of the evenings. After a stuffy day the roof garden is much better than an ordinary theatre.[241]

That, I think, is about all, except that the steamer which brought us back from Coney Island took us up along the docks which fringe the Hudson River. They, the docks, are really splendid, as is the Riverside Drive which follows. We walked back along the drive after leaving the boat.

We – that is Bridgman and I – have to thank Chicago for one thing. That is our cabin on the *Mauretania*. At first we were told she was full, but we were lucky enough, on calling at the Cunard office at Chicago, to find one just fallen vacant. It is on Deck E (even that though is well above the water line) and is inside. Consequently for the first two nights it was almost unbearably hot. However, as any cabin, almost, on the *Mauretania* is an expensive luxury, we were fortunate in getting ours for the comparatively low sum £25 10s each. The Chairman, who has a cabin on Deck B, has had to pay £100 for his!

Certainly the *Mauretania* is a wonderful ship. All the 'living rooms' are exactly like hotel rooms – very spacious, extremely well furnished, and even with open fireplaces. They must be delightful in winter. After our latest experiences in the way of ships, the size is immense: it is about a quarter of a mile round the promenade deck.

And she romps along at 24 knots, with hardly any vibration. The only comment I have really to make is that she does only 550 knots a day whereas I had rather expected 600.[242]

---

241. Central Park, originally on the city's northern outskirts, had been laid out to a design by Calvert Vaux (1824–95) and Frederick Law Olmstead (1822–1903) and opened in 1869. The Metropolitan Museum had been founded in 1870 and its main building opened in 1902. Coney Island had developed as a pleasure resort with amusement parks, especially after the completion in 1875 of a rail link to the city centre. There was a large amusement park at the White City at Shepherd's Bush in London: the site had been developed particularly for the Franco-British Exhibition of 1908 which celebrated Empire as well as the recently signed Entente.

242. The Cunard Steam-Ship Company had been operating a transatlantic service since 1840, and employed 19 ships by 1910. *Mauretania* was one of its large, fast and prestigious vessels: 31,950 tons, 762 feet by 88 feet, capable of 26 knots, built by Swan Hunter on the Tyne, and, like her sister ship *Lusitania*, launched in 1907. She could carry 560 first-class passengers, 460 second and 1180 third. She survived her war service as a troop transporter and hospital ship and sailed until 1935.

There hasn't been much of interest during the voyage. It was very hot the first two days – in fact hotter and damper than anything we had on the Pacific. Since then there has been just the ordinary breeze, and occasionally fog, but we haven't slowed for that.

On the whole my impression is that the Atlantic is bigger than I thought it would be. After our other voyages, I imagined this last one would be a trifle. It isn't.

I have been working most of the time, and haven't made many acquaintances. But there are some interesting people on board – Marconi, a leading American suffragette, Garey the head of the Steel Trust, Lady Constance Richardson the dancer – and, last but not least, an American journalist who is starting to make a tour of the world in 35 days and expects to be back in New York on August 5th! I admire and do not envy him.[243]

Here, I think, is the point to stop. I will assume, for the sake of completion that we get to Fishguard in the ordinary way, and that I arrive in London sometime in the night of Monday.

A tour of the world is interesting. Taken in six months, it is apt to dull one's impressions towards the end. I shan't mind if during the next six months I go no further from London than – Margate.[244]

Ever your loving son
E. J. Harding

---

243. Guglielmo Marconi (1874–1937) succeeded in sending wireless telegraphy signals across the Atlantic in 1901, and thereafter developed a system for commercial and Royal Navy use. (Harding would return home to find that Lloyd George had just escaped political extinction when he was found to have invested in the Marconi Company of America while the government was awarding contracts to the Marconi Company of Great Britain: a Select Commitee of the House of Commons produced a critical report in June 1913.) The American suffragette would be a woman with a grievance: energetic lobbying had secured votes for women in only 11 American states before the war and not for federal elections until 1920. Elbert Henry Gary (1846–1927), corporation lawyer and financier, had been entrusted by J.P. Morgan with a major role in organising the U.S. Steel Corporation: he was chairman of the board 1903–27. Lady Constance Mackenzie had married Sir Edward Austin Stewart-Richardson in 1904: she published *Dancing, Beauty and Games* in 1913, and died in 1932. But who was the journalist who planned to travel round the world faster than Phileas Fogg?

244. Margate, with a permanent population in 1911 of 27,085, was a popular seaside resort for Londoners, easily accessible by road, by rail or by steamer (4½ hours from Swan Pier).

Second Journey

To South Africa,
February–April 1914

R.M.S. Kinfauns Castle
About in the Latitude of Gibraltar
Feb. 10th 1914

My dear Father,

I have just discovered that the English post, which will go off at Madeira, closes at 8 this evening, so I must get my letter finished at a sitting – not that it will take long, for there is really nothing to tell you, except that we have had a somewhat dismal voyage so far.[245] It has been cold and rough and generally disagreeable, and all except the stalwarts like Vincent, Bateman and Lorimer have been more or less *hors de combat*. Personally I spent most of Sunday in bed, and was extraordinarily sleepy yesterday. However, I am now recovering.

I wasn't actually seasick, but perilously near to it, so near that I wish I had been!

We had a nasty cross sea, and a heavy swell, and the boat has been rolling continuously – is in fact rolling now so that you must excuse any deficiencies in writing. I am writing in the 'study cabin' which is small, but quite comfortable. The only drawback at present is that it has been too rough to open the portholes and that the 'sarcophagi' have a tendency to slide about.

---

245. The Commission party with Harding consisted of Vincent, Bateman, Garnett, Lorimer and Tatlow – five of the six United Kingdom representatives, Haggard would join them *en route* – plus Campbell (Australia), Sinclair (New Zealand) and Bowring (Newfoundland), together with Bridgman and various Commissioners' wives. Langerman (South Africa) would meet them on arrival, and Glenny from the Board of Trade would join them later in Cape Town. Owing to the pressure of parliamentary business, Foster (Canada) was absent.

Kinfauns Castle.   *Postcard franked 24 September 1904*

In fact the whole ship, save for the tendency to roll aforesaid (which appears somewhat excessive), is quite habitable – and will be more so when we get into warmer weather.[246]

We just caught a glimpse of Finisterre,[247] otherwise the land has been conspicuous by its absence, but there have been quite a lot of ships passing, many more than on the Pacific where, so far as I remember, we saw three in 3 weeks.

Cribbage has begun, also deck quoits and deck golf – but so far as I am concerned they are in their infancy, as inclination and opportunity hasn't been very great so far.

The passengers outside the Commission party (who form about one-third of the whole) look extraordinarily dull.

Which also is this letter – but, as I said at the beginning, there is really nothing to say.

Ever your affectionate son
E. J. Harding

---

246. *Kinfauns Castle*, 9700 tons, 515 feet by 59 feet, was built for the Castle Line by Fairfield on the Clyde and was launched in 1899. The ship could carry 250 passengers first class, 200 second and 136 third. During the First World War she served as an armed merchant cruiser, an experience

R.M.S. *Kinfauns Castle*
At sea
Between Teneriffe and Cape Verd
Thursday, Feb. 12th 1914

My dearest Mother,

Today we have had something of the fragrance of the Pacific – blue sea and sky, a fresh breeze, and a glimpse of the Peak of Teneriffe – it came out of the mist to greet us as we went by early this morning, and very beautiful it looked, just like an enormous cone, with a little snow at the top.[248]

If we have a succession of days like today the rest of the voyage promises well. Anyhow, I am encouraged to begin a letter to tell you about Madeira, even if I don't get very far this evening.[249]

We got there yesterday about noon, several hours late after our experiences in the Bay.[250] But the lateness was an advantage really, as the usual practice is to arrive about seven in the morning and leave at twelve.

There is no harbour, just an open anchorage, and the boat lies out about 300 yards or so from the shore, where she is immediately surrounded by dinghies with diving boys and the usual sellers of wares. Unfortunately it was rather misty, so that we couldn't see to the top of the hills, but we could see enough to show that the island is extremely beautiful – it is built up in terraces, full of vines, sugar canes and bananas, while Funchal, the capital, nestles at the foot.

---

she survived. She was finally laid up in 1922. The Union Line, established in 1853, and the Castle Line, 1863, merged as the Union-Castle Line in 1900. The company operated 41 vessels by 1910 and became part of the Royal Mail Group in 1912. Royal Mail steamers left Southampton every Saturday for South Africa, £28 7s 0d first class, £23 2s 0d second class and £10 10s 0d third class. The voyage was scheduled to take 17 days to Cape Town and 22 days to Durban, from where return journeys began. The Commissioners had sailed on Saturday February 7.

247. Cape Finisterre on the north-west coast of Spain is a landmark for voyagers going south.

248. Teneriffe, one of the Canary islands, with its distinctive mountain peak of 3718 m., lies off the coast of what in 1914 was the Spanish colony of Rio de Oro. It was first settled from Spain in 1496. This is where Horatio Nelson (1758–1805) lost his arm, in an unsuccessful naval attack in 1797.

249. Madeira, off the coast of French Morocco, had become a Portuguese colony in 1419. The British temporarily occupied the island on two occasions during the Napoleonic wars but returned it to Portuguese control. It had a population of 148,263 by 1900.

250. It sounds as though the Commissioners had another rough crossing of the Bay of Biscay.

I was very much reminded of Locarno and the country above it, and when one landed there was very little to dispel the illusion, except that all the names are Portuguese instead of Italian.[251]

We spent, I regret to say, most of our time in 'Cook's Tourists' fashion, that is to say we paid a lump sum down, and were taken the great round of the place in motor car, train and 'toboggan'.

The programme starts with a terrifying ride in a motor car from the quay to the funicular railway station. The car whizzed through the narrow streets and round corners in a way that might well frighten anyone, much more those who had just emerged from four days shaking in another way.

However, we reached the station safely, and proceeded to climb in a funicular some 3000 feet to a chalet hotel which is said to have an extraordinarily beautiful view. I say 'is said', because by the time we got there we were well into the mist, and there was nothing at all to be seen. However, the journey was worth the trouble, for one climbed past delightful shrubs and flowers (bougainvillea and the like) and had glimpses of the peasants in their cottages and all the rest of Madeira life.

The chalet at the top provided us with a very acceptable lunch (rather marred by the time which it took to get the first few courses) and after it we started down in the time-honoured way by toboggan.[252] But this really is so curious as to need detailed description – which I will leave over till another evening. We have 13 days without a call, so there should be plenty of time!

Saturday, Feb. 14th

The promise of the Atlantic is being fulfilled. We passed Cape Verd this morning – at least I suppose we did though we weren't near enough to see it, and so now we are steaming past, say, the mouth of the Gambia.[253]

It doesn't at all fit in with my presuppositions of West Africa. I imagined very damp oppressive heat and a murky sky. Instead we have clear sky and a fresh breeze and weather not at all unduly hot. In fact,

---

251. Locarno is in the Italian-speaking Ticino district of Switzerland.
252. Probably Terreiro da Luta, from where *carrinhos de cesto*, wicker sledges invented by English settlers, descended to Funchal.
253. The French occupied Cap Vert in 1857 and established a settlement at Dakar, from where French colonial control expanded through Senegal into the Sahara, particularly after 1879. A British trading post had struggled to survive at the mouth of the Gambia since the 17th century. A formal colony was defined during the 19th century, and this was extended in 1894 to include a protectorate over part of the hinterland.

though we shall be crossing the Equator in a day or two, I have by no means come down to the thinnest possible clothes.

After all this prelude, I will now go back and tell you of the toboggans of Madeira. They are like ordinary ones in that they have steel runners. They are unlike them in that they are broad enough to hold two or even three people sitting down, with a back to lean against and a ledge for the feet. And they are steered, not by the occupant, but by two 'natives' who have each a rope and turn the toboggan this way or that as the exigencies of the descent require. The descent itself is really great fun. The road goes down some 3000 ft. in a mile or two. It is much steeper and more 'hairpinny' than any Swiss road I have seen, and it is constructed of a series of minute ledges of stones in such a way that they look (sideways) like this ⌐ (I fear this illustration isn't very illuminating – but it is the best I can ⌐ do, and may anyhow serve as a recollection for myself!).

How the guides succeed in keeping the pace down to anything reasonable is somewhat of a mystery, but they do somehow, though the process is a heating one and requires them to stop half way down for a drink at the expense of the occupant of their toboggan.

Our other stoppages were for an occasional beggar and a photograph or two. The people (I mean the villagers) that one passes are extremely picturesque, and the local means of conveyance are chiefly mules and oxen. We had half an hour or so when we reached the bottom to poke about Funchal. It is of the ordinary type of southern European town, I imagine, with a market place, a not very interesting cathedral, and several houses with walled gardens. The most interesting thing to look at in the shops is the drawn thread work.[254] I purchased a small table cloth which I hadn't time to send home, but which I shall hope to have the honour of presenting, when I get back, to the new house. (It occurs to me as I write that perhaps you have, after all, had a hitch in the negotiations).

We sailed almost immediately after getting back – and found on reaching the ship Haggard with his wife and daughter already on board.[255] They had apparently enjoyed their fortnight, and were full of

254. It is reputed that an Englishwoman, Elizabeth Phelps, had opened a needlework school in Funchal in 1850 to provide a living for families experiencing economic hardship when disease struck the vineyards.
255. Haggard, accompanied by his wife and youngest daughter, had spent a couple of weeks on the island to escape the English winter and to revisit some of the scenes he had described in his ludicrously melodramatic first novel, *Dawn*, published in 1884. Madeira toboggans are described in book II chapter XXVIII.

the Blandys and their works. I had hardly realized that they (I mean the Blandys) had been in the island for a century or so and are the English people of the place. They specialize, I gather, in Madeira wine.[256]

One rather interesting thing Haggard pointed out to me. Right up the mountain side, and looking down over the town, stands a large building, something like a hospital. This is the famous building which the Germans put up a few years ago, nominally as a sanatorium for German consumptives, but really for use as a barracks when they should have completed their plan of taking over Madeira from the Portuguese! The plan, apparently, was frustrated by our Foreign Office at the last moment. The building remains as a 'might have been'.[257]

Sunday, Feb. 15th
Nearing the Equator

Today it has been real tropics – or doldrums – or whatever the proper term is – a perfectly calm sea, a misty and somewhat 'sticky' looking sun, and very considerable heat, so that one has now come down 'with a run' to the coolest possible clothing.

We have a Bishop on board, the Bishop of Nyasaland, a somewhat rotund and very cheerful looking cleric who is on his way back to his diocese, and he has been conducting services. But as he didn't preach in the morning, and the evening was rather stifling, I haven't heard him discourse on his diocese. I know a good deal about it though, having of course had to do with the Protectorate in my first years at C.O., and I find that I have some common acquaintances with him amongst the officials.[258]

Most of the day has been spent lolling on deck and watching flying fish which now appear for the first time – I don't remember seeing them on either of the 'Australian' voyages. The study cabin (which, by the way, is very well fitted up and is quite cool and comfortable) has been deserted for the time being.

Friday, Feb. 20th

I don't seem to have written anything for some days – and even now there is not really very much to say. We are over the Equator and 'under' the sun – I took some photographs yesterday of various people standing on their own shadows, which should be interesting if they come out.

Today is really the first cooler day we have had – ever since Sunday it has been hot, damp and rather trying. Tomorrow we are promised 'wind and sea', but I don't know if they will come off.

I have got through a good deal of work, but on the whole have taken it pretty easy. Work after dinner is unknown, and I spend my evenings playing bridge with Sinclair (the New Zealander), Lady Haggard and Mrs. Garnett. Very amusing the games are too. Mrs. Garnett I have described before I think, and you probably know of Sinclair too – he is a good fellow but rather 'opinionated' and, of the members of the Commission, the one who gives most trouble. As to Lady Haggard, she improves greatly on acquaintance. She is stout and placid and what might be called an 'outdoor person' – very practical and full of commonsense – just the reverse of Haggard.

The other members of the party who are new for description purposes I will leave over till another evening. Here I will just add that the usual games, athletic sports and the like, fill in the rest of the time. Everyone likes the ship, I think – and personally I find the voyage much too short.

Sunday, Feb. 22nd 1914

The last thing I wrote almost needs contradiction today – it is getting much colder, also rougher, and as I haven't been working, and deck games aren't allowed on Sunday, the day really has seemed quite long enough. However, I won't take back the principle that, with a lot to do, the voyage is all too short.

I will go on to describe the other new additions to the party.

Miss Haggard is a curious mixture of her Father and Mother – she has some of the placidity of the one, and some of the nervousness of the

---

256. The wine trade with Great Britain had been first stimulated by an Anglo-Portuguese commercial treaty in 1660, and British merchants and settlers acquired considerable economic and political influence in Madeira during the 18th and 19th centuries. John Blandy (died 1855), a former quarter-master in the British army, established the dynasty which came to exercise most power, not only through the wine business but also through catering for tourists, servicing ships in the port and controlling water supplies.

257. The power and arrogance of British settlers help explain the initial local support for a German attempt, beginning in 1904, to break the British monopoly. In addition to constructing the sanatorium, a German company also aimed to establish a coaling station and a new mail steamer route from Europe which would by-pass English ports. These efforts, aggressively pursued, ultimately generated Portuguese opposition and had failed by 1909. The belief that the sanatorium was really planned for use as a German barracks is indicative of pre-war English paranoia.

258. Nyasaland, now Malawi, had been busy with Scottish missionaries since the 1870s before becoming a formal British protectorate in 1891.

other: the result is rather nondescript, and I don't feel able to give at all an accurate description. Anyhow, she is quite good fun, whatever one's final opinion.[259]

Mrs. Lorimer is also a mixture. She doesn't appear to fit very well with the rest of the female contingent (they laugh at her a good deal), and is rather voluble and flattering, neither of which qualities go down very much. Still she seems very pleased with, and devoted to, old Lorimer – which is to her credit – and she seems likely to relieve me a good deal of trouble. More than that I can't say at the moment. (I seem, by the way, to have done very imperfect analyses of the newcomers.)

The greatest acquisition to the voyage is really Just. He started, so I was told at the C.O., with the greatest fear of being indiscreet. This attitude he kept up for the first few days on board. Thawed by the genial influence of the Commission, he now has reached a stage where he writes topical poems (I send you one with this letter for the 'collection'), plays bridge a good part of the day, and begins to learn the Tango. Altogether he is great fun, and has caused much amusement by the aforesaid thawing process.[260]

Monday, Feb. 23rd 1914

We are due in early tomorrow – and the usual Marconigrams are beginning to arrive with invitations for lunches etc. So I will get this letter done and post it, being doubtful how much more I shall have time to write before Saturday when the mail starts for home (we passed last week's one last night, the first steamer we had seen for 10 days).

There is no one very exciting on board beyond the Commission party. The best are a Miss Samuel, who has developed the zest for the Tango in Just, Jewish, but quite nice, and decidedly clever;[261] a certain Lady Helen Mitford with a delightful child of three or so (the 'Rosemary' of Just's poem);[262] and the Bishop of Nyasaland whom I have already pictured. The boat is really rather empty – which has made it the more enjoyable.

So now to close.

Ever your loving son
E. J. Harding

259. Lilias Rider Haggard (1892–1968) became her father's first biographer: *The Cloak That I Left* was published in 1951.
260. Sir Hartmann Just (1854–1929) had joined the Colonial Office in 1878. He became assistant private secretary to a sequence of ministers before moving up the office hierarchy to become ultimately assistant under-

ALPHABET OF THE D.R.C. (written with a J pen).

A for Sir Alfred whom figures do cheer,
B is for Bridgman, the old marinere.
C is for Campbell, Australia's boast,
D for the dungeon, of duty the post.
E for Sir Edgar, Apollo so spruce,
F for the food which he brought for his use.
G is for Garnett, most courtly of men,
H is for Harding's right diligent pen.
I for Lord Inchcape, whose loss we regret,
J for Sir Jan, who has not joined us yet.
K for the *Kinfauns*, which this trip is making,
L for the ladies, all five very taking.
M for the minerals – Lorimer's quest,
N for Newfoundland, and Bowring, its best.
O for the ocean we're traversing now,
P for the porpoise that plays at our prow.
Q for the Quinta, a farm in Madeira,
R for Sir Rider's yarns, queerer and queerer.
S is for Sinclair, whose law never fails,
T is for Tatlow, our expert on rails.
U for the Union – Castle, our line,
V for the voyage for which we combine.
W for whales, which spout and pass by,
X for the cross on our quoits and the sky.
Y for Young Rosemarie, witchingly curled,
Z for New Zealand, the pick of the world.

February 18th 1914

---

secretary 1907–16, in which capacity he was responsible for the affairs of the dominions and for organising Imperial Conferences: he was knighted in 1911. He had acquired more overseas knowledge than most officials, having already visited South Africa in 1902–03 and Canada in 1910. He was not a member of the Commission but was travelling with them as far as the Cape *en route* for Australia and New Zealand on a six-month tour which would bring him home via Fiji and Vancouver.

261. Mild anti-semitism was a common cultural characteristic of Great Britain's pre-war upper middle class.

262. Lady Helen Mitford had married the son and heir of the 1st Baron Redesdale in 1909: she was soon to be widowed when he was killed in action on 13 May 1915. Her daughter Rosemary was born in 1911.

Civil Service Club
Capetown
Feb. 28th 1914

My dear Father,

What with heat – and work – and other preoccupations I couldn't bring myself to start another diary letter which stood any chance of catching the mail which went today. But I really must begin tonight as there seems such a lot to say, and I shall get hopelessly behindhand unless I make a start.

Impressions are thick and all are totally different to what one expected them to be.

First of all a word or two as to Capetown.[263] I thought it would be older-looking than it is. As a matter of fact, save for one or two older houses, it might be Perth or Adelaide, and its outskirts in particular are hopelessly shoddy-looking. What does strike one is that where the buildings are new, they have, most of them (I except the City Hall which is very 'modern England'-looking), a distinct character of their own.[264] It looks as though the country might develop a distinctive architecture. I have seen no sign of that in our previous wanderings.

---

263. A settlement was established at the Cape by the Dutch in 1652. This was overrun by the British because of its strategic importance on the route to India, first in 1795 and then permanently in 1806. Cape Town then became the capital of Cape Colony, receiving responsible government in 1872. The movement of the Dutch, known as the Boers, into the hinterland from 1833 generated further conflict. Natal, for example, became a Boer settlement in 1838 but it was claimed by the British and annexed in 1843, initially as a dependency of the Cape and then in 1856 as a separate colony: responsible government was granted in 1893. Meanwhile, Boer republics were established in the Transvaal and Orange Free State, but conflict continued, and the British tried unsuccessfully to control these territories in the late 1870s, actions which were rebuffed in the First Boer War of 1880–81. Annexation was, however, effected after the Second Boer War of 1899–1902. However, Transvaal and the Orange River Colony were then granted responsible government in 1906 and 1907. Finally, in 1910, the British colonies and former Boer territories were merged into the Union of South Africa, a unitary state with a two-chamber parliament (a House of Assembly and a Senate). There was a registered electorate in the four provinces of 346,161, but all except 24,347 in the province of the Cape of Good Hope and just 326 in Natal were white. Cape Town was the political capital of the Union.

264. The City Hall was designed in Italian Renaissance style with classical facade and central campanile, built from sandstone imported from England, and completed in 1905. Other notable buildings included the

Cape Town, City Hall.   *Postcard*

Secondly, the climate. We arrived to find Table Mountain in mist – the clouds covering the top and pouring over it exactly like a waterfall. This was very attractive, and our first day was comparatively cool. But apparently this particular phenomenon (I mean the clouds pouring over Table Mountain) is a prelude to a 'South Easter' – this means a vicious hot wind which blows intermittently, chiefly at night, and leaves one to swelter by day under a particularly dazzling sun. Capetown makes no provision against heat – at least this Club certainly doesn't, comfortable as it otherwise is – with the result that I have felt the climate somewhat severely. The Club is right in the middle of the town, and the town itself being directly under Table Mountain, and having the heat refracted from it, is hotter than anywhere else. One holds on, and hopes for better things.

Thirdly, the people. Arriving with the fact well in view that the white population is in a minority of one to six in South Africa, one is surprised to find what a big show the whites make, in Capetown at any rate. No doubt the disproportion is less here than elsewhere, and there is a large admixture of 'coloured' people – i.e. those of mixed race, as opposed to

old Supreme Court (1799–1815), Houses of Parliament (1886 with a new wing for the use of the Union Parliament in 1910) and South African Museum (opened 1897).

Cape Town, View of City
and Table Mountain.

Photograph,
Cape Government Railways, c.1910

the 'Kaffirs' proper. Still one can't fail, I think, to be impressed.[265]

Next the race cleavage.[266] Of course, it is rather early to judge. Still I put down the view for what it is worth – that is that amongst the politicians one has met there is no particular race feeling. 'His Majesty's Opposition' here – as typified say by Smartt, the leader, whom I sat next to at dinner the night we arrived – seems to be on the best of terms with 'His Majesty's Government' as exemplified say by Botha.[267] Vincent who, of course, has

---

265. In 1911 the population of Cape Town was 161,759 (53% white), of the Cape of Good Hope 2,564,965 (23% whites), and of the Union of South Africa 5,973,394 (21% white). There was a marked distinction between the urban areas in the Union, where according to the 1911 census whites formed 45% of the population, bantu 34% and mixed and other coloureds 21%, and the rural areas where the proportions were 14%, 78% and 8% respectively. Kaffir, derived from the Arabic word *kafir* meaning infidel, was the term commonly used to describe black Africans in southern Africa.

266. Here the word race is used to describe the two principal European 'tribes', Britons and Boers (or Afrikaners).

267. Sir Thomas Smartt (1858–1929) was the leader of the Unionist Party, representing in particular British settlers. He gave evidence to the Commission on Wednesday March 4. Louis Botha (1863–1919) was an ex-Boer commando leader, but his South African Party was prepared to cooperate, on terms, with the British imperial system: he had been prime

Cape Town, Adderley Street.   *Postcard dated 1918*

seen a good deal of both sides since he came, confirms this observation.
(On the other hand a certain good lady whose name I don't remember,
with whom I have travelled some 90 miles in a motor car today, did give
me very strongly the idea of narrow race feeling of British against Boer.)

Vincent's own view is (and he is very clear sighted in these things) that
there would be a combination of the 'official' Government party and the
'official' opposition against the combined forces of Herzog and Labour,[268]
only both sides are afraid to propose it – or, in other words, that the effect
of the war on the Dutch was as 'broadening' as a University education is
commonly supposed to be. Again an 'upsetting' view to one's precon-
ceived ideas – but, all the same worthwhile, I think, to set down.

minister of Cape Colony 1907–10, was chosen as prime minister of the
Union by the Governor-General in May 1910, and won the first general
election in September.

268. Harding's arrival followed the resignation of Barry Hertzog (1866–1942)
from Botha's government in 1912 and his foundation in January 1914 of
the National Party, which professed to represent the interests of the
Afrikaner community. He eventually became prime minister from 1924 to
1939. The Labour Party aimed to speak for labour among both white
communities. Vincent's assessment was pretty good: the co-operation of
the Unionist Party and the South African Party was close during the First
World War, and they merged in 1920. Nationalists and Labour also found
opportunities for electoral co-operation after the war.

Two more general observations, and then I have done (I fear I shall be writing what you will find boring). The first, that the strike is no longer a a topic of general conversation, only the 'aftermath' in that a small obstructionist party has caused two 'all-night' sittings in the Legislative Assembly this week. People appear to be much more interested in the 'fiasco' (so called) of the arrival of the deportees in London.[269]

The second, that everywhere Botha seems popular and acclaimed. This possibly is the result of his action over the strike which practically everyone endorses. As to Smuts, the 'second in command', he is feared rather than loved.[270] Smartt described him to me as a 'personality without a following' and suggested that he is 'intellect' without 'soul'. As I haven't spoken to him, I can't venture to assent or dissent. But everyone else says much the same, though in a less striking way.

Sunday, March 1st

It is hotter than ever in Capetown – but I escaped for the day and have been by the sea, so that I have come back tolerably cool. I will go on to describe some of our doings since we got here on Tuesday.

Certainly things are very well arranged here, infinitely better than in Australia and almost better, I think, than in New Zealand. Frank Robb, the man who has been my correspondent and is arranging things generally, is a Railway and Harbour Official, age about 50 or so.[271] He is

---

269. The Transvaal Federation of Trade, created in 1911, brought 19,000 mineworkers out on strike by 5 July 1913. A settlement was only temporarily effected, and the Federation proclaimed a general strike (mainly of miners and railway workers) on 13 January 1914. The government declared martial law and sent in troops: nine strike leaders were deported on 30 January.

270. Jan Christian Smuts (1870–1950), another ex-Boer commando leader and currently Minister of Defence, had sent in the troops and introduced legislation restricting trade unions. He became a member of the British War Cabinet in 1917, and succeeded Botha as prime minister in 1919, serving until 1924. He returned to office in coalition with Hertzog in 1933, and together they formed the United Party in 1934. He was again prime minister 1939–48. Vincent records that whereas Botha was charming, Smuts was called 'a head without a heart'.

271. Frank Robb (born 1864), the Commission's South African agent, worked first for the Cape Government Railway Department but moved to the Harbour Board in 1890, became Dock Manager in Table Bay in 1908 and Superintendent of South African Railways in 1911.

very thorough and has got everything well in hand – down to such details as the 'franking' of letters and the delivery of luggage. Which is a comfort and great relief, especially in view of the climatic conditions.

Moreover, we haven't had nearly so much fuss over the Commission as there was in Australasia – I mean in the way of journalists and the like. There have been no interviewers yet, I think, and only one photographer. As it happens, just now there are a lot of counter excitements – if you can call the Commission an excitement – and anyhow Commissions etc. from home are much more frequent here than in Australia.

Nevertheless, both the Government and all sorts of private and public people and institutions have been extremely kind. The Government sent one of the Ministers to meet the Commission when the *Kinfauns Castle* arrived – true, a 'minor star', one Senator Graaff by name,[272] but then we arrived at 7 a.m. and the House had been sitting all night.

They also gave a dinner in the Commission's honour, on the Tuesday evening, which was held (rather a strange fashion) in the public dining room of the Mount Nelson Hotel, with all the ordinary (sic) people finishing their dinners at surrounding tables. It felt as though we were beasts being fed in public. My neighbours were Sir Thomas Smartt, leader of the Opposition whom I have mentioned already – a clever and very amusing Irishman – and Sir N.F. de Waal, Administrator of what is now the Cape Province (since Union the Provinces take a much less prominent part than do say the States in Australia) – a Dutchman, quite genial and pleasant to talk to.[273] I was introduced, of course, to a lot more people but didn't talk much to any. Still the impression left on my mind (here again I give it for what it is worth) was that politicians of both shades, in intellect, manners and culture, rank much higher than those of Australia and New Zealand, particularly Australia.

Our other function on Tuesday was a visit to an Agricultural show, some four miles out from the centre of the city, and lunch there. The

---

272. Senator Jacobus Graaf (1863–1927), a former businessman, was elected to the Cape Legislative Council in 1903, became a senator when the Union government was created, and was appointed Minister without Portfolio. He was a protectionist with a strong concern for 'poor whites'. He was knighted in 1917.
273. Sir N. Frederic de Waal (1853–1932) was born in Holland, emigrated to South Africa for reasons of health in 1880, became a journalist, entered the Cape Parliament in 1898, sided with moderate Afrikaner opinion, acted as Colonial Secretary at the Cape from 1908, and finally served after the Union as Administrator of Cape Province 1910–25.

show was quite interesting – particularly the stock. I was pleased to come back to my friends the Holstein and Ayrshire cattle, and there were some quite good horses too.

By contrast with Tuesday, Wednesday and Thursday were quite uneventful. We started the taking of evidence (here I may say that we are excellently housed for 'official' purposes in a place called Huguenot Buildings – where I believe Kruger's body lay in State when it was brought back from Holland), and on Thursday afternoon inspected the harbour in a launch, in preparation for hearing the evidence of the Harbour Engineer.[274]

Friday, on the other hand, was a good deal more interesting. There was evidence till about 4 p.m. (I forgot to say that, at lunch, I had to go to a party given by Sir Thomas Smartt in the House of Assembly dining room and sat next to Sir Lewis Mitchell, one of the Directors, I think, of the British South Africa Co.),[275] and after it was over we all drove out to a garden party given by Mrs. Louis Botha – the Prime Minister's wife – at Groote Schuur. This is the house (and estate) built by Rhodes, and dedicated by him to be the home of the first Prime Minister of United South Africa.[276] It is in the old Dutch Style, with a 'stoep' (i.e. a verandah) both back and front, and filled with all sorts of curiosities – old chests, silver, china and whatnot. I am very glad to have seen it. As to the garden party, I will say no more. As you know I never find such functions[x]

---

274. 'Oom Paul' Kruger (1825–1904) had been the President of the Transvaal Republic 1882–1900 and political leader of the Boer resistance to the British prior to the Boer War. He went to Europe in 1900 to seek support and died in Holland. The Commission arrived in Cape Town on Tuesday February 24 and thereafter collected evidence from 35 witnesses over 8 days, beginning on Wednesday February 25, having a weekend break, and concluding on Friday March 6.

275. The British South Africa Company, which was commercially and politically active throughout southern Africa, had been largely the creation in 1889 of Cecil Rhodes (1853–1902). He had also been a Director of De Beers, Premier of Cape Colony 1890–96 and an imperial visionary. Sir Lewis Michell (1842–1928), an early biographer of Rhodes, worked for thirty years with the Standard Bank of South Africa as well as being a director of the British South Africa Company, of Rhodesia Railways and of the Mashonaland Railway and chairman of De Beers Consolidated Mines. He had also been a minister in the Cape Colony government.

276. Groote Schuur had originally been a barn, built in 1657. It was turned into a residence in the 1790s, but was much rebuilt for Rhodes to a design by Herbert Baker (1862–1946), later the architect (with Sir Edwin Lutyens) of New Delhi.

exhilarating – still less so are they when one knows practically nobody.

The house has a park all round – dedicated by Rhodes to the public, and containing all manner of strange beasts – and in this park is the famous Rhodes Memorial, which we went to see on our way back into the city. This is really impressive – a long flight of granite steps flanked by sculptured lions on either side, at the top a small pillared building also of granite, with a bust of Rhodes, his head on his elbow, looking out, down the steps, towards the north. The building lies high up just under Table Mountain, below which there is a plain of perhaps 20 miles across. When one stands where the bust is and looks out to the Drakenstein mountains across the plain, the effect is splendid.[277]

After this, it seems rather an anticlimax to add (still I will do it as the last of this evening's instalment) that they are making a new road out of Capetown to the Groote Schuur park, which lies well up on Table Mountain and has splendid views over Table Bay and towards the mountains. I mention it for this reason, that it is being made by convict labour – they were working, as we went along, to the accompaniment of a string of wardens with loaded rifles. Truly a sight which British democracy would not tolerate!

ˣ *Note*. I apologize for the smudge which is due to my having made an unsuccessful slap at a mosquito.

Thursday, March 5th 1914

The heat has now gone – temporarily at any rate – not so the work. Still I have a spare half hour this evening, and will try to push on with my story. I got as far as Friday in last week. On Saturday we had a holiday, and proceeded at the invitation of the Mayor of Capetown to go out in a 'team' of motor cars to see the fruit and vine districts in the (comparatively) near neighbourhood of Capetown. It turned out that we had a drive of 90 miles or so, I should say. It began at 10 and ended just after 6 – and would have ended later, save that the car I was in had a 'Jehu' who cared little for his springs and was an absolute terror to chickens.[278] Still, we had a most excellent day. Our objective was the most 'settled' part of Cape Colony – I beg its pardon, I mean the Cape

---

277. The Rhodes Memorial was similarly designed by Baker and built in white granite. The bust of Rhodes was by J. M. Swan.
278. '...the driving is like the driving of Jehu, the son of Nimshi; for he driveth furiously', II *Kings*, ix, 20.

Groote Schuur, Rondebosch,
Cape of Good Hope.

Photograph,
Cape Government Railways, c.1910

Province – where there are several old Dutch farms – I mean 100 years old or more, with roomy and delightful interiors, and a vine covered 'stoep' outside. One is rather surprised to find the houses so old and the industry so new (they have only begun to export fruit to England within the last few years). I suppose the explanation is twofold – the invention of cold storage on the boats and the natural disinclination of the Dutch farmer to exert himself more than he need.[279]

Anyhow, one couldn't but draw comparisons (I expect I shall be doing this a good deal) between the 'houses' in Australia on the fruit farms and those we found here. And certainly the comparison did not go in favour of the former. The first farm we went to on Saturday had the best collection of Nankin China in S. Africa, and Old Dutch cupboards to form a setting. The last (which belonged to Merriman one of the leading politicians here)[280] was also full of curiosities, old engravings and

---

279. Fruit was first exported to Britain in 1888; serious trade only began in the 1890s. Fresh fruit exports were worth £34,714 in 1910 but £93,049 in 1914. Exports of dried and canned fruit were just beginning.
280. John X. Merriman (1841–1926) was a minister in several Cape Colony governments from 1875 and the last prime minister of Cape Colony from 1908 until the Union in 1910. He remained in Parliament, a supporter of Botha, Smuts and the South African Party.

Groote Drakenstein, Cape of Good Hope,   *Photograph,*
Packing Fruit for Export.   *Cape Government Railways, c.1910*

the like. Which reminds me to say that almost all the politicians here seem to have farms not far from Capetown to which they retire for weekends. But whether this practice is a historical relic or whether they, as the phrase goes, 'farm with a cheque book' I don't feel competent to say.

Certainly the farms themselves are delightful, and one (or rather a cottage) which belonged to Rhodes, where we had a picnic lunch, had also a magnificent outlook – a broad valley, full of fruit trees in the foreground, and a long line of high and rather jagged peaks standing up in the sunlight behind. I fancy that the Tyrol must be rather like this part of South Africa.

We drove back through Stellenbosch – the 'Oxford', I gather, of the Cape – a quiet little town with tree-lined streets and rivulets to divide the pavements from the road.[281]

Sunday was also a 'day off' and provided two quite new experiences. Bridgeman and I were asked by Robb (he, as I said before, is the South African in charge of our arrangements) to go down to his house at

---

281. Stellenbosch had been settled in 1679. Its population in 1911 was 6152 (44% white). Its reputation as an educational centre began with the establishment of Stellenbosch Gymnasium in 1866. This became a college of the University of Cape of Good Hope in 1881, and, after a struggle, an independent university in 1918.

Muizenberg, which is a seaside suburb of Capetown,[282] make the acquaintance of his wife and family (he has in fact 4 children, of no particular interest), and experiment in surf bathing. This we did – it was a great relief to get out of Capetown which was quite unbearably hot by that time.

Surf bathing is even more attractive than that which we had seen in the Sydney suburbs. Here people use boards, three feet long or so, and get so expert that a big roller will carry them in – board and all – for perhaps thirty yards. I experimented twice (bathing was the one cool thing we had had for days), but I am bound to confess with singular want of success. I only barked my knees. We spent the time when we weren't bathing (or eating) in trying to make up for the sleep missed on previous nights, and in the evening came back to Capetown, making a stop at the Observatory (about half-way). Here the Astronomer, whose name I have forgotten, had a special 'séance' for the Commission, and showed us Mars and Saturn and various other solar celebrities through the big telescope. It was all very fascinating.[283]

Altogether I started work on Monday much revived by two day's rest. As the heat suddenly vanished on Monday evening (it had really been very bad though – it must have been 100 or near it for four days in succession), this week has been comparatively easy.

But I think I shall close this letter here, and leave our doings this week for the next one. I will only add that, if you want to get the photograph of us taken on the *Kinfauns Castle* at Southampton, buy a copy of *South Africa* of Feb. 14th, which contains it. The whole party looks frozen – I wish they could have published a second photograph showing our condition last week!

Ever your affectionate son,
E. J. Harding

---

282. Muizenberg developed from a military outpost into a convalescent centre during the Second Boer War and thereafter into a resort and suburb of Cape Town, much encouraged by the railway link completed in 1883.

283. The Cape had been valued since the 17th century as a site for astronomical observations in the southern hemisphere. The Royal Observatory had been founded in 1820, and it was visited by Sir John Herschell (1792–1871) in 1834. The astronomer in 1914 was Sydney Samuel Hough. The passage of Halley's comet in 1910 had been a recent stimulus to local amateur observers.

E. J. Harding indistinctly photographed (back row right) with members of the Dominions Royal Commission on *Kinfauns Castle*.

From South Africa, *14 February 1914, p.325*

R.M.S. *Kildonan Castle*
Between Capetown and Port Elizabeth
March 11th 1914

My dear Father,

We have 'finished' at Capetown and are on our way to Port Elizabeth in various ways, most of the party in a special train which left on Monday night and is stopping by the way at Oudtshoorn to inspect ostriches,[284] and the remainder – that is, Vincent, Bateman, Glenny (who turned up yesterday), Lady and Miss Haggard – by boat.

We arrive tomorrow morning, a few hours ahead of the land party. And whatever joys they may have had over their ostriches, we at least

---

284. These Commissioners also formally collected evidence in Oudtshoorn from 5 witnesses on Tuesday and Wednesday March 11 and 12. This was the centre of a prosperous agricultural district and boasted a population in 1911 of 10,930 (50% white). Its railway link to Cape Town had been completed the previous year. Victorian fashions had turned the negligible early 19th-century export of ostrich feathers into a major industry. Commercial farming began in 1867. In 1913 there were over 750,000 birds, nearly all in Cape Province, and over 1 million feathers were exported, worth nearly £3 million. A breeding pair of ostriches could be sold for £500. But at the time of the Commission's visit the peak was past, fashions had changed, and the business collapsed during the First World War, never to recover.

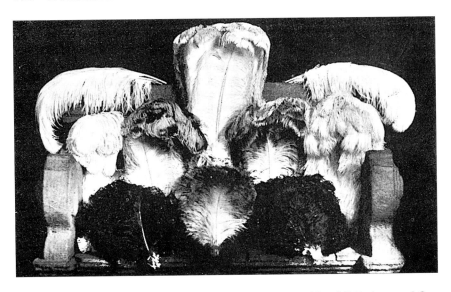

Prime Ostrich Feathers.   *Postcard issued by A.J.Pudney and Co.,*
                                           Feather Merchants, Port Elizabeth

have it cool – also smooth. As we passed Cape d'Agulhas this morning, where there is usually a good deal of sea, we are lucky.

As usual, we have had a good many letters to write on board – but those are done for the present, so I will get on with a diary letter. I think last time I got to the end of the 'heat wave' at Capetown (and very glad we were to see – or feel – the last of it).

Our second week was pretty busy, one way and another. We had evidence every day till Friday, and interspersed dinner by the Chamber of Commerce on Tuesday, another with the Governor General on Friday,[285] and various lunches in between.

Did I say before – at any rate it bears repetition – that everyone has been extremely kind at Capetown and that the heads of the various Departments have gone out their way to help me in getting all the information which I wanted?

The Chamber of Commerce dinner was rather amusing – the Menu card (I have had to keep this, it won't go in) and the newspaper cutting

---

285. The Governor-General was Herbert John Gladstone (1854–1930), the younger son of the prime minister. After a career in British politics, concluding as a reforming Home Secretary 1905–10, he was made Viscount Gladstone and served as South Africa's first Governor-General 1910–14.

will illustrate it for you, and so will a flashlight picture which I sent to Eva by last mail. There were no speeches, and after dinner one talked to all and sundry, collected miscellaneous information, and bespoke a witness or two.

The G.G.'s dinner was also amusing in its way – more formal, of course, but happily less so than in Australia. There were no curtseys by the ladies, and when Vincent and Haggard sat down on a sofa while the G.G. was still standing, nobody seemed to mind! I had the A.D.C. at me on questions of precedence of the members, but that is an old question now, and I find no difficulty in answering the various conundra.

I might as well say, by the way, that though Government House, where one signs one's name in the Visitor's book, is in Capetown, the G.G. lives some miles outside, at a place called Newlands beyond Groote Schuur (that, as I think I said in the last letter, is where the Prime Minister lives). It is quite a 'small house in the suburbs' comparatively – nevertheless distinctly comfortable.

The G.G.'s dinner further reminds me to say that I hear that neither he nor the 'Governess' is exactly popular in S. Africa. In fact – I trust you won't be shocked! – he is known as 'Lord God' and she as 'Lady God'. Need I say more?

We had two more 'diversions' in the course of the week – one a 'moonlight excursion' by tram taken by Just, Bridgman and me, to one of the bays the other side of Capetown called Camp's Bay – thus

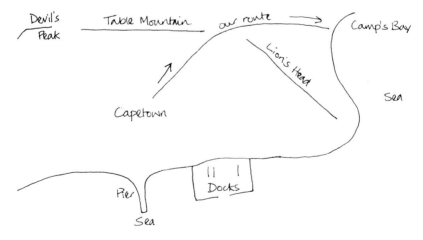

There is just a narrow neck between Table Mountain and the Lion's Head, and from it there is a magnificent view, all over Capetown on the one side and on the other over the mountains at the back of Table Mountain (known as the 'Twelve Apostles') and down to the sea. Just as

we reached the ridge the sun was setting, so the sea was gold and the clouds over the 'Twelve Apostles', a series of jagged peaks, purple. It was really a magnificent sight.[286]

We descended to the bay – rather like a Cornish cove – and had dinner there at the hotel. Of the dinner I can only say that the soup and the cheese were quite eatable!

On Saturday there was a grander excursion, our host being the Administrator of the Cape Province. He provided us with motor cars which took us a drive round the coast of the Cape Peninsula (the map will show you how we started) and so to lunch at Groote Constantia – the Government Wine farm – and to tea at his own house.[287]

The scenery was splendid – a good deal of it rather like Wales – and Constantia is a charming old Dutch farm which has been built nearly 250 years. It has the usual 'stoep' – and enormous wine cellars – and secret passages, and all sorts of other delights. Also the vines and fruit trees outside are distinctly pleasing.

The day was rather marred on the way home by a collision which ended in Mrs. Tatlow falling out of her car and getting concussion of the brain – she is better now, fortunately, but has to stay in Capetown, and won't join the party again until Kimberley.

On Sunday I had another shot at surf bathing at Muizenberg, and very nearly mastered it (I wonder if there will be any more at Port Elizabeth). Also Bridgman and I went on in the afternoon to Simonstown, and had a look at the Admiralty Dock. The weather was hot, the place dusty and the dock dull – so I needn't dilate on that. Still I am glad to have seen the Dock – think of the learning I shall be able to show about it when I get back to C.O.[288] Between Muizenburg and Simonstown (about half an hour's run by train) there are a series of

---

286. The seaside residence of the Governor of Cape Colony had been established at Camps Bay since the early 19th century.

287. As noted earlier, the Administrator was de Waal. Groot Constantia, named after the wife of an early Dutch governor of the Cape, became a government experimental vineyard about 1885. Viticulture had been introduced into the fledgling Dutch settlement in the 17th century, and French Huguenot immigrants brought in extra expertise. Exports of South African wine to Britain reached 1 million gallons by 1859, greatly encouraged by preferential tariffs. Their removal by the British government, in the interests of free trade and of commercial ties with France, devastated the industry as seriously as the phylloxera which struck in 1886. By 1914 exports were only 48,492 gallons, but soared during the war, reaching 452,428 gallons in 1918.

Cape Town, Houses of Parliament.   *Photograph,*
                              Cape Government Railways, c.1910

villages or 'seaside resorts' or whatever you care to call them, all either with sandy beaches or with bathing pools made by convenient rocks. Certainly the whole coast is a paradise for the Capetowner.

Monday and Tuesday we spent in clearing up and in seeing a few things in Capetown itself – e.g. the Museum which has some excellent 'Bushmen' casts, and the castle which is almost as good as a 'Chateau' in Normandy – it has dungeons, Dutch coats of arms over the doorways, an old picture or two, and various other delights.[289]

The only other 'episode' that I need mention is that on Monday night I went to the House of Assembly – i.e. the lower Union house – and sat

---

288. Simonstown, with a population in 1911 of 4751 (61% white), 35 kilometres by rail from Cape Town, had been the winter anchorage of Dutch East India Company ships. It became the major base of the Royal Navy in the southern hemisphere and the headquarters of the Cape and East Coast Naval Squadron. Harbour extensions, capable of docking vessels of the Dreadnought battleship class, had been opened in 1910 and new fortifications completed.

289. The Museum had been first founded in 1825, and its new buildings, costing £19,000, were opened in 1897. The Bushmen (or San) were probably the hunter-gatherer descendants of the Late Stone Age inhabitants of southern Africa, but they and the allied Khoikhoi were largely dispersed northwards by the arrival of Bantu-speaking peoples and European settlers. The castle, built 1666–79, was the oldest monument in Cape Town: it had housed the centre of adminstration and court of justice in the 18th century.

out the third reading of the Indemnity Bill. The debate itself was poor, but all the speakers, of course, were interesting to me, and one couldn't but admire the very small 'Labour party' contingent who had fought the Bill for weeks and never yielded an inch.[290]

I think this narrative brings me, so to say, 'up to date' – but I must add just a word or two about things in general in South Africa.

First, one has been lucky in having the opportunity of hearing about the Indian problem from the Indian side. Sir Benjamin Robertson and his secretary (who by the way I found to be a contemporary of mine at 'Wrens') were staying at the Civil Service Club, waiting for the report of the Commission on the Indian question which they had been sent over to 'watch'. Both of them were quite willing to talk, and I heard the 'Indian' view very emphatically put (the South Africans neither love the Indians nor are loved by them).[291]

Secondly, while Capetown has the politicians of both sides, and one has heard new views of the English-Dutch problem (which I tried to tell you about last week), it isn't, at least I imagine it isn't, at all the place to get any light on the relation of the 'whites' to the blacks. One hopes for more in the subsequent wanderings of the Commission, so I won't anticipate matters. Still, it may be just worth saying that Capetown does not reflect South Africa on this particular question.

---

290. The Indemnity and Undesirables Special Deportation Bill, passed against the opposition of the Labour Party, made legitimate Smuts's actions in deporting the strike leaders in January.
291. Indians had been brought into Natal as indentured labour to work on sugar plantations from 1860: this practice continued, with a gap 1866–84, until the Government of India stopped it in 1911. Many Indians remained after the completion of their contracts, and other non-indentured Indians joined them, especially as traders, and they spread to other parts of South Africa. They were made increasingly unwelcome, for example losing their voting rights in Natal in 1896, being subjected in the Transvaal to compulsory finger-printing in 1907 and facing many other restrictions on their civil liberties. Mohandas K. Gandhi (1869–1948), who had been in South Africa since 1893, led the campaign against such discrimination. The passive resistance movement he had launched reached a climax in 1913. It obliged the Union government to appoint a Commission of Enquiry into Grievances of Indians. Sir Benjamin Robertson (1864–1953), Chief Commissioner of the United Provinces 1912–20, gave evidence on behalf of the Government of India. In the event, only some restrictions were removed by the Indian Relief Act of 1914. Gandhi returned to India in July, and began a yet more ambitious campaign.

Oh, I forgot to add one 'episode' when I was describing our week's doings and I may as well finish up this letter by telling you about it. As we drove back on Saturday from 'Mrs. Administrator's' garden party we stopped to look at the animals on the Groote Schuur estate (I think I told you about them last week). There was the baboon – leaning over the back of his cage, with his arms folded and his head gazing meditatively towards the north, in exactly the same position as the Rhodes bust in the Memorial on the mountain side above. I thought it quite the funniest thing I have yet seen in South Africa.

> Best love
> > Ever your affectionate son
> > > E. J. Harding

DOMINIONS ROYAL COMMISSION
Beach Hotel
East London
March 15th 1914

My dear Eva,

I think it is your turn for a diary letter. It seems only a day or two ago that I finished the last one – but as we shall be travelling all next week, I don't see much chance of further writing for some days, so I will start tonight.

Certainly, for the last few days, we have had no heat to complain of. At Port Elizabeth, where we were from Thursday to Saturday, it rained most of the time: last night in the train it was quite cold: and today has been just like an English summer day, hot sun, a few clouds, and a cool evening.

I left off, I think, when we were coming up the coast from Capetown. The *Kildonan Castle*, on which we travelled, is the sister ship to the *Kinfauns* – only not quite so comfortable.[292] As we were only on her two nights, we hardly made an acquaintance, so I needn't elaborate the voyage.

We woke up on Thursday morning to find ourselves anchored in Algoa Bay, just opposite Port Elizabeth. There is just an open roadstead with a jetty or so where small steamers can lie; the Mail steamers lie outside and land their passengers in tugs. We were honoured with a

---

292. *Kildonan Castle* was launched hastily in 1899 to serve as a troop transporter in the Boer War, before becoming a commercial liner in 1901. Like her sister ship, she was requisitioned during the First World War, first as a hospital ship and then as a liner-cruiser. She was restored to commercial use after the war and operated for Union-Castle until 1931.

Port Elizabeth, Cape of Good Hope, Main Street, Looking South.
Photograph dated July 1906

special one, and got ashore just about 10. Our headquarters were The
Port Elizabeth Club, which lies well back from the business part of the
town, up the hillside. We were very comfortable there. It is a big place,
with a semi-tropical look about the architecture. Most of the bedrooms
open on to verandahs.

Port Elizabeth, as a town, improves largely upon acquaintance. From
the sea it looks merely a series of houses built on a low hill. Really it has
some good streets, public buildings and monuments (including one – a
drinking trough – to the memory of the horses killed in the Boer war,
with a really excellent inscription) and looks thoroughly prosperous.[293]
You may be interested to hear that it is a great centre for ostrich feathers
– to the purchase of which the Commission largely succumbed!

293. Port Elizabeth, 680 kilometres by sea from Cape Town, was founded by
     British settlers in 1820 as a commercial centre. It was named by the acting
     governor in memory of his wife, 'one of the most perfect of human beings'.
     It became the second city of Cape Province, with a population in 1911 of
     37,063 (54% white), even though its plans of 1904 to construct a sheltered
     harbour had not yet been effected. The monument to which Harding
     refers was sculpted by Joseph Whitehead: the inscription reads: 'The
     greatness of a nation consists not so much in the number of its people or
     the extent of its territory as in the extent and justice of its compassion'.

Port Elizabeth, Horse Memorial.   *Postcard franked 20 December 1907*

The party which had travelled via Oudsthoorn (the real centre of the ostrich industry) turned up an hour or so after we did. They reported a strenuous and interesting time but a hot one – apparently they had spent most of their time, outside the train, motoring in a temperature of 100, whilst in the train it was as hot or hotter!

Thursday afternoon was spent in discussing matters informally with the local Chamber of Commerce, and Friday in taking the usual evidence – not of any particular interest.[294]

But one thing is borne out by all the evidence we have had hitherto – that is, that there is no room in South Africa, quite apart from the racial question, for any immigration of the type that goes to Canada and Australasia. There aren't the facilities and there isn't the water. No one without considerable capital would stand a chance to start farming.[295]

---

294. Five witnesses were questioned in the Town Hall in Port Elizabeth on Friday March 13.
295. The Immigration Regulations Act of 1913 effectively limited immigration to Europeans, but in 1914 new arrivals totalled only 9047 (including minors), of whom 6523 were British subjects. Of the total, 28% were classified as leisured, professional or business, a higher percentage than for other British colonies of settlement, and just 11% were skilled workers. Opportunities for the unskilled, except female domestic servants, were much restricted by the presence of cheap black labour.

This by the way. I go back to the story of our travels. Saturday morning was utilized for 'clearing up' and for getting Lorimer and Langerman, with their respective wives and with Glenny, off to Kimberley in advance of the main party. Saturday afternoon was holiday – I was taken off in a motor car, with Robb and his wife, to see some of the country round Port Elizabeth.

It isn't extraordinarily interesting, but very pleasant, and the roads were beyond reproach for most of the way (comparing them with others we have seen – or felt – in South Africa). 'Shoemakers' Kop (I can't spell the Dutch word) was our first halting place, a little seaside resort, with splendid surf and rocks. Then a 'tea gardens', for a hasty tea (the flowers in the gardens were better than the tea, especially a big bush of flaming hybiscus). Then a hot spring, the other side of the town (which they say would make anybody's fortune if only it happened to be in Bath – it comes up from 4000 feet down with a temperature of 132, and tastes disgusting). And finally another village or township called Zwartkop, with a river alongside, of no very particular interest.[296]

I was sorry to leave Port Elizabeth, but the journey we have had since then is almost sufficient to drive its recollection out of my head altogether.

A word or two first about our train. We have, as I think I said in my last letter, a special train which is to take us round the country. It has showerbaths, and a special dining car, and a compartment apiece for all the party, all mercies to be thankful for, so we travel in comfort not to say luxury. As the gauge is narrow and the curves many, the pace is never very great – *ergo*, there is no particular reason for getting tired.[297]

Now for the journey itself. If you look at the map, you will see that the railway from Port Elizabeth to East London first goes north, and then strikes east. When we woke up this morning, we had finished the north going and had gone east some way. I had my bath when we were waiting at Fort Beaufort (the name is a survival from the early Kaffir Wars), and a little later on we came to Alice where is 'Lovedale' – a very famous mission station and training school.[298]

---

296. Schoenmakers Kop and Zwaartkops were modest resorts close to Port Elizabeth.
297. Railway construction began in South Africa in 1859, with government taking a prominent role from the 1870s when lines were pushed inland from the coast. By 1914 there were 14,400 kilometres of track, mostly of 3 ft. 6 ins. gauge.
298. A more direct line from Port Elizabeth to East London was currently under construction. Lovedale, a Prebyterian mission station, was named after John Love (1757–1825), secretary of the Glasgow Missionary Society. It

During the Kaffir wars, the Kaffirs were steadily pushed northwards, till they reached what is now known as the Transkei territories, where they were left in peace.[299] But a number of them must still remain further south, possibly as tenants of the few white settlers who now live in the districts we went through. Anyhow, we had the experience of passing through village after village of Kaffir Kraals – with patches of mealies and Kaffir corn, herds of cattle and flocks of sheep and goats, and of seeing the Kaffir children running out to see the train in the hope of an occasional penny.

The children are delightful – they haven't much clothing, very often none at all, but they are beautifully made, and their 'action' when running would warm a sculptor's heart. The women weren't so much in evidence. Where we saw them, they favoured a form of blanket, of a colour between orange and vermilion. It looked decidedly 'striking'. The men also wear a blanket sometimes, but more often disreputable-looking and tattered European clothes. They remind me of 'distressed colonial subjects' – so I pass them by. The Kraals look attractive from some distance away – they are round, with walls of mud and a thatched roof. I daresay that on closer inspection the 'vision would fade away'.

I fancy I told you, in an earlier letter, that Capetown was not the place to get an impression of native South Africa. We look to be in a fair way to get the necessary corrective.

East London Station
March 16th

I go on with this in my compartment in the special train. We are sleeping here and starting for Kimberley early tomorrow morning – a procedure which has caused much disgust among some of the members of the party, notably the Chairman, who complain of sleeping in a station. Not having been responsible for the arrangements, I merely listen with amusement!

We reached East London yesterday just after lunch and drove down to a hotel on the beach (some little distance away from the town) which has not much to recommend it beside its position. But it was full all the same,

---

was first established beyond the frontiers of European settlement in 1824, and after its destruction it was rebuilt in 1841. The territory was annexed in 1847 and the municipality of Alice was created in 1852.

299. However, the political annexation of the Transkei territories by the Cape had been completed by 1885. Traditionally, nine Kaffir Wars between Cape settlers and the Xhosa people have been counted between 1779 and 1877.

East London, Cape of Good Hope, Buffalo River and Harbour.
Photograph, Cape Government Railways, c.1910

so full that I had to sleep in a 'dependance' a little way up the road.

East London is just a small seaside town with a business: it has a harbour of sorts, with a particularly dangerous entrance, and heavy surf rolling in. It has also a first class beach with bathing pools and surf bathing, which must be the delight of thousands in the season.[300]

We had a walk in the evening along the beach and then up to the downs behind: they are so like the South Downs that one would think oneself at home, save for the different kinds of vegetation that are seen.

Today's evidence, which lasted for the morning only, partook of the nature of the picnic which we had in Tasmania, that is to say 7 witnesses were 'bowled out' in 2½ hours.[301] Everyone was most friendly.

We adjourned to a lunch given jointly by the Town Council and the Chamber of Commerce, another quite pleasant ceremony, and afterwards to an inspection of the harbour, and the Buffalo River which forms it. There was quite a big party – Town Councillors, members of the Chamber of Commerce and all the rest of it. I fear these functions become increasingly boring.

---

300. The port of East London was founded in 1848, but it grew slowly, and from 1886 its harbour required constant dredging. Nevertheless it had attracted a population of 24,606 (61% white) by 1911, it had become an important commercial centre in Cape Province, and it was raised to the status of a city on 1 June 1914.

301. The session was held in the East London Town Hall on Monday March 16.

Only one other episode needs mention: sandwiched in between the lunch and the harbour inspection was a visit to a wool sale, where 'lots' of wool are sold by auction among a crowd of excited buyers who shout against one another in eighths of a penny in an effort to catch the ear of the auctioneer.[302]

I think my tale is done: the harbour excursion ended in a tour up the Buffalo River for a couple of miles or so – it has wooded banks that remind one of the Dart [303] – then returned to dinner and to packing, and so up to the train where, as I said, I am writing this letter.

> Best love
> Ever your affectionate brother
> E. J. Harding

> Hotel Edward
> Durban
> March 23rd 1914

My dearest Mother,

We are here in luxury but limpness! That is to say, this hotel is delightful, compared with a good many which we have struck in South Africa, but the place is hot and steamy to a degree which, as you can imagine, is not to my liking. As it is the first stopping place for more than a week at which we are for more than one night, you can imagine that my time for writing has been very limited for some days. Generally, we have had to travel by night and take evidence by day, and everyone is becoming rather exhausted. Personally I have been 'liverish' during the last few days, spent most of yesterday in my bed in the train – a new kind of birthday experience – and am only now recovering.

However, that there is some justification even for the hardiest to feel the strain will, I think, be clear when I give you just the outline of our doings since we left East London, whence I think I wrote last:

17th Tuesday. Train all day. Slept in train.
18th Wednesday. Arrived 11 a.m. Kimberley. Lunch with Mayor and

---

302. Wool production in Cape Colony began in the 17th century, but it expanded rapidly only in the 20th century: there were an estimated 33½ million sheep in South Africa by 1911, and wool exports reached 174 million lbs, worth £5,770,000, by 1913–14.
303. Another reference to one of Harding's favourite English counties: the Dart flows from Dartmoor to Dartmouth in Devon.

Chamber of Commerce.

Evidence all the afternoon.

Full dress dinner given by the De Beers Directors in evening.

19th Thursday. Evidence all the morning.

Visit to De Beers Mines and Compound in the afternoon. Left for Bloemfontein 11 p.m. Slept in train.

20th Friday. Arrived Bloemfontein about 8 a.m.

Meeting with Chamber of Commerce 10.30 a.m.

Evidence 11.30 a.m. to 1 p.m.

Lunch with the 'African Club' and listened to Haggard making a speech.

Evidence 2.30–4.30.

Dinner by the Mayor and Town Council.

21st Saturday. Evidence all morning.

Tea party by Victoria League in afternoon,[304] then a motor drive of 10 miles or so to see a destructive insect pest on a farm. Left for Durban 10 p.m. Slept in train.

22nd Sunday. In train all day. Stopped at Ladysmith and Colenso to see some of the battlefields. Slept in train.

And for the unfortunate Secretary who has all the arrangements for evidence in hand and has to keep an eye on the general arrangements (often a good deal more than an eye), even a 'liver' is perhaps not too much to expect. However, as I said, I am recovering – and fortunately everyone else who has had ailments (and they are the majority) has got over them pretty speedily.

We have a certain amount of trouble – or amusement, according to the point of view – with the ladies of the party.

The Haggards have not been seen since Port Elizabeth. They came on by sea to Durban, and left for Maritzburg (where they are likely to 'rejoin') before we arrived here.

Lady Langerman, who is, or appears to be, quiet and domesticated, went off at Kimberley and won't reappear again till Johannesburg. (I can't remember, by the way, whether I told you that Langerman, the newly appointed South African member, is turning out quite an acquisition.)

---

304. The Victoria League was established in London in 1901 in memory of the Queen who had died that year and to foster friendship between parts of the Empire. It also had an immediate task, to alleviate the distress of refugees from the Second Boer War and to assist Boer families imprisoned during the war in concentration camps. Branches opened throughout the dominions. Most members were women.

But Mrs. Garnett, Mrs. Tatlow and Mrs. Lorimer stick close to the main party. Mrs. G. and Mrs. T. get on splendidly, both with each other and the male members of the party. Mrs. L. hates them like cats – a compliment which they return. So one has to be careful in one's doings.

As I lay in bed yesterday, and meditated on my liver and my birthday, I made up the following doggerel, which I will reproduce so as to show you how even the Commission can't wholly occupy my thoughts! This is how it runs –

> Fair lady one is simply fun.
> Fair ladies two give a lot to do.
> Fair ladies three – well, do not agree.
> Fair ladies four are distinctly a bore.
> Fair ladies five are the devil to drive.
> Fair ladies six are a still worse mix.
> Fair ladies seven give the staff ——

Well, as this is a family letter, I will leave a blank, and simply say that the rhyme is not what you might naturally suppose.[305]

March 24th

Today is still limper than yesterday: in fact everyone thinks it as bad as Colombo or worse, and I feel like a super-saturated sponge. But the mail goes tomorrow, so I must defy the moisture and go on with this letter tonight.

Our two journeys – from East London into the interior and back again here – should have given us a pretty good idea of a good deal of S. Africa, I fancy: first of all comes the coast belt – rolling, green and very beautiful country – rather reminiscent of the English southern counties, particularly Wiltshire; then the high lands, 3000 feet and more, where the mountains begin to close in, and the vegetation gets thinner and browner; and finally the high veldt which is flat, and desolate, and, as we saw it, very barren. There has been a three years' drought, and the veldt looked like nothing but a succession of large antheaps, with an occasional tuft of very sickly-looking grass.

Undoubtedly, the time to see the veldt of this kind is in the evening, as we saw it at Bloemfontein last Friday. We climbed a hill on one side of the town, and looked down over the houses to the veldt and the sunset

---

305. What *can* it be? Suggestions to the Editor, please.

beyond. The barrenness disappears then in the haze, and the mountains in the distance look like fairyland. There really was a view then that I shan't soon forget.

I must go back to the story of our doings. Our two days at Kimberley, Wednesday and Thursday of last week, were some of the most interesting we have had since the Commission commenced.

The town itself is very little.[306] The streets are built round the sites where the first miners put up their shanties, so the place isn't much in the 'town-planning' line. Nor can you say that it has any particular architectural characteristics. Its whole centre is in the De Beers Company which is fabulously rich, and the Company's riches depend on the vanity of mankind, particularly of 'feminine mankind', if I may put it that way. There are immense works, enormous machines, some thousands of workmen employed, most elaborate devices for checking fraud. The net result of all this, the output say for a week or even a month, is seen on one shelf in one room – a handful of stones which look like rubbish and for which I personally wouldn't give a farthing. I tell you that the whole paraphernalia induce the most melancholy reflections on the folly of human nature. *Liberavi animam meam*.[307] Having said all this, I proceed to say that the De Beers Co. maintain a first class hotel, quite the best in South Africa, where they entertained all the Commission sumptuously. I also feel bound to confess that the machine which separates the diamonds from the dross in the last stage of washing, known as the 'pulsator', is fascinating. The diamonds with all sorts of other stones come through a machine and down a 'shoot', which is covered with some species of wax, is constantly moving with a kind of 'quiver' and is continually flushed with water. Someone, not so very long ago, discovered that the diamonds stick to the wax, whilst the water washes everything else down. The result is almost uncanny.

---

306. Kimberley was created by the discovery of diamonds in 1870, and brought under British control by the annexation of Griqualand West. The population in 1911 had reached 44,433 (39% white). A rail link to Cape Town was completed in 1885, extended to Johannesburg in 1906 and to Bloemfontein in 1908. The De Beers Company, founded in 1888 after a merger of other mining companies by Rhodes and Alfred Beit (1853–1906), dominated production. It was here that the 3024¾-carat Cullinan diamond was unearthed on 25 January 1905. At the time of the Union in 1910, South Africa accounted for 98% of the world's production of diamonds. The Commission held its formal sessions in the Town Hall, questioning 5 witnesses, including the Assistant General Manager of De Beers.

307. 'I have freed my soul.'

Kimberley, Cape of Good Hope, General View of De Beers' Workings.
Photograph, Cape Government Railways, c. 1910

Kimberley, Inside a Compound. *Photograph,
Cape Government Railways, c. 1910*

Very interesting too was the 'compound' which we saw. The Kimberley mines are worked on a system which doesn't allow the native any contact with the outside world so long as he is under contract with the De Beers Co. The compound itself is perhaps 5 or 6 hundred yards square – with living rooms for the men, shops where they can buy their food, a large space for exercise, a hospital and so on. But they go straight down an underground passage from the compound to the mine shaft. They mayn't go out, and they mayn't see their families till their 'spell', generally four months, is up. It is really a case, temporarily, of *Lasciate ogni speranza chi entrate qui*[308] – and it seems incredible to modern notions that the men should stand it. That they do, and that they like it, is undoubted. Work on the De Beers mines is about the most popular, apparently, among the natives in the whole of the Union.[309]

The only other point I need mention about Kimberley – and it seems extraordinarily unimportant besides the essential 'parasitism' of the place – is the kindness of the welcome we got, and the extreme geniality of the inhabitants. Possibly this is due to the 'De Beers' atmosphere, which breathes wealth and therefore hospitality. Possibly it is the result of early 'miner' days. Anyhow, we had a crowd at the station to meet us, and quite a lot to see us off; and everyone we met went out of his or her way to help us.

I must just add a particularly good story with which someone entertained me at dinner apropos of the Semitic origin of the presiding Kimberley race. A stranger went to the Golf Club there, and finding no one about, asked the Secretary whether he could get a game. The Secretary replied, 'Well, I don't know: there's Oppenheimer here, there's Wirtzheim here and – let's see – yes, there's Hoggenheimer here'.

---

308. 'Lasciate ogni speranza voi ch'entrate': 'Abandon all hope whoever enters here': Dante, *The Divine Comedy: Hell*, canto 3, line 9.
309. The popularity of working for De Beers was mainly a reflection of the poverty of alternatives for Africans subjected to hut taxes and poll taxes and largely deprived of land by the legislative sequence beginning with the Squatter Acts of 1878 and 1884 and culminating in the Natives Land Act of 1913 which massively restricted African landownership. The policy was consciously designed to provide the diamond and gold mines with migrant labourers. They were hired in the tribal areas normally on short-term contracts of up to 10 months which ensured that they remained essentially unskilled and not a threat to white skilled miners. Their control within isolated compounds for reasons of security against theft and to prevent the organisation of labour became the norm in the diamond mines from 1885, a practice subsequently emulated on the goldfields.

Bloemfontein, Orange Free State.   *Postcard*

'Look here', said the stranger, 'I asked for a game of golf, I don't want the wine list!'[310]

Bloemfontein, after Kimberley, is a great change. It is just a sleepy small country town, decidedly unprogressive, and (probably) very anti-British. Its Mayor is a German piano seller – that is to say he finds no market apparently for English pianos. Most of the men one met, either casually, or at the various functions, seem to have been deported as 'prisoners of war' or at least to have fought against the British. They still do not love the British officer (this opinion, though, I find is not confined to the Boers in South Africa), and their allegiance is mainly on account of the fact that the Orange Free State is now part of the Union.

We haven't met latent disloyalty before (though there has been certainly no demonstrative loyalty such as we had in Australia), so the experience was interesting. I am bound to say that, both in kindliness and what one may call 'temper', these Free Staters were quite the equal of anyone we have seen in South Africa. Let us hope that the ones we met were not exceptional.

---

310. The Jewish origins of mining company directors like Beit and Oppenheimer provoked anti-semitic comment, particularly at the time of the Second Boer War: critics often blamed its outbreak upon Jewish capitalists.

Bloemfontein as a place is attractive enough. It has a big market place, and some good public buildings – amongst them the Raadsaal where we had our sittings. It has ambitions, I gather, to be the capital of the Union. But I fear they won't be realized.[311]

It is getting late – and this letter is becoming long, and I am afraid, boring. So I will pass over our journey down from Bloemfontein to the coast. As I told you at the beginning, I was in bed for most of the day, so I haven't much to say anyhow. I didn't get out at Ladysmith at all, and I didn't go as far as the others did when we stopped at Colenso. But so far as I could judge, knowing nothing of the matters, the battle of Colenso must have been singularly ill advised on the British side. It seems to have been just an advance over a level plain against strongly defended hills. And, as one looked at the hills round Ladysmith – Caesar's Camp, Waggon's Hill and all the rest of them – it looked as though it would have been quite easy to 'rush' the town after a month or two. So perhaps one can credit both sides with equal folly.[312]

> Best love
> Ever your affectionate son
> E. J. Harding

> Pretoria Club
> Pretoria.
> March 31st 1914

My dear Eva,

I can't for the life of me remember whose turn it is for the diary letter – anyhow it doesn't matter much, and this one is likely to be short. We have had a lot to do here in a limited time, and are likely to have the same thing and rather more so in Johannesburg, whither we go tomorrow.

I think I left off the last letter just after we arrived at Durban – and described ourselves as living in luxury but limpness. It was a description all too true. One day the humidity was 100%. I don't know exactly what that means, but the effect is appalling. And on the day we left, when the temperature had dropped to the lower eighties, it felt quite cold! As to the hotel, it was well out of the town, and close by the sea. Durban is fortunate in having on its beach, first, a bathing enclosure (I mean an enclosure protected by netting against sharks – where the proper 'surf bathing' can be indulged in) and, secondly, quite the finest open air swimming bath I have ever seen. It must be at least 100 yards long. You can imagine that, with the heat what it was, we spent as many minutes as we could get 'off' in the bathing enclosure or the bath.

I must go back to the hotel. It was clean, well run, and airy – a contrast in all three ways to some we have struck. It is also almost wholly staffed by Indian servants – another nearly new experience (not quite, as we had the same thing at East London, but there the service was bad).

Durban is semi-tropical and very attractive.[313] It has a first class harbour, entirely dredged out of what was once a shallow (and no doubt malarial) lagoon. It has good public buildings, particularly a modern Town Hall. It has broad streets, tramways, electric light – in fact all the appurtenances of a modern civilized town. But the real charm of the place is that there are at least two civilizations conflicting with the white – if you can call them 'civilizations'. There are the Indians – who have a separate quarter, through which I found time to walk – gaudily dressed for the most part, particularly the women, and no doubt busily engaged in undercutting the white man. And there are also the natives, I suppose Zulus or akin to them. They are fine-looking men, and were presumably fierce warriors not so very long ago. Now they seem to find their chief amusement in doing housemaid's work – or else in drawing a 'rickshaw'. For the latter occupation they adorn themselves with extraordinary head dresses of feathers, horns and what not. As they run up in anticipation of a 'fare', and cut capers of delight at the prospect of obtaining one, the proceedings savour strongly of the barbaric.

---

311. Bloemfontein was probably first settled in 1840. It was selected as the capital of the Orange Free State in 1854 and began to develop as an administrative and commercial centre. The rail link to Cape Town and to Johannesburg made it also a railway centre and workshop. It became the judicial capital of the Union while remaining the political capital of the province of the Orange Free State. But its population in 1911 was still only 26,925 (55% white) out of a provincial total of 528,174 (33% white). The old government offices had burnt down in 1908, but had been rebuilt in 1910–11. The Raadzaal was built in 1892, with classical columns and a domed tower, at a cost of over £57,000. It was here that the Commission questioned its 8 witnesses.

312. The journey back to the coast was taking Harding through scenes made famous in the recent Boer War, especially Colenso, a tiny settlement which British forces took until 20 February 1900 to capture, and Ladysmith, whose siege by the Boers was finally ended on 28 February 1900.

313. Durban was founded in 1835 and named after Sir Benjamin D'Urban (1777–1849), Governor of Cape Colony. It became the principal town and port of Natal. Its population in 1911 had reached 89,998 (39% white). The harbour works, crucial for Durban's development, were begun in 1855, and a graving dock had been added shortly before Harding's visit. The town hall, with its splendid dome, was opened in 1910 and cost £300,000. Here over three days the Commission collected evidence from its 20 witnesses.

Durban, Mail Boat at Wharf.   *Postcard*

I wish you could have seen Vincent and myself returning in one of these conveyances in the evening in pouring rain, to the accompaniment of lightning and thunder, and apparently in imminent danger of being shot backwards on to the road, owing to the mud, and our own weight. (Vincent, as you know, is not exactly light.) I used to shake with laughter.[314]

I fancy I gave you, in last week's letter, a sort of diary of our doings. I am going to do the same in this – so that you may see how our 'progress' has got on.

Monday March 23rd
  Arrived Durban 8.45 a.m.
  Met by the Mayor and local celebrities.
  Evidence 10.30 a.m. and in afternoon.
  Reception by the Mayor and Mayoress in the evening.
Tuesday March 24th
  Evidence all morning.

---

314. Vincent, too, described to his wife the 'picturesque ricksha runners ... who leap and dance about like the youngest of colts.' He added: 'They are said to die in 4 years but a merrier crew of condemned men never lived'.

Rickshas and Pullers.   *Postcard dated 9 May 1922*

Visit to Harbour in afternoon. (We saw the *Ceramic*, the biggest boat in the Australian service, and in fact assisted, as a 'tug', in getting her away from the quay.) [315]
Evidence of Harbour authorities afternoon.
Dinner by Chamber of Commerce in evening. (I ought to say that I 'cut' the dinner on the plea of recovering from my liver attack, and went instead to sports at the swimming baths aforesaid which were doubtless much more amusing!)
Wednesday March 25th
Evidence morning and afternoon.
Lunch by Mayor at Durban Club.
Thursday March 26th
Packing up.

---

315. The White Star Line had been a major force in transatlantic shipping since 1871, but its attempt from 1899 to break into the Australian traffic via South Africa met with only partial success. *Ceramic*, 18,500 tons, 655 feet by 69 feet, was built by Harland and Wolff in Belfast and launched in 1913. She had accommodation for 800 emigrants. She served as a troop transporter in both world wars, but was finally sunk on 6 December 1942 off the Azores with the loss of all her mainly civilian passengers.

Durban, Natal, Town Hall and South Street.   *Postcard*

Left for Maritzburg 4.15 p.m.
Dinner in Train.
Arrived 8.30.
Met by Mayor and taken to Hotel in Municipal Charabanc.
Friday March 27th
Evidence morning and afternoon.
Dinner by Administrator in evening.
Saturday March 28th
Special train in morning to a farm called 'Nels Rust'[316] where the
Commission took evidence in the drawing room of a farm (another
nail, by the way, in the coffin of Bateman's precedents) while I, when I
got bored with listening, went out and inspected the farm and the
Indian 'location' on it. Motored back to Maritzburg, about 18 miles,
and arrived 2 p.m. Went off in another motor at 3 p.m. along appalling
roads, with Lorimer and Bowring, to inspect an iron deposit some
8 miles away. Got back just after 5, and went down to a Mayor's
reception which, fortunately, we found just over. Tea at the local
cricket ground, and then taken off to see an old Dutch Museum.
Left for Pretoria by special train 11 p.m.
Sunday March 29th
In train all day on the way to Pretoria, arrived 9 p.m.

It really is too much of a rush, and I shall be devoutly thankful when we are 'through' Johannesburg, and start back for home. One has constantly to be on the 'qui vive' to see that things don't go 'wronger' than can be helped. Still, though I feel getting rather tired out, I can't say that I have felt this tour such a *strain* as the Australian one was. Whether one is more used to it, or the arrangements are better, or what the reason is, I don't really know. I expect there are several causes.

Now to go back again. If I could do nothing in Durban, I should like a long stay. As it was I was glad to get away. But on the morning we left a curious thing happened. I came down to breakfast to find Mr. and Mrs. Bray sitting placidly at another table – last seen on the *Medina* on the way to Port Said. Now, it appears, they are touring South Africa for 3 months. I can't but suspect that old Bray is watching the many insurances that various members of the party have effected with him! Still they appeared quite pleased to see me.

After Durban, Maritzburg seemed quite bracing. Also we had a cool and rainy day which was very refreshing. But we had a pretty strenuous time there, as you will see on reference to the timetable above!

The people were extremely friendly, a shade more so if that be possible than those in the other places we have been to, and I really enjoyed our stay very much. Unfortunately I couldn't find time to see Lady Goodrich's brother, though I heard about him a good deal.[317]

Maritzburg is an extremely pretty place – that is its position is pretty: it lies within a circle of green hills, and it is very well laid out.[318]

Which reminds me to say – I don't remember whether I said it before – that all these South African towns seem to me to be better laid out and, for want of a better word, more 'distinctive' than the corresponding towns we saw in Australia (even New Zealand also, I think). One

---

316. This was the home of Joseph Baynes (1842–1925), who had been a settler since 1862, Minister of Lands and Works in Natal 1903–4 and a member of the Legislative Council.

317. Lady Goodrich was the wife of Admiral Sir James Goodrich (1851–1925). Her brother Geoffrey Gladstone Helbert (d.1934) had been on the staff of the High Commissioner in South Africa and became a Lieutenant-Colonel.

318. Pietermaritzburg, 114 kilometres inland from Durban, was by 1911 a town of 30,555 people (48% white) and the capital of the province of Natal, population 1,194,043 (only 8% white). The settlement had been founded in 1838 by Boer trekkers from the Cape and named after Pieter Retief and Gerrit Maritz, their leaders. British control was imposed when Natal was annexed in 1843. Here, in the Provincial Council Buildings, the Commission spent March 27 interrogating 12 witnesses.

wonders whether the difference is climatical or temperamental, or whether merely the wealth of the mines has ramified itself into the provincial towns.

Rand Club
Johannesburg
April 1st

I must finish this letter tonight, as the mail goes tomorrow. You will see we have safely 'got' here – but I shan't attempt to describe either Pretoria or the Rand. I will just finish about Maritzburg, and our journey up to Pretoria.

As I said before, I enjoyed Maritzburg very much. It was, of course, distinctly 'provincial'. The loan of the 'municipal charabanc' to take us to and from the hotel caused us much amusement, and the Mayor's garden party (which I just missed) must have been great fun. But it is the capital of Natal and prides itself not a little, being particularly jealous of Durban, which is larger and I suppose rather richer. The Administrator's dinner party (the Administrator, as I possibly explained before, is the 'Pooh Bah'[319] of each Province) also provided me with considerable entertainment. I tried each of my neighbours (one was the daughter of the 'Provincial Secretary' of the Natal Government – the other I know nothing about) to find out their views on the native question generally and the Indian question in Natal in particular. They were distinctly 'limited' in each case – that is their ideas seemed confined to making the native work as much as possible and to keep the Indian indentured. I say 'limited', but I think it is quite possible that if one were here for long and could really study the conditions, one's ideas would be much the same. Certainly it must be very irritating for white people to find themselves undersold by the Indians if they start retail shops, and to feel themselves up against a native race whose only concern is to work long enough to get money for an extra wife or two![320]

---

319. Pooh-Bah, 'The Lord High Everything Else', appears in the light opera *The Mikado* by W.S. Gilbert (1836–1911) and Sir Arthur Sullivan (1842–1900), first performed in 1885.

320. Vincent at this time was writing to his wife: 'The key to advance would be to get the native to work – but this he won't do – preferring to enjoy life in his own way'. Meanwhile, Haggard jotted down in his diary: 'The native is both the greatest asset and greatest curse of the country. Latter because when white man comes he thinks the native should do the work, not he'.

But I am becoming 'reflective' again, and must go on with our doings. The experiment of holding a sitting of the Commission in a drawing room was quite a success. The hostess originally wanted to have the evidence taken while the members sat round in armchairs and drank morning tea! This was altogether too much for Bateman who was in the chair, Vincent having gone off to Johannesburg. No sitting could be held without at least a pencil, and a table. He insisted on both!

The farm was right up in the hills, and very jolly the country was – a certain amount of woodland, rolling hills, and rich pasture. Certainly Natal deserves its title of the Garden Colony.

We left Maritzburg, as I said before, late at night. We woke up to find ourselves getting near the coal area of Natal[321] – not very enlivening country – and spent the rest of the day first climbing up to the plateau where the Transvaal begins, and then running slowly through it. We stopped a minute or two at Majuba of many memories – the hill itself is a bold kopje, and commands the countryside – but otherwise didn't 'call a halt' for any length of time.[322] The day didn't seem too long though. We seemed always passing by some township or other, and when we weren't there was always cattle, or maize, or Kaffir corn – or at any rate the bare veldt to amuse oneself with.

Whatever demerits the constant travelling has, it certainly has given us the opportunity of seeing a lot of the interior of the Union. I must say that I still find Australia suffers by the contrast, but I doubt whether I should like perpetual sunshine and heat, which most of the country seems to be favoured with, as a permanent possession.

I was late last night and must stop. It seems curious to think that the next mail should bring myself as well as my letters home!

> Best love
> Ever your affectionate brother
> E. J. Harding

---

321. Coal in Natal came, appropriately, from the district near Newcastle. The province's output had risen to over 2¼ million tons by 1910. Coal production was even greater in the Transvaal. A committee of the Commission, made up of Haggard, Garnett and Bowring, had already visited Newcastle on Monday 23 March and gathered evidence from 4 witnesses.

322. On 27 February 1881 the defeat of British troops under General Sir George Colley (1835–81) on the summit of Majuba Hill by a smaller force of attacking Boers practically concluded the First Boer War, leaving the Boer republics with an uneasy and temporary independence.

R.M.S. Edinburgh Castle
(1 day out from Capetown)
April 12th 1914

My dear Father,

If I am to finish a 'diary' for this tour I must certainly begin now, or else I shall have forgotten all my recollections of South Africa. And even if it gets to you more or less at the time I do myself, I daresay you won't mind reading it.

I think I left off the last letter when we had got to Pretoria from Maritzburg. That was a fortnight ago, and it seems like several months – such a lot seems to have happened since.

However, I remember enough of Pretoria to say that the town has quite a character of its own, that the Union Government Buildings – which lie on the slope of a hill a mile or so outside – are palatial and put 'Downing Street' hopelessly in the shade, and that it has a Zoo of no mean merit which I stole half an hour to see.

It has also a Church Square, which has seen a lot of history. It is now well laid out with a fountain in the middle, and fine public buildings all round.[323] Haggard told us that when he first went to Pretoria – some thirty or more years ago – he 'outspanned' for several days on the site of the present square, and was driven away because of malaria. That was the time when the British annexation of the Transvaal was first proclaimed, when Haggard himself hauled up the flag and assisted in reading the Proclamation, and when the present Administrator of the Transvaal, Johannes Rissik (after whom, by the way, Johannesburg is named), admits that he would have liked to have shot him.

This same Rissik by the way – *quantum mutatus ab illo*[324] – entertained the Commission at a garden party, and was generally most friendly.[325]

---

323. By 1911 Pretoria had a population of 57,674 (62% white) and the Transvaal 1,686,212 (25% white). The town was founded in 1855 and named after the father of Mathinus Wessel Pretorius (1899–1901), the first president of the Transvaal Republic. It was in turn the capital of the state, the colony and the province of the Transvaal and from 1910 the administrative capital of the Union. The Union Government Buildings were designed by Herbert Baker in classical style and built at a cost of £1,180,000 in 1910–12. The zoological gardens were established from 1899. Church Square stood in the town centre, faced on one side by the three-storied Transvaal Government Buildings, surmounted by a statue of Liberty and containing the meeting hall of the Provincial Council. Here, over three days from Monday March 30 to Wednesday April 1, the Commission questioned 13 witnesses.

324. Virgil, again.

Pretoria, Transvaal, House of Parliament.   *Photograph, c.1910*

For the rest we had the usual scramble of evidence and entertainments for the 2½ days we spent in Pretoria. Haggard was in his element, and made lots of speeches. 'Jess's' cottage is in Pretoria. In one of his speeches he suggested that it might be bought up as a municipal – or even a national – possession. Not having read *Jess* I feel quite cold – nor did I notice a very strong feeling in the way of adopting the suggestion.[326]

I don't think I have much more to say about Pretoria. We stayed at the Club which is rambling and comfortable, and we had a black 'boy' as valet – very useful and hardworking he was too.

Wednesday April 1st saw us on the move again – this time a short spell only, from Pretoria to Johannesburg, about an hour's run. It was the last of our 'special' train which we left with great regret, as considering the

---

325. Haggard had accompanied Sir Theophilus Shepstone (1817–93) to Pretoria where on 12 April 1877 British annexation of the Transvaal was declared. Local resistance subsequently triggered off the First Boer War. Johannes Rissik (1857–1925) was born in Holland and emigrated to Pretoria in 1876 where he joined the government service, became Surveyor-General for the Transvaal in 1895, served under Botha's command during the Second Boer War and in his Transvaal government from 1907, and became the first Administrator of the Transvaal province after Union from 1910 until 1917.
326. Some of the central episodes of Haggard's novel *Jess*, published 1887, are set in Pretoria when the town was besieged by the Boers in the war of 1880–81.

nights we had spent in it, it was the best home we had had for the last three weeks. All the members of the party solemnly met and dined on the train on the Wednesday evening. The chef nearly burst himself in trying to provide a super excellent dinner. The Chairman ended the proceedings by presenting envelopes, with suitable enclosures, to all the train staff. So we parted with protestations of mutual goodwill.

Johannesburg beggars description.[327] Thirty years ago it was pure veldt. Now there is continuous double track railway for 60 miles or so along the reef from Randfontein to Springs. All the way along there are chimneys and shafts and huge white dumps – which Vincent graphically describes as the 'icebergs of the veldt'. There is a heterogeneous collection of 150,000 natives or so from all parts of South Africa who toil for 2/6 a day. There is a large collection of white people – much the largest in South Africa and mainly discontented.[328] There are houses of all kinds from the hovel to the palace. And in Johannesburg itself, there are public buildings which London might envy – all built on the proceeds of a gold reef which in actual production per ton of ore is, I suppose, one of the poorest in the world.[329]

In the streets the raw native jostles, so far as he is allowed to, the latest Paris fashions. Shops that might rival Harrods are within a stone's throw of shanties where nothing is sold but 'Kaffir truck'[330] and (probably) illicit liquor. The Carlton Hotel with its Tango Teas and the Rand Club with marble pillars have as counter attractions Kaffir dances and compounds where the native lives and sleeps in the most approved of overcrowded conditions. I could go on with similar contrasts for quite a long time, but I won't bore you further! Anyhow, for me certainly, the place had an extraordinary and growing fascination. I started by finding it somewhat repulsive in comparison with the rest of South Africa. I ended by wanting to see more and more of it.

Outwardly, our visit was neither more nor less than those to the other towns. There was the same round of entertainment – perhaps rather less

---

327. Johannesburg leapt into existence following the discovery of gold in 1886. Its growth was spectacular. By 1911 the population was 237,104 (51% white), making it outstandingly the largest city in South Africa and indeed in Africa south of the Sahara.
328. It was here that the general strike of 1914 erupted. The Labour Party in March won a majority of seats in the Transvaal Provincial elections.
329. South African gold production was valued at £6010 in 1885 and £37,372,949 in 1914.
330. Cheap goods sold to black families on low incomes were known as 'Kaffir truck'.

Johannesburg, Transvaal, Fox Street.   *Postcard*

for us, because there was so much work to do in a limited time, and rather more for the ladies. There was the same kindness from all the people whom one came across. And there was the same atmosphere that one has got to associate with Africa – blue skies, clear air, and a hot sun.

But on one evening, as it happened with hardly any warning, there was a heavy storm, vivid lightning, and torrential rain. I think it is emblematic of the inner history of Johannesburg. One felt somehow all the time that there might be another sudden outburst to follow the many they have had. Or, to put it in another way, that the place is built on the top of a volcano.

The truth is that the gold industry came in too quick, and has developed too soon, for its organization to correspond with its needs. The financiers who have supplied the necessary cash for development don't live in the country, and don't understand it – or if they have lived in the country have been financiers only and not administrators. The people who run the industry locally have, naturally, a tendency to look after the dividends of their employers rather than the well being of those they employ. The result is that the white mining population is unstable and discontented – it wanders from mine to mine in search of higher wages and wrings concessions by being able to agitate. The black population is voiceless, but still discontented. At present it hasn't agitated – but it

'East Coast Mine boys showing their passes in the Witwatersrand Native Labour
Association's Compound'.   *Postcard*

probably will do so soon.[331] And then there is likely to be much more
trouble than ever there was in the disturbances of last July and January.

Curiously enough, one heard very little of the last disturbances.
I suppose the mining people are bored, and the agitators momentarily
cowed. But I can't think that the quiescence will last very long.
Repression isn't the way to success when there are, as far as one can
gather, very serious grievances which remain untouched. I won't go into
the grievances now, as I think all the members of the Commission were
extremely dissatisfied at the present position of affairs, and will have not
a little to say about it.[332] But I shall always be glad to have seen
Johannesburg – and really I shan't be surprised at anything that may
happen there within the next few years.

I will go on to describe the various things we did there.

---

331. The South African Native Congress was formed in 1909, renamed the
     South African Native National Congress in 1912 and the African National
     Congress in 1923. African mineworkers joined in strikes in 1913 and
     1914. Neither political nor industrial agitation made much headway
     before the 1920s.
332. The Commission's *Third Interim Report*, pp.11–27, contains observations
     on industrial conditions in the mining industry.

'The Musicians (Piano Players) at Native War Dance, Johannesburg'.
Postcard franked 28 December 1907

We divided forces, so far as accommodation went, between the Carlton Hotel and the Rand Club. The Carlton is a caravanserie of the approved London type – noisy, large and not too comfortable. Personally I went to the Rand Club which I liked much better – though it was as solemn, almost, as I always understood the Athenaeum to be.[333] Its occupants afforded scope for amusement and study. The Semitic type is prominent – and one might fairly call the crowd, according to the words of the *Interim Report*, 'hybrid and cosmopolitan'.[334]

We worked very hard from Thursday to Saturday morning, but between that and Monday morning there was an interlude.

Saturday afternoon was spent by Glenny and myself in visiting the local Zoo,[335] much inferior to the Pretoria one, and in walking across country, thence to Vrededorp, some four miles across 'semi-veldt' – I use the term because it would obviously be built over in a few years' time. Vrededorp is the home of the poor whites and lies two miles or so

---

333. The Athenaeum had been founded in 1824 as a London club for eminent men of science, literature and the arts.
334. As noted later, Harding was already drafting the *Third Interim Report* on the voyage home.
335. Johannesburg zoo, based on a private collection of animals, was opened in 1904.

to the right of Johannesburg as one looks at it from the north. There was nothing to see there, so I needn't waste words over it.[336]

On Sunday we had the special honour of reserved seats in Church in the evening, and a sermon in which the Commission was specially mentioned by name. Indeed a final dignity – or indignity! – the preacher spluttered a good deal before he got the name right, and my gravity was badly strained in consequence. In the morning we had been to a Kaffir dance in one of the Crown Mine compounds – which I think would have made a great impression upon all of you, particularly Eva. The Chief musician, or conductor I should say perhaps, performed mainly lying on his back clasping a Kaffir piano, about a yard long, with outstretched legs. If the photographs which I took of it only come out they must clearly go to M.J.V.W., Dr. Allen and Sir Henry Wood.[337] The performers, in every variety of costume, indulged in marches and countermarches and various antics and grimaces – more than once they made the ground tremble with their stamping. There were also subsidiary dances in various parts of the compound at which we had a look, but which won't bear detailed description. And the dust and odour were not a little trying.

We escaped to lunch with the Mine Manager close by. He had a charming house and garden in strange contrast with the neighbouring compound. I evaded a similar entertainment (I mean a tea party, not another Kaffir dance) in the afternoon, and had a walk in the midst of mine shafts and dumps, in order to absorb the better the atmosphere of the place.

The evidence for Johannesburg ended – with rather a scramble – on Monday afternoon.[338] Most of the members went off to Capetown the same evening, but as there was a lot of clearing up to do in preparation for the voyage home, I and the rest of the staff stayed until Thursday

---

336. There was, in fact, much to see, little of it pleasant. The Transvaal government had opened up Vrededorp as a settlement for unemployed ox-wagon drivers, made unemployed in their hundreds by the arrival of the railway in 1892, but the area degenerated into a slum.

337. M.J.V.W. is Margaret Vaughan Williams. Dr Hugh Percy Allen (1869–1946), knighted 1920, was the organist at New College, Oxford, 1901–18, the conductor of the Bach Choir from 1907 and Professor of Music at Oxford from 1918. Sir Henry Wood (1869–1944), conductor and minor composer, founded and conducted annual Promenade Concerts from 1895 until his death.

338. The Commission had questioned 18 witnesses from Thursday April 2 to Monday April 6. At the same time, a committee of the Commission, consisting of Haggard and Garnett, had been questioning 8 further witnesses on April 2, 3 and 4.

Robinson Deep Gold Mine, Johannesburg.   *Postcard*

morning April 9th, and only reached Capetown on the morning of the
day that the boat sailed.

We did our 'clearing up' successfully, and also found time for one or
two more experiences. On Tuesday evening Bridgman and I had a look at
the East Rand where we saw apparently quite 'raw' natives bathing in the
'dump' water, and shaking themselves like dogs after their ablutions.[339]
And on Wednesday morning we, with Lorimer who had also stayed
behind, were shown over the Crown Mine. This was not the least strange
of our many adventures in our wanderings. We went down to the 2000
foot level, had a scramble down the 'stope' where the men are at work (the
'stope' is the actual place where the reef is opened up, and is perhaps 3 ft
high and 200 ft in width), and finally when we got back safely to the
surface had a look at the engine rooms, the batteries, and the various sets
of machinery which turn the gold-bearing ore into gold blocks. The
'stope' in particular, and all the various underground workings, were most
fascinating – especially the sight of the (to my mind) unfortunate natives
who have to struggle with hammers or machines or whatnot for eight
hours a day for a paltry two shillings or so. I envy neither them nor the
white man who only 'supervises', but who gets say ten times as much.

---

339. The East Rand Proprietary Mines Company declared a dividend of 12½ %
    in August 1913.

Just north of the Equator
April 19th 1914

I must 'round off' the tale of our doings in South Africa. We left on the morning of Thursday (April 9th) on our 40 hours journey to Capetown. Lorimer, as befitted the supplier of most of the engines for the South African Railways, had extracted a special car. We, that is Glenny, Bridgman and I, had ordinary compartments in the train, but 'fed' with Lorimer and his wife in the private car. As we were in the middle, and their car at the end, our journey provided some amusing experiences. As meal times approached, we had either to wait for a stop, and if there were one dash along the line to get in to the end carriage, or if there seemed no chance of a stop make a pilgrimage along the corridors.

Some of the carriages were for natives only. The elder ones spent their time looking out of the windows: their babies blocked the corridors. It was a trying business anyhow to get through, and it generally ended in finding the luggage van so blocked up with luggage that a little Alpine climbing had to be resorted to before getting to one's destination.

We came down by way of Kimberley, Fourteen Streams and De Aar.[340] The names are historical, the country not so interesting as one would expect. In fact, it is really very dull, mostly flat and, all through the 'Karroo' as it is called, apparently desert.

It can't be desert really – for at one small wayside station in the middle of sandy scrub we had the experience of seeing a girl get down, being met by a buggy and driving off into apparent nothingness, but presumably towards a farm. So I will just say that the experience of a day and a half of this kind is not exhilarating: the redeeming feature is the sunsets which are splendid.

We landed at Capetown at 7 in the morning, had a hasty breakfast at the Civil Service Club and a rush to do various things that needed doing. By 12 we were on board this steamer, and we sailed just before lunch.

A good many of the original party on the *Kinfauns* – having planned to go up to the Victoria Falls and then foregone the trip through fear of malaria – couldn't get cabins and have had to wait a week in Capetown. The party consists only of the Chairman, Sinclair, Glenny, Bridgman and myself.

---

340. Fourteen Streams developed as a railway junction from 1890. De Aar was settled when the railway first arrived in 1881: the author and feminist Olive Schreiner (1855–1920) lived there 1907–13.

We have been hard at work collecting our thoughts about South Africa and putting them down on paper for the Report. So I needn't record final impressions. But I may as well just say this, that in spite of S. Africa's extraordinarily good climate and sunshine and the beauty of a good deal of it, I would much prefer New Zealand as a place to live in, though not, according to my recollection of it, Australia. On the other hand, South Africa seems to me to have more problems even than Australia has and still less adequate means of solving them in spite of, as far as I could judge, a higher level of intelligence amongst its citizens!

I have got very little to say about the voyage so far. The ship is very full, which means that it is harder to get to know people, and, as we have been at it pretty strenuously, we haven't had much time even to begin to make acquaintances.

Fortunately, I have got an outside cabin to myself on the shady side. We have also got a study cabin next door. But that is an 'inner' one, and not at all to be recommended in the tropics.[341]

We got over the Equator yesterday – and the Southern Cross is sinking. I wonder if I shall see it again! The sea has been almost continuously smooth, and the weather is now getting cooler after two days of particularly vile humidity. That I think, completes all I want to say just now.

April 26th
In the Bay of Biscay

I had better finish off this letter tonight, as we shall be 'in' with luck by tomorrow evening, and I shall have packing to do.

We are pluming ourselves for having finished the first draft of another Report. Now will begin the weary business of getting it printed, discussed and issued.

We have certainly been extraordinarily lucky over our weather. It has been cool ever since last Sunday, cooler in fact in the tropics than further north. Also, until today the sea has been particularly kind. Even today we have nothing worse in the Bay than a strong breeze and that to the accompaniment of continuous sunshine.

---

341. *Edinburgh Castle*, 13,350 tons, 570 feet by 65 feet, designed to carry 800 passengers in three classes, was built by Harland and Wolff in Belfast and launched in 1910. She was used as an armed merchant cruiser during the First World War and as a depotship in the Second, after which she was scuttled.

Apart from these somewhat uninteresting facts, or at any rate facts of passing importance only, one might really say nothing about the voyage. We have enlivened work with some exciting games of cribbage – Bridgman has extraordinary luck despite the fact that he plays to a running comment of criticism and even abuse by the Chairman. We also play deck quoits and deck golf in the usual fashion, besides deck tennis and a new game with a stuffed football. We also have made acquaintance with a certain number of fellow passengers, particularly some people called Craig – Americans but quite exceptionally good specimens.[342]

That, I think, completes the story.

Even of Madeira, I have nothing much more to say, as I told you all about it when describing the voyage out. We didn't experiment on the tobogganing again, but wandered about Funchal, and amused ourselves with buying lace and chairs and various local products. My chief comment is that returning to a Latin civilization was particularly attractive after 13 days of sea, and 7 weeks even of a country like South Africa which is only partially 'new'.

We had one experience at Madeira which is worth recording – a visit to a new German liner, the *Cap Trafalgar*, on her way home from South America.[343] Certainly she has reached a pitch of luxury which none of the English liners I have been on – even the *Mauretania* – has yet achieved. The big dining saloon reminded one of the Carlton – I mean the London one.[344] There were delightful lounges, drawing rooms and smoking rooms. And when one got to the top deck of all – where on the *Edinburgh Castle* one finds nothing but boats – there were a swimming bath, a gymnasium, a conservatory, and even dog kennels! We came away much impressed.

Three months' absence isn't like six months. One doesn't feel out of things to the same extent, nor do I feel so 'sated' with new sights as I did

---

342. Mild anti-Americanism was another cultural characteristic of the upper middle class of pre-war Britain.
343. *Cap Trafalgar*, 18,509 tons, was built by the Vulkan Werke in Hamburg for the Hamburg–Amerika Line and launched in 1913. With the outbreak of war she was converted into an armed merchant cruiser with two 4.1-inch guns, and almost at once, on 14 September 1914 in the South Atlantic, she engaged and was sunk by the similarly transformed Cunard vessel *Carmania*, 19,650 tons, eight 4.7-inch guns.
344. The Carlton Club had been founded by the Duke of Wellington (1769–1852) in 1832 and became the principal club in London for members of the Conservative Party.

when we got back last year. Still I shall be glad to be home.[345] I will add one thing to this letter, a poem by Vincent giving his impressions of the situation at Johannesburg. I think it is extraordinarily clever – and it certainly sums up extremely well one aspect of the South African position!

Ever your affectionate son
E. J. Harding

THE MAGNATE AND THE MINER.
A CONTRAST.

1907

Magnate (loq.).
Wandering miner, whither art thou going?
Art thou an exile from a soulless country?
Was it for loafing, or for agitation
That they discharged thee?

Miner.
No, Sir; the fact is I know naught about it;
Tramming and lashing, blasting and machine-work
All are one to me, Sir; for the simple truth is
I can do nothing.

Magnate.
Wandering miner, do we seek the skilful?
Count we the cost who work for Greater Britain?
Do we need handcraft; is not voice sufficient?
Thou art a voter.

What is the output, what the cost of working,
What the amalgam, little reck we of it
So thou can'st strike a blow for me and freedom
At the election.

---

345. The Commission recorded 26 days gathering evidence in South Africa; 141 witnesses had been questioned; numerous official visits had been completed and many formal functions attended.

1914

Magnate.
Lazy and thriftless, insolent and drunken,
Ignorant of minecraft, brutal to the native;
Who can abide thee, anarchistic idler,
              Phthisical outcast.

R.M.S. Edinburgh Castle
23rd April 1914

---

346. A previous letter is missing, describing Harding's voyage across the Atlantic. The Commissioners had sailed from Liverpool on Monday July 17, but were delayed by fog. The party with Harding consisted of Bateman, Tatlow, Haggard, Garnett, Lorimer (representing the United Kingdom), Sinclair (New Zealand) and Langerman (South Africa), plus Glenny, Bridgman and miscellaneous wives. Bowring (Newfoundland), Foster (Canada) and Campbell (Australia) were awaiting their arrival, and the Chairman (who had become Baron D'Abernon on 2 July) planned to join them later in Quebec. The inquiries in Newfoundland and Canada were scheduled to be completed by early November 1914.

347. *Alsatian*, 18,481 tons, 571 feet by 72 feet, had recently been built by Beardmore on the Clyde, to carry 263 first-class passengers, 596 second and 976 third. Haggard described her as ' a beautiful ship ... all furnished in Jacobean oak ... with old engravings on the walls, open fire places in the great saloons....' Her maiden voyage began from Liverpool to Halifax, Nova Scotia, on 17 January 1914. She was converted into an armed merchant cruiser on the outbreak of war in August, and was renamed *Empress of France* after the war. The origins of the Allan Line's Canadian service go back to 1819. Eventually the company was unable to compete with newcomers to the North Atlantic. Although nominally retaining a fleet of 28 vessels, in 1909 the company had been secretly taken over by the Canadian Pacific Line (disclosed in 1915). The Canadian Pacific Railway had been operating steamships from its western terminus across the Pacific to the Far East since 1887, but only began transatlantic services in 1903, after buying up Elder Dempster's Beaver Line. C.P.R. operated 65 vessels under its own flag by 1910. *Alsatian* would have approached Canada south of Cape Race, Newfoundland, obliging the Commissioners to transship at Rimouski halfway along the St Lawrence seaway and to return across the Gulf of St Lawrence to Newfoundland. *Earl Grey*, 265 feet by 48 feet, 2357 tons, had been built by Vickers in Barrow, Lancashire, in 1909.

Third Journey

To Newfoundland and Canada, July–August 1914

Canadian Government Steamer *Earl Grey*
Nearing Cape Race
July 27th 1914

My dear Father,

We ought to have been in St. John's on Saturday evening.[346] It is now Monday evening and we are still the 'wrong' side of Cape Race. However, if it keeps as comparatively clear as it is now, we hope to get in sometime tomorrow morning. Meanwhile we have our first experience of a 'private steamer' for any distance. It is quite comfortable, though after the *Alsatian* not exactly luxurious. As a matter of fact, it is a steamer built particularly for icebreaking – and spends its time in winter in fulfilling that function. In summer it does 'official' trips of this kind.[347]

The end of our voyage on the *Alsatian* was quite exciting. We had a perfectly clear run from Cape Race to Rimouski and went at a great pace. On the Saturday morning, just as the St. Lawrence began to narrow up, we sighted the Canadian Northern steamer *Royal George*, hull down ahead of us.[348] She, as I think I told you in my last letter, left two days before us and had also been delayed by fog. We gained on her little by little, and after a time it became apparent that we might or might not get up to Rimouski ahead of her. Finally we just did it, but only in the last mile. The point of the race was that whichever arrived first got the mail tender, discharged her mails, and was off first to Quebec – a gain of an hour or so.

We ourselves transferred our persons and our baggage to the said tender, called on the *Royal George* to pick up her mails also, and then steamed off to this boat. We started at once, and since then have been

Footnotes appear opposite and on page 239.

R.M.S. Alsatian, Allan Line.   *Postcard*

leisurely proceeding towards Newfoundland – with frequent slowings on account of mist and soundings. Really this must be one of the most treacherous bits of sea in the world. We passed quite close to the place where the *Empress of Ireland* lies – it is marked by a sloop and a series of buoys, but nothing can be seen of the *Empress* herself. It seemed incredible, as we came up in bright sunshine over perfectly smooth water, that a tragedy could possibly have happened there. Campbell, who had travelled by New York and was 'held up' for two days in Rimouski village, told us though that it was impressed vividly on him. Practically all the people in the village were engaged in making coffins, and the quay was piled with 40 or 50 of them – waiting.[349]

Government House
St. John's
Newfoundland
July 30th 1914

You will see from the address that we have 'arrived' in Newfoundland.[350] We got in on Tuesday morning, the ship being 'dressed' in honour of the occasion as we neared St. John's. The coast line, seen as it should be seen (too often it is searched for in vain – or found when not wanted), is quite attractive. There are rugged cliffs with gently sloping hills behind them, and a fishing village here and there. Altogether I was reminded very much of Cornwall and the Irish Coast. St. John's itself lies inside a narrow entrance which widens out into a considerable harbour. The town itself is like Dartmouth, on a hill of a good height, sloping steeply to the sea. There is no 'promenade' – all the shore is covered with wharves and sheds, no doubt for sufficient and historic reasons. The most picturesque things about the port are really the erections known as 'flakes' on which the fishermen dry their cod, preparatory to salting them. The town has lots of churches – the denominations vie with one another in erecting them – but is otherwise

348. The company and the ship had a disappointing history. The Canadian Northern Railway began in 1910 an unusual transatlantic service, known as the Royal Line, sailing from Avonmouth near Bristol (a terminus of the Great Western Railway), mainly transporting emigrants. But its ships were requisitioned for the war in 1914 and were subsequently bought by Cunard in 1916 when C.N.R. became insolvent. *Royal George*, 11,150 tons, 526 feet by 60 feet, was built by Fairfield on the Clyde in 1907, originally for the Egyptian Mail Steamship Company and named *Heliopolis*. That venture failed, and its ships were laid up until purchased by C.N.R. Because of her lack of stability in bad weather *Royal George* became known as 'Rolling George'. Cunard used her in Cherbourg from June 1920 merely as an accommodation ship for emigrants.

349. *Empress of Ireland*, 14,191 tons, 550 feet by 65 feet, built by Beardmore on the Clyde and launched in 1906, had been one of the Canadian Pacific Line's prestige liners. Shortly after midnight on 29 May 1914, in fog, she was struck by a Norwegian collier and sank in 20 minutes with the loss of 1014 out of the 1477 people on board.

350. The first English settlements in North America were established in Newfoundland. Early English contacts resulted mainly from the fishing industry: John Cabot's landing in 1497 generated much publicity. The island was claimed as an English colony in 1583. (The poet John Donne (1572–1631) addressed his mistress: 'Oh my America, my new found lande....', *Elegie: To His Mistris Going To Bed*). English and French settlers continued to contest ownership, but British sovereignty was confirmed by the Treaty of Utrecht in 1713, and thereafter French interests were largely eroded. Meanwhile, by 1829, the native Beothuck Indians had been hunted to extinction. Like other colonies in British North America, Newfoundland was granted responsible government, in 1855, but chose not to join the other colonies when the Dominion of Canada was formed in 1867. The constitution consisted of a Governor, representing the crown, an Executive Council of nine ministers, and a legislature made up of a nominated 24-member Legislative Council and a 36-member elected House of Assembly.

St. John's, Newfoundland, Landing Seals.   *Photograph c.1910*

ultra plain. Most of the houses are of wood, and fires are frequent.[351]

I found myself, with Bateman and the Langermans, allocated to Government House, so I have had at least all the comfort that the town can afford. (I forgot to say that there is no decent hotel in St. John's – all of the party who aren't staying with people are quartered at a private boarding house, some 3 miles out.)

The Governor is one Sir Walter Davidson – he was once in the Transvaal, and latterly of Seychelles, where I used to come across him when doing 'Eastern' work in the C.O. He is somewhat heavy, and rather casual – certainly not a 'flier', but he seems to get on pretty well in the Colony.[352]

---

351. St. John's was the capital of the colony. It had developed as a centre for the fishing industry during the 16th century, but disputed possession led to frequent conflict with the French. Development was slow until the 19th century. The frequent fires to which Harding refers also caused setbacks: a severe one in 1892 destroyed half the city. The population by 1918 was 34,045.

352. Sir Walter Davidson (1859–1923) had joined the Ceylon civil service in 1880, became Colonial Secretary in the Transvaal 1902–4 and Governor of the Seychelles 1904–12. (This Indian Ocean colony had been secured by Britain from the French in 1814.) He served in Newfoundland 1913–17 and ended up as Governor of N.S.W. 1918–23. Not a bad career for a 'non-flier'.

His wife has the brains of the two. She, I find, is a daughter of old Lady Louisa Fielding who lives at Betchworth – so that you will have a topic of conversation when next you call, or are called upon.[353] She is the Governor's second wife and they have two daughters aged about 5 and 3, quite charming, but somewhat shy. A fledgling A.D.C. (very excited over the war prospects) and another of very mature age (Harry, I fancy, knows about him) complete the ménage.[354] Obviously neither of these worthies has any but the remotest idea of staff work.

Government House is substantial, unpretentious but comfortable. Two cows graze peacefully in what one would expect to be the front garden.

Sydney Hotel
Sydney
Cape Breton
August 3rd 1914

This is the first opportunity of writing which I have had for some days, and now everyone and everything is so full of wars and rumours of wars that I don't feel much inclined to go on.[355] Still I will do my best.

Our days in Newfoundland were as strenuous as any we have had in our travels, and the people were extraordinarily kind. I will just give you an outline of our days, so that you can see how they were filled.

Tuesday July 28th
  Arrived 1 p.m.
  Evidence all afternoon.
  Dinner with one Sir Joseph Outerbridge.[356]
Wednesday July 29th
  Evidence morning.

---

353. Betchworth, near Dorking in Surrey, was close to the Harding family home in Coldharbour. Lady Louisa's husband, General Sir Percy Feilding (1827–1904), late of the Coldstream Guards, had been a veteran of the Crimean War of 1854–56.
354. The Great War was imminent. Crown Prince Franz Ferdinand of Austria had been assassinated at Sarajevo on June 28; Austria-Hungary had declared war on Serbia on July 28; Russia began to mobilize her armies on July 30.
355. Germany had declared war on Russia on August 1 and on France on August 3.
356. Sir Joseph Outerbridge (1843–1933) was born in the British colony of Bermuda (under British control since 1612) but moved in 1862 to Newfoundland and to a career in business and public service: he had been knighted in 1913.

Motored 12 miles to lunch at Bowring's house at Topsail (a fishing village).

Drove back to St. John's and went to a 'garden party' (otherwise and vulgarly a 'beanfeast' at a Roman Catholic Orphanage).

'State' Dinner Government House.

Thursday July 30th

Evidence, morning and afternoon.

Dinner with Chamber of Commerce and Municipal Committee – some 3 miles out. Back about 11.30 and packed.

Friday July 31st

Started by motor 10.30 a.m. for Portugal Cove (another fishing village). Yacht thence to Bell Island (about 6 miles) famous for its iron ore.[357]

Lunch with one of the companies operating there (the Nova Scotia Iron and Steel Co.). Went down their mine, 1300 feet below sea level, and 2 miles under the sea! Dinner with the other company (the Dominion Steel Co.). Drove to wharf and joined yacht, and sailed to Holyrood, a station on the Newfoundland Railway. Found special train waiting there, and slept in it on the way to Grand Falls.[358]

Saturday August 1st

Stopped for breakfast 8.30–9.30 a.m. (the train shakes so much that this was imperative). Arrived Grand Falls about 1 p.m. Lunch with Manager of the 'Harmsworth' paper mills.[359] Inspected mills all afternoon. Tea. Evidence. Dinner, and speeches. Slept in train.

Sunday August 2nd

Train across country to Port aux Basques (in the south west corner of Newfoundland). Stopped about one hour (for lunch at a 'Log Cabin' Hotel) and again for tea. Arrived about 8 p.m. Left by special steamer for Sydney, Cape Breton.

---

357. Portugal Cove and Bell Island are in Conception Bay, north west of St. John's. The island contained unusually high grade ore, 50% iron.

358. The 874-kilometre narrow-gauge Newfoundland Railway was built between 1881 and 1897 and operated by a private company until 1923. Grand Falls, with a population of about 2500, lay almost half way between the termini of St. John's in the east and Port aux Basques in the south-west.

359. Harmsworth was the family name of the newspaper magnates better known as Lord Northcliffe (1865–1922) and Lord Rothermere (1868–1940): they revolutionised the British popular press by launching the *Daily Mail* in 1896 and the *Daily Mirror* in 1903. Northcliffe also bought *The Times* in 1908 and restored its circulation. To provide newsprint, Northcliffe's Anglo-Newfoundland Development Company consumed 50,000 tree trunks daily: its forests covered an area about half the size of Wales.

That is the bare outline, and means little. I will try and give an impression or two of Newfoundland.

First, that it is obviously a 'Crown Colony' and should be governed as such. Davidson, as a matter of fact, told me that he was beginning in this direction. The 'best' people in the Island don't go into politics, and those who do play for their own hand, and aren't too 'clean-handed'.[360]

Second, that the Island isn't, as I had supposed, dreary and fog bound. The impression that I come away with is rather that of Switzerland. There are lots of wild flowers (the wild calmia conspicuous among them, you may be interested to hear),[361] upland pastures, cows with tinkling bells, fir trees in infinite quantities, waterfalls and even an occasional patch of snow.

Third, that there are only three things worth speaking of in the place – the fisheries, the pulp industry and the minerals. Of these the fisheries stand in the same position as the mines of South Africa. They provide practically all the exports and most of the revenue. The Government attitude is similar also – it is one of absolute neglect!

Fourth, that the railway is a scandal and a laughing stock. It is in private hands – and its owners appear to subsist mainly on the money which was paid to them for its construction and not spent on the building. The track is so badly laid that the trains go off the line most days, and the shaking is so bad that two nights in the train have reduced most of us to complete exhaustion! We were told too that sometimes in winter the snow is so bad that trains get held up for weeks at a time.

Fifth, that the Colony, as a Colony, is much more English than any other we have been to except possibly New Zealand. This is partly due to the fact that a lot of the boys go to school in England. But it seems largely due to mistrust, not to say dislike, of Canadians and Americans. Newfoundland only 'toys', I believe, with confederation with Canada – though it is talked about a lot, and was being actively discussed when we were there.

---

360. The financial stability and political reliability of Newfoundland remained a problem: in 1934 during the depression the government became bankrupt and the constitution was suspended at the request of the local legislature. Newfoundland became in effect once more a crown colony under Colonial Office control. In 1949 the country regained self-government and joined the Canadian federation as the 10th province.

361. Kalmia, named after Pehr Kalm (1715–79), a Finnish traveller, naturalist and pupil of Linnaeus, is an evergreen shrub, first introduced to British gardens in 1734.

Grand Falls, Newfoundland, the Harmsworth's Pulp and Paper Mills.
Photograph c.1910

Sixth, that the pulp mills, and the iron deposits are both very remarkable. I should think that it must be quite unique to mine two miles underneath the sea. We found the iron mine almost entirely dry, and it was almost more thrilling to reach it than to go down the Rand Mines. As to the pulp mills, the Harmsworth energy and thoroughness is reflected in the management – even though the place is 200 miles from anywhere. The mills are entirely up to date, there is a town with a town hall, picture palace, and other delights dear to the soul of the *Daily Mail*, a country house in the English style for Lord Northcliffe's use during his 'hustling' visits, and all this in a wilderness of pines, spruces and water – only pierced by the disreputable and ramshackle railway.

So much for impressions – I need only add a line or two more. I found quite a number of 'acquaintances' in St. John's. J. S. Munn, now in the exalted position of President of the Board of Trade and the managing partner of Bowring's firm, was at Oxford (and also at Hertford) during my first two years. He got a cricket blue, but was forced to retire (to Marcon's Hall I think) owing to inability to pass Smalls! [362] Now he has blossomed out a good deal, is clearly making lots of money, and seems an extremely good fellow. I found also an uncle of Grieve – Harry will remember both him and Munn at Hertford – and finally might have seen the Bartons, but did not. I called at their house but found them away on holiday.

I end up with what I began – that the kindness and hospitality of the people were enormous. I tremble to think of the condition I should have been in if I had drunk all the champagne and other intoxicating liquors which they tried to press on one in our five days. I escaped with some little weariness, due mainly to the Railway, and hope for better things if we carry out our tour in Canada.

Oh – I forgot to say that we had a quite unique 'local officer' in the shape of a certain P. T. Magrath, member of the Legislative Council and editor of a local evening paper. His energy was boundless. He nearly broke the telephone with his messages during the days we were in St. John's and ended up with a voice midway between a foghorn and a shriek. But certainly he had got things ready remarkably well.[363]

Ever your affectionate son
    E. J. Harding

Steamer D.H. Thomas
Bras d'Or Lakes
Cape Breton
Aug. 4th 1914

My dear Eva,

Though I only finished my last letter last night, there is nothing like seizing the golden opportunity to begin another, and that opportunity certainly exists today. We are steaming down the Bras d'Or Lakes on a

---

362. 'Smalls' or 'Responsions', later replaced by 'Prelims', were the first of the three examinations which students at that time had to pass to obtain the degree of B.A. John S. Munn entered Hertford College in October 1899, but failed his examinations in September 1900 and on three subsequent occasions, for the last time at Easter 1901. Marcon's Hall was probably a 'crammer', supposed to coach such failures. Munn was actually Edgar Bowring's stepson as well as, since 1908, a director of the firm. Tragically, he was among those who drowned in February 1917 when the Bowring ship *Florizel* was driven on to a reef off Cape Race during a snowstorm.

363. Patrick Thomas McGrath (1868–1929), who acted as the Commission's local agent, was a journalist and author as well as politician. He became a member of the Legislative Council in 1912 and later its President, and was knighted in 1918. Because the Commission's arrival in Newfoundland had been delayed by fog, he had been obliged to rearrange the summoning of witnesses in St. John's: 25 were called in three days, Tuesday July 28 to Thursday July 30. A committee made up of Foster, Lorimer and Tatlow, had lightened the load by seeing 9 of them. The Commission had also called 2 witnesses at another formal session in Grand Falls on Saturday August 1.

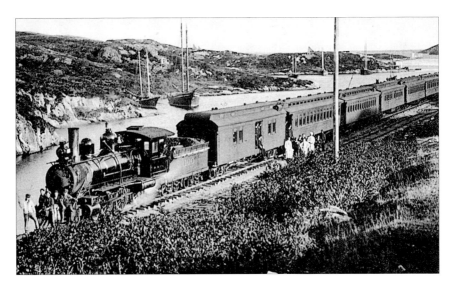

Port aux Basques, Terminus of Newfoundland Railway.   *Postcard*

steamer lent for the purpose by the big steel company at Sydney. It is a perfect day – bright sunshine and a fresh breeze, and the shore on either side is just near enough to be attractive. There is nothing to do but look out, talk, read or write, and to wonder what the war news is! [364]

We got to Sydney early yesterday morning after a passage from Port Aux Basques which upset some of the party but fortunately not me. Two nights in the Newfoundland Railway had been more than enough. I went to bed immediately after we had started, and slept like a log.

We landed at Sydney before breakfast, and went to the hotel. [365] Our first experience was receiving an address from the Mayor and the Board of Trade – a document in an imposing pink wrapper which unfortunately had omitted the names of some of the members. I had hastily to rectify the omission. The reading of the address, and the more or less appropriate reply, was followed by a round of handshaking – the absurdity of which was obvious, and forcibly expressed by Lorimer in one of his loudest whispers.

We were then rushed off to inspect the Harbour and the Steel Works which lie alongside. The former is excellent, and as yet quite undeveloped. The latter were as interesting as anything we have seen in our travels.

We had seen the crude ore in Newfoundland. We now watched the smelting and rolling operations which result in the finished products such as steel rails or wire nails. The diabolical looking machines which crush red hot ingots into steel rails are particularly fascinating and almost human. Lorimer, of course, was always on the go, and relays of officials were employed to answer his manifold questions.

The rest of the day was more peaceful – I stayed in and worked all the afternoon. The evening was enlivened by another harbour trip accompanied by a band, and prominent citizens of Sydney. It was, in theory, to have been by moonlight. In fact, there was pouring rain. We returned hastily, and the band played patriotic airs outside the hotel!

Today has been quite a holiday. We had to make an early start – getting up at 6 and starting at 8. Since then we have been travelling successively by ferry, by carriage, and by this steamer. The country looks delightful. There are low wooded hills on either side with farms and pastures on the lower slopes. At one point, the lake narrows up and the railway goes across. We stopped at this point for lunch – which was given us in a 'summer hotel' in the village. Newly caught salmon, wild strawberries, and buttermilk were the staples, and excellent they all were.

Aug. 10th 1914
Pines Hotel
Digby
Nova Scotia

We finished our day on the Bras d'Or lakes with great success at a village called St. Peters – rather French-looking with the usual wooden houses (anything else but wood for the houses is the exception in this region), green pastures and pinewoods. The only drawback was that we had an

---

364. Harding may have been less at ease had he known: Germany invaded Belgium on August 4 and the British ultimatum expired unanswered at midnight.

365. A committee of the D.R.C. began work at once in Sydney, calling 4 witnesses on Monday August 3. The town had been founded in 1784 by United Empire Loyalists, who had migrated north after rejecting the American revolution against British imperial control. The town had a population of 17,723 in 1911, much dependent on the Dominion Iron and Steel Company established in 1899. It was also a port commanding the north of Cape Breton Island in the Canadian province of Nova Scotia. Nova Scotia had formerly been part of the French colony of Acadia. It had been briefly claimed by the English in the 17th century, and was finally largely annexed in 1713 by the Treaty of Utrecht, Cape Breton being added in 1758. The colony obtained responsible government in 1848 and became a founding province of the Dominion of Canada in 1867. Its population in 1911 was 492,432, nearly 7% of Canada's total population of 7,206,643.

extremely early 'tea dinner' on the steamer about 6 o'clock, and nothing else till a very late breakfast at Halifax next morning. Unfortunately, the special sleeping cars, which met us at St. Peters and conveyed us to Halifax, hadn't a corresponding restaurant car. I shall remember our journey down the Bras d'Or Lakes for some time. It and an almost equally delightful journey yesterday, which I shall come to later on, were interludes in a very trying week.

Wednesday morning brought the news of the declaration of war. Since then we have been immersed in the wildest of rumours spread broadcast by an irresponsible Press. There are all sorts of messages – almost all contradicted in the next issue. A sober paper doesn't exist in this part of Canada. All these rumours, as you can imagine, sorely excite all the members of the party – most of them already anxious enough over their own affairs and homes in England.

Added to this has been extreme uncertainty about what the Commission is to do. We started with a meeting, immediately after arriving at Halifax, to discuss the situation. This was pretty heated – as the Dominion members wanted to go on, and the U.K. ones to go back, if they could go back. It ended in the usual compromise – a decision to go on for the present, to give up all 'public' functions, and to telegraph to the Chairman to know how the land lay, and whether he was coming out.

Next day, there was an even more stormy meeting. A telegram arrived from the Chairman – suggesting (on the advice of the C.O.) postponement of the tour, but that we should wait in Canada for a few days until the 'sea was clear'. It wasn't at all clear whether this telegram was in answer to ours (as it turned out it wasn't). Anyhow, the result was a two hours' wrangle, which left me quite exhausted, and the members more 'jumpy' than before. Net result again a compromise. Bateman has telegraphed for further instructions, saying that the Dominion members want their Governments consulted, and has added that Haggard and Lorimer want to get home at once. To this telegram we await an answer. Meanwhile, in the words of – I forget who it was – παντα ρετ [366] but our journeys continue as arranged. The consequence of all these heated discussions superimposed on not too comfortable travelling is a state of nerves amongst all the party which outdoes anything I have seen in the somewhat chequered career of this Commission throughout the world. Personally, I am fairly immune so far – only fairly though. If the tension continues, or increases, I really shudder to think what may happen.

---

366. 'Everything is in flux', Heracleitus (540–480 B.C.).

Halifax, Nova Scotia, The Old Clock Tower.   *Postcard*

I put all this down, as a record of what is going on. No doubt it is
small compared to the troubles you must be having in England. But it
looms large here – and is aggravated by the absence of news.

I go on to more ordinary matters.

We stayed in Halifax on Wednesday, Thursday, and Friday.[367] It is a
dingy town, and the hotels are more than mediocre. They were worse
than usual, possibly, because a Firemen's 'parade', or some such Festival,
was going on when we were there. Bateman returned one evening to find
one fireman in his room dead drunk and lying asleep with his boots on
over both the beds. The usual duties of a Secretary of a Royal
Commission had an addition that night – that of 'chucker out'.

There is a 'Citadel Hill' above Halifax, and it has a quite magnificent
harbour. Those are its two redeeming features. The *Cedric* and the
Mauretania came in while we were there escorted by the cruiser *Essex*.
There was immense excitement – it was the first visible sign of war in

---

367. On these days 27 witnesses were interrogated at sessions held in the
Provincial Government Buildings. Halifax, the capital of Nova Scotia, had
been founded in 1749. Its population by 1911 was 46,619. Sadly, many of
them would be killed on 6 December 1917 when a munitions ship
exploded in the harbour, taking the lives of 2000 people and devastating
much of the city. This is reckoned to have been the largest man-made
explosion before the dropping of the atomic bomb on Hiroshima.

Halifax, and also the *Mauretania*, under the influence of (real or supposed) German pursuit, had made a record run across the Atlantic. This fact was seized upon by the city as proof conclusive that their port was better than New York.[368] (Incidentally, I think it is – except that it is more liable to fog and ice.)

Considering the conditions, we got through fairly well as regards the evidence at Halifax, and I don't think it lost very much in value. Social functions were mostly abandoned – the only ones left in were a private dinner at the Halifax Club, and an excursion to view the harbour which we thought to be purely business, but which turned out to be a sort of 'beanfeast' of the citizens of Halifax, their wives and daughters, organized by the local Chamber of Commerce (they are called 'Boards of Trade' in Halifax – Bateman considers the use of the term almost sacrilege).

Our experiences yesterday and today have compensated a good deal for the anxieties of the week. Yesterday we came down from Halifax here – today has been spent in this Hotel (quite the most comfortable we have yet struck) 'lazing' in the most approved fashion, walking, writing and – a little – working.

Yesterday's travel was mostly by motor car (or rather cars as there were three 'relays') – some 100 miles or more out of a total of 150. The route lay down the famous Annapolis Valley – I say famous though I must confess to complete ignorance of it before coming here – because it has mile after mile of apple orchards, and the farms look as smiling and prosperous as do those of Kent, which they most resemble. I can think of no better compliment. The valley is 10 miles wide or more, and is 'settled' all the way along – that is, there is a succession of farms with frequent villages and quite a considerable number of little country towns.

We saw it all in ideal conditions – as each motor car had a local celebrity (more or less) in it so that one could glean all the information possible. Thus I had as companions the Archdeacon of the Province, the 'local member' in the Dominion Parliament – one Foster (if Will

---

368. Halifax was the nearest mainland North American port to Britain (3400 kilometres) and a railway terminus. Harding had sailed home from New York in the *Mauretania* in 1913. *Cedric*, 21,000 tons, 681 feet by 75 feet, was a White Star liner, built in 1903 by Harland and Wolff in Belfast. She was shortly to become a liner-cruiser and later a troop transporter, but survived the war to serve the White Star Line until 1931. *H.M.S. Essex* was a County class cruiser, built in 1903–4, 9800 tons, 440 feet long, capable of 23 knots, carrying fourteen 6-inch guns and other armaments, with a complement of 540 and costing £750,000.

Skilbeck should happen to see this he will be interested in hearing that this same man defeated Sir Frederick Borden),[369] a barrister who kept a sheep ranch, a solicitor interested in a silver fox farm, and the wife of a hardware merchant. All were interesting in their several ways.

I suppose I ought to add (though it conveys very little to me – I fear) that part of the country we came through was the 'Evangeline' country. If ever I get to a stage where general reading becomes possible again, I must begin to study Longfellow.[370]

Digby – from which I am writing – is a little seaport on the Bay of Fundy.[371] From it we are to cross tomorrow to St. John, New Brunswick. The hotel is out of the town, and justifies its name 'The Pines'. It has a delightful outlook over the inlet – and five minutes walk takes one to a lane where grow wild raspberries, and even wild cherries, just at their prime.

I must stop and go to bed.

> Best love
> Ever your affectionate brother
> E. J. Harding

> Victoria Hotel
> Charlottetown
> Prince Edward Island
> August 16th 1914

My dearest Mother,

Our fate is settled. We hold our last 'sitting' here tomorrow, return to Quebec, and thence sail for England, taking our chance of a German cruiser on the way. So, with luck, you may see me back some time in the first part of September. I shall try to get up to Ottawa, or certainly Montreal, before we start, and the dates of steamers are, of course, very much 'in the air'.

---

369. The parliamentary career in Nova Scotia of Sir Frederick Borden (1847–1917) had run almost without a break from 1874 until his defeat in 1911. William Skilbeck (1864–1919) had been the editor since 1908 of the periodical *The Nineteenth Century and After*.

370. Henry Wadsworth Longfellow (1807–82) was born and brought up in Maine, the American state across the border. His narrative poem *Evangeline*, written in hexameters and published in 1847, centres on the English expulsion of French settlers from Acadia in 1755.

371. Digby, with a population which even by 1921 had reached only 1300, was famous for its cherries and for its smoked herrings, known locally as 'Digby chickens'.

For some reasons I shall be very glad to have it over. The mental atmosphere here remains sultry, not to say electric. What with war excitement, and the constant travelling in conditions not of the best, one is hard put to it to keep one's temper, let alone the peace. Then, too, of course I want to be home at this crisis.

For other reasons I am sorry. What we have seen so far isn't Canada as I imagine it, or as what I believe it to be. It is settled, somnolent and self-satisfied – if you will forgive the iteration. It is the Victorian England of 50 years ago, as I understand that that was.

If war could penetrate into these regions or get as near as it is to England now, I believe it would do a world of good. You will think I am somewhat pessimistic – if I am, please put it down to the general strain of the situation.

Now to return to our doings. Our respite of last Sunday at Digby was over all too soon. We were at it again on Monday morning – inspecting the town by motor car, going over a fish factory, and generally 'acquainting ourselves with local conditions'. By the afternoon we were off again, bound for St. John across the Strait of Fundy, some 45 miles away. The steamer ran into a dense fog the moment we got into the open sea. She continued at practically full speed, and 'made' St. John all right, but deviated sufficiently to touch ground in shallow water. We were delayed a bit in getting off, but otherwise suffered no harm.

The fog continued for the whole of the first day we were at St. John.[372] It is a dingy place – worse than Halifax to my mind, without the counterbalancing advantage of a first class harbour. The 'commercial men', as we saw them, were the stupidest lot, I think, that we have met in the whole of our wanderings. Altogether my impressions were very poor.

---

372. The Commission met in the Board of Trade Offices in Saint John, questioning 12 witnesses over three days, Tuesday to Thursday, August 11–13. The town had been first established by the French in the 1630s, and it later became the principal port for New Brunswick on the Bay of Fundy. Its population in 1911 was 42,511. This province, with Nova Scotia, had formerly been part of French Acadia: it was confirmed as British in 1763, became a separate colony in 1784, obtained responsible government in 1854 and was another founding province of the Dominion of Canada in 1867. Its population in 1911 was 351,889, about 5% of the Canadian total. Its most famous son (in Britain) was Max Aitken (1879–1964), another newspaper owner, who left the province in which he was raised in 1910, developed the *Daily Express*, became a force in British politics and took the title for the peerage he obtained in 1917 from a small place in New Brunswick called Beaverbrook.

Saint John, New Brunswick, The Falls and Bridges.   *Photograph,*
Fisher Collection, 1909

When I tell you that I was located in a comparatively comfortable hotel whilst most of the others were in a hostelry, their description of which is quite unreproducable, you can imagine what *their* impressions were.

Our stay was enlivened, if that is the proper word, by the presence of a large number of 'Knights Templars' – or a fraternity of that description – of Americans from Boston (in Canada, we find, you call it 'Boreston'). They spent most of their time in parading the streets in uniforms and cocked hats – resembling those of the fifth class of the Civil Service. As they were, for the most part, more than middle aged and very stout, the effect was queer. Their wives and other female belongings were of the most heterogeneous kind.

This seems the proper place to say a word or two about Canadian hotels as we have found them in the Maritime Provinces.

The entrance hall, as a rule, is like the inside of a shop with large plate glass windows and chairs instead of goods on show. In these chairs the visitors sit, and spit, most of the day. When they are not engaged in either of these occupations, they are gobbling a meal in an insufficiently large dining room where the service is slow and extremely bad. I had to interview the Manager, and speak many winged words, before I could get a table reserved for us at St. John. He explained that if he tried to reserve one, it would probably be seized by any stray visitor who saw an empty seat. Late dinner, as we understand it, is unknown. High tea is the evening meal (sometimes it is called 'lunch'). Cruets and sauces are found in great abundance. Boots are not cleaned except under severe pressure. The usual thing is to enter a 'shine shop' where, for the trifling consideration of five cents, they are cleaned to the accompaniment of a gramophone. At the last hotel where we were (the 'shine shop' being unavailable as we were setting out too early) I sent my boots down. I had finally to pursue them in my socks, and succeeded in retrieving them, after a long wait, one done, one untouched. In this 'garb', I travelled all day.

If the hotels are bad, the transportation facilities aren't much better. We have had to travel in several steamers – lake, river and sea. Most of them – well, I will say only that they weren't built yesterday. One, which conveyed us up the St. John river, had a 'beam engine', if you know what that is, and had obviously crumbling wood work. As to the trains – well, we have done better since Sir George Foster left us (he did that three or four days ago) as we persuaded the Manager of the Intercolonial Railway to give us his own car,[373] but before then Foster seemed to think that a policy of doing without meals, or 'taking one's chance', was good enough for the Commission. Well, I don't want to be captious, but when people have to travel at the rate we do, it isn't!

Enough of grumbling – and anyhow we have only got two days more of it. I wanted to let you know that the Maritime Provinces of Canada aren't the up to date places you might otherwise believe. Now for the other side of the picture.

St. John has a fair harbour, and quite a good park. It has also a curious natural phenomenon in the shape of what are called 'reversible falls'. That is, the St. John river, coming down, falls into the sea at low tide. At high tide, the sea falls into it.

On Friday we went a long way up the river – more than 80 miles – as the guests of the New Brunswick Government in the 'beam engine' boat which I have described already. It was really delightful. There are little settlements along the banks, and quite often one met a steamer towing down a 'lumber raft' – that is several thousand logs, perhaps, fastened together. Some of the reaches quite reminded me of the Upper Thames – only the atmosphere was rather that of a deserted country. Lots of the people have left New Brunswick and gone west.

---

373. The Intercolonial Railway was completed in 1876, at the expense of the government of Canada, to link the maritime provinces with the political centre of the Dominion: this commitment had been a precondition for federation.

Log Burling, King's County, Nova Scotia. *Photograph, Fisher Collection, 1909*

Our destination was Fredericton, which is the capital of the Province. With the possible exception of Charlottetown where we now are, it is quite the pleasantest town that we have struck in Canada. In the course of centuries, it might even resemble Oxford! Its streets are broad and tree-shaded. It has good buildings, and a really beautiful Cathedral. The St. John river flows alongside, so that the picture may be complete.[374]

Fredericton, as a matter of fact, is the head of navigation of the St. John River, and a few miles above it all the logs which are 'floated down' from the regions above (New Brunswick is a heavily timbered country

---

374. Fredericton was redesigned and extended following its selection as the capital of the new colony of New Brunswick in 1784. By 1911 its population had reached only 7208. It was noted for its elm-shaded streets, its university (built in 1828) and the 180-ft. spire of its gothic Christ Church Cathedral (built in 1849).

and lumbering is its main industry) are sorted, measured, and 'packed up' into rafts. We inspected these operations, and very interesting they were. The men get as agile as monkeys in climbing and jumping among the floating logs. Also, we were told they fall early victims to rheumatism. Incidentally we had a look at the 'bothy' (only it is on a large scale) where the lumbermen sleep and eat. The food was better than at most of the hotels (I can vouch for that because I ate some) and the sleeping accommodation just as clean if somewhat less private.

We left Fredericton again early next morning, and after devious wanderings reached here at 11.30 p.m. But I will leave over any account of Prince Edward Island. I will only add that at a dinner, to which we went at Halifax, Haggard distinguished himself by making a speech which some people think the extreme of pessimism, and others a 'trumpet-call'. So that you may judge for yourselves I send you the cutting. Personally, considering the navy question has been the most burning political question in Canada, I think the speech in the worst of taste. But Haggard prides himself on his diplomacy![375]

> Best love
>   Ever your affectionate son
>   E. J. Harding

> Chateau Laurier
> Ottawa
> August 23rd 1914

My dear Eva,

Possibly this letter will come by the *Royal George* by which we purpose sailing on Tuesday – possibly it will go by another boat and get to you even if the much talked of German cruiser catches us in mid Atlantic. Anyhow, I will begin, as the diary is a week behindhand – I fancy that I wrote last from Prince Edward Island, but said nothing about it.[376]

---

375. This was indeed a highly sensitive topic. The Canadian government had long been under pressure from the British government and from Canadian imperialists to respond to the German naval challenge by contributing to the Royal Navy, but this had been resisted particularly by French Canadians. The Naval Services Act, passed in May 1910, established the Royal Canadian Navy (based at first upon the former Fisheries Protection fleet) but placed it under the control of the Canadian government except in an emergency when control could be assumed by the British Admiralty. This compromise satisfied no one, it contributed to the defeat of the Liberal government in 1911 and it left Canada with just two warships

It is commonly known as 'The Island' – and it is 'dry' throughout. By which cryptic saying I mean that wine and spirits are officially taboo. They can be got, but only *sub rosa* and with difficulty. At the official luncheon with which we were entertained at Charlottetown, we had the unusual experience of seeing the waiters carry off the glasses solemnly and return with them filled with water.[377]

This reminds me to tell you a story concerning the state of Maine, U.S.A. A man went in to a hotel – say at Portland – and demanded a whisky and soda. The proprietor replied that he was sorry but that he could only serve it if his customer had a snake bite. The man made a bee-line for the nearest snake shop. The proprietor there replied that he also was sorry, but said that the snake was booked up for the next six months!

(I apologize for the diversion – but Campbell told it to the wife of the P.E.I. premier who gave us the aforesaid luncheon and she failed to see the point; this must be my excuse for mentioning it.)

Though sadly handicapped by this defect, and by general deficiencies in hotel accommodation (I went into those last week so won't refer to so sore a subject again), Prince Edward Island is really delightful.

---

when war broke out. Haggard had been disturbed by the apparent local lack of concern at the outbreak of war. He therefore spoke of the Empire's peril and of the need for Canadians to rally to England's cause: 'The Angel of Death appears in a dawn of blood'. In explicitly condemning the 'little navy' party in Britain he had implicitly criticised their Canadian equivalents. He preserved in his diary a report from the local *Daily Telegraph* which described him as 'deadly pale' and speaking with 'repressed fervour'. The silence which followed his remarks was broken by the mayor leading a singing of the National Anthem.

376. The first European colonists of the island in the early 18th century had been French, but in 1763 the island was formally ceded to Great Britain by the Treaty of Paris after the Seven Years War. It became independent of Nova Scotia in 1769, and was named Prince Edward Island in 1799 as a compliment to the then Duke of Kent, father of the future Queen Victoria. It secured responsible government in 1851. In 1911 it had a population of just 93,728, barely over 1% of the Canadian total. Perhaps the island's most famous resident was Lucy Maud Montgomery (1874–1942): her novel *Anne of Green Gables* was published in 1908.

377. Temperance campaigns began in Canada in the 1820s. By 1850 many reformers were insisting upon legislation to impose total prohibition. Their pressure led to an act of 1878 which allowed for local government areas by popular vote to make the sale of alcoholic drinks illegal. In 1900 prohibition was imposed in P.E.I.: this was extended in 1915 and 1916 to all provinces except Quebec, but restrictions were largely reversed in the 1920s.

Its soil is as red, and as fertile, as the eyes of any Devonshire man could wish. It is 'intensively' cultivated, so that hardly an acre remains which is not producing a crop of some kind. It is undulating, and breezy and warm – 'smiling' in fact, is the epithet for it as we saw it. And it is so unsophisticated that, until the last year or so, motor cars were forbidden altogether by law. Even now they are only allowed on certain roads and on three days in the week.

But, alas, a wave of commercialism is threatening to engulf the Island. Some years ago a native genius discovered that its soil and climate were particularly suited for breeding the black fox – an animal with a skin which, in normal times, would fetch fabulous prices. The result is that the peaceful paths of agriculture are being deserted, that everyone is starting to breed the black fox, or better still (or worse) is floating wild cat companies for purchasing and breeding, and that ranches, as they are called, are springing up all over the Island. Let us hope that the war and its effects will bring the people concerned to their knees and their senses.[378]

In the meantime we had furs and pedigrees and prices dinned into our ears, and were hauled out on visits of inspection to the ranches nearest Charlottetown. The foxes are attractive little beasts (one got friendly enough to eat a leaf out of my hand), but I can't think that there will either be fashion or money enough in the next generation to justify a tithe of the money which is going into the industry.

There isn't much more to say about Prince Edward Island. Charlottetown, the capital, (where we stayed) is a nice little place and well laid out, but with inhabitants, and a Government, more than suburban in appearance and intellect. Its chief fame, I think, lies in the fact, that it was the 'cradle of Canadian confederation' – that is, the first of the conferences which led to Confederation was held there in 1864. There had been great preparations to celebrate the jubilee of so great an event. But the war closed them all down.[379]

---

378. Black and then silver-grey foxes had been introduced from 1878. By 1920 over 500 farms and 23,000 animals were satisfying the bizarre desire of city-dwellers to wear the pelts of dead animals.

379. However, P.E.I. chose not to join the Dominion of Canada until 1873, when impending bankruptcy persuaded the islanders of its advantages. Charlottetown supported a population of just 11,198 in 1911. Its most distinguished building (1843–7) housed the provincial legislature, and it was here on Monday August 17 that the Commission met 9 more witnesses, the last on this trip.

Charlottetown, Prince Edward Island, Government House.   *Postcard*

The Prince Edward Island Railway is narrow gauge, at present. I say 'at present' because a 'car ferry' is being built which will bring over trains from the mainland, and this will involve alteration, and it winds about in a most snakelike fashion through comparatively level country. The explanation, we found, is this. The contractors who built the railway were paid so much per mile of line constructed, and were given power to deviate from the straight course up to one mile on either side. They used their privilege to the fullest extent! [380]

The other thing that I shall remember about the Railway is that the chairs in its cars are the slipperiest and most uncomfortable that I have ever struck.

Did I tell you in the last letter that, egged on by the futility of Foster's arrangements for travelling, we 'made representations' to one Gutelius, the manager of the Intercolonial Railway, who gave evidence at St. John? The result was seen when we got clear of Prince Edward Island and reached the mainland en route for Quebec. We had a special train all the way to Levis (the station on the St. Lawrence opposite Quebec, which is reached by ferry) and travelled in comparative comfort. I say 'comparative' because, even so, the travelling wasn't up to the South African standard.

---

380. The construction of the railway 1871–4 was also bent by the constituency demands of the politicians.

The tour has ended officially at Quebec. I must say, looking back on it, that I am much relieved. What with quarrels between the ladies of the party (to which those in South Africa were as nothing), quarrels amongst the members, grumbling at the travelling arrangements, and the general state of 'nerves' the tension was getting pretty bad – and I don't think we should have got through Canada without very serious trouble.

As it is, if we come back again – and I think the 'if' is a very large one – we shall have learnt some lessons which should be useful. One of them will be to make a dead set against taking any female belongings! And another not to trust Sir George Foster!

Since we got to Quebec, things have been comparatively quiet. My two days there were mainly spent in arranging for passages home. We got off half a dozen by the *Virginian* on Thursday.[381] Some of the party were in an arrant state of nerves, and I hear that I fell foul of Mrs. Lorimer because I did not telegraph to the Admiralty for a super Dreadnought to be detached to convoy the Commission home! Seriously, she seems to have thought that I ought to have telegraphed specially to inquire if the Atlantic were clear. And she added two codicils in her will, leaving them in Quebec to be posted on a subsequent ship, with the idea that the *Virginian* would be taken and she perish.

The remainder of my time has been spent in exploring Quebec and Ottawa (whither I came on Friday in order to see Foster and find out what he thought had best be done when we got back). Both are singularly pleasant places and give one a quite different idea of Canada than does the 'backwash', as I am fain to call the Maritime Provinces. Quebec will be familiar to you from photographs, so its externals need no description.[382] The site is absolutely magnificent – river, hills and

---

381. *Virginian*, 10,700 tons, 520 feet by 60 feet, was built for the Allan Line by Stephen on the Clyde in 1905. Soon she would be operating as a liner-cruiser. After the war she was bought in turn by several companies and went to the breakers only in 1955.

382. Quebec had been established by Samuel de Champlain (1567–1635) in 1608 and became the capital of French Canada. The city and the colony were captured by the British during the Seven Years War and ceded by the Treaty of Paris in 1763. The colony was renamed Lower Canada in 1791, but was united with Upper Canada in 1840: the whole colony formally acquired responsible government in 1849. Quebec was revived as a province when the Dominion of Canada was formed in 1867. The province had a population of 2,003,232 in 1911 (28% of the Canadian people) and the city 78,710 (116,850 by 1920). Nine-tenths of the city's population was French.

Quebec, General View.   *Postcard dated 22 September 1912*

ramparts combine to make an exquisite picture. Internally, it is extremely quaint and very French. Only one shudders sometimes at the grafting of the Canadian accent to French speech, and on the addition of the 'shoe shine parlour' to the cafe.

In contrast to Quebec, Ottawa is cold, but imposing.[383] It has a fine pile of Parliament Buildings built up on a bluff above the river. It has good parks and open spaces, and modern houses of a quite attractive pattern. It hardly shows up well in comparison with Melbourne – or even Johannesburg – and it is 'upstart' of course compared with Quebec. Still, it is a wholesome contrast to the towns of the Maritime Provinces. One begins to think, after seeing it and Quebec, that there may be something after all in Canada other than a third-rate effort to copy the United States.[384]

---

383. Ottawa had been founded in 1827 where the Rideau Canal was being constructed to link Lower Canada with Lake Ontario. The still very modest settlement was chosen in 1857, supposedly by Queen Victoria, as the least divisive site for Canada's new capital, much to the astonishment of superficially more obvious claimants. The construction of the Parliament buildings, in sandstone to gothic design, took from 1859 to 1876. The central section had to be largely rebuilt to the same plan following a disastrous fire in 1916. The city population in 1911 was 87,062.

384. In fact, Canadian fears of absorption by the U.S.A. were a fruitful stimulus to national identity.

Ottawa, Ontario, Parliament Hill.   *Postcard franked 29 August 1912*

> *R.M.S. Royal George*
> At sea
> August 30th 1914

After all this letter has come by the *Royal George* – though not, as I had thought, in a mail bag. It has also come in safety so far. We have only had one mild excitement – this afternoon when we sighted a mysterious vessel (the first since leaving the other side) which might have been a torpedo boat, but turned out a tramp.

In two days more we should be in the Bristol Channel, so it behoves me to finish tonight the story of our Canadian visit.

We were in Quebec from Wednesday morning until Friday. Then, as I told you last week, I went up to Ottawa. The railway run is quite short – that is comparatively so, it actually takes eight hours or so – but is interesting. Most of the way along you see the old French system of cultivation – that is very long and narrow strips forming each farm, and all the farm houses close together along a road. The only other item of interest was our dinner at the Grand Trunk Station at Montreal where we had to change.[385] By 'we' I mean Campbell and myself. The room

---

385. The Grand Trunk Railway Company had been established in 1852, had completed the link between Toronto and Montreal by 1856 and then expanded its operations by takeovers and further construction.

was dirtier even than most of the hotels we have come across and the waitress started operations by 'chucking' the menu at us.

Saturday morning was spent partly in interviewing Foster and his 'deputy' O'Hara (who had in hand all the local arrangements for our evidence and tour)[386] and partly in having a look at the Canadian Houses of Parliament, and in listening for a few minutes to the House of Commons in the special 'war' session. They have there the system of 'desks' for members, such as we found at Capetown: otherwise, as the House was in Committee, there was nothing of interest except to look at the notabilities, Borden and Laurier in particular. Laurier looks stouter than he did in 1911 when I last saw him.[387] Borden looks a very fine fellow.[388] My interviews with Foster and O'Hara, which continued at intervals till I left on Monday, were chiefly interesting as showing that the two hate one another like the proverbial poison. O'Hara took every opportunity to 'crab' Foster, politically, as an administrator, and as connected with the arrangements for the Commission, the shortcomings in which he attributed (I am fain to think rightly) to his parsimony and general incapacity. Foster, on the other hand, obviously doesn't consult O'Hara unless he can possibly help it, and then only at the last moment.

This being so, one is surprised that we got through as well as we did. I wonder what would happen if the relations between the President and the Permanent Secretary of the Board of Trade were those between Foster and O'Hara.

Incidentally, one has got some interesting sidelights on Canadian politics, which cause one greatly to wonder.

---

386. Francis O'Hara (1870–1954) had a long and distinguished career in the Canadian civil service: he was Deputy Minister of Trade and Commerce 1908–31 and the D.R.C.'s local representative in Canada.
387. Sir Wilfrid Laurier (1841–1919) was born in Quebec, became a Liberal minister in 1877, leader of the Liberal party in 1891 and prime minister in 1896: the first French-Canadian and the first Roman Catholic to be appointed. Harding had seen him when he attended the Imperial Conference in 1911, shortly before the fall of his government. He was a supporter of the Empire while being also an insistent advocate of self-government within it. While he supported Canadian entry into the war, he was an opponent of conscription, an issue which split the Canadian Liberal party, as it did the British Liberal party.
388. Sir Robert Borden (1854–1937) was born in Nova Scotia, became leader of the Conservative party in 1901, overturned Laurier's government in 1911 and became prime minister until 1920, leading Canada into the First World War and organising her mobilisation.

After so excited a mental atmosphere, the other incidents of my visit to Ottawa seem quite tame. Campbell and I were taken a tour of the place and its surroundings by O'Hara in a motor car on Saturday afternoon. And on Sunday afternoon, being then by myself (Campbell having gone off to Niagara), I went up by a tram car up the Ottawa river and had a walk there.

So I have got a fair idea of the amenities of the place which are considerable without being thrilling. There are two nice clubs, the 'Rideau Club' and the 'Country Club' (to both of which we went) and the 'Chateau Laurier', where we stayed, is quite first class.

One incident, which I shall remember, is our visit to Sir Joseph Pope who is the Dominion Secretary for External Affairs, and whose name was very familiar to me from C.O. papers. I found his office to be over a barber's shop.[389]

I came down to Montreal on Monday afternoon, boarded the *Royal George* which was due to sail early on Tuesday morning, and then went back to dinner in the town. For my last night on Canadian soil I thought I would experiment with the 'Ritz Carlton' and did so. It hasn't quite the luxury of the similar hotels in New York and London, but was quite comfortable enough – the prices being extremely moderate too considering the range of Canadian tariffs. I was surprised at paying only $1.50 for a very excellent dinner.

Then I went on to a Music Hall – the chief point of which was large notices inviting the audience not to whistle or make cat calls if they disapproved of a turn – and so back to the ship and to bed. We sailed at 5 in the morning.

I had no idea that we should be such a time on the St. Lawrence. As a matter of fact we didn't get clear of it until quite late on Thursday evening. On Tuesday the river was comparatively narrow and we got down as far as Quebec (where we took on the majority of the party – the full complement consists of Bateman, the Langermans, the Tatlows, Campbell, Glenny, Bridgman and I). On Wednesday we were off Anticosti – an island which is larger than Prince Edward Island and has a population of some 400 only. On Thursday we had the Labrador coast to port and Newfoundland to starboard, and came through the Straits of Belle Isle. The coast line of Labrador is rather attractive, and not too bleak. You may gauge the dangers of the passage from the fact that at

---

389. Sir Joseph Pope (1854–1926) entered the Canadian civil service in 1878. From 1882 to 1891 he was private secretary to the prime minister Sir John Macdonald (1815–91) and from 1909 to 1925 he was Under-Secretary of State for External Affairs.

Royal Canadian Regiment, Officers Ante-Room, Wellington Barracks, Halifax.
Photograph, Fisher Collection, 1909

one time we could see no less than 20 icebergs.

By midnight we were clear away from ice, and since then we have had an extraordinarily good passage – very calm, but rather cold, in spite of lots of sun. The ship is also good – she was built for the Mediterranean service, and, as that proved a non-paying proposition, was bought up cheap by the Canadian Northern Railway. Cabin passengers are conspicuous by their absence (there are less than thirty of which we contribute ten). To make up we have 700 reservists, 200 French and 500 English, so we should be quite a good prize![390]

Everything connected with the Commission being rather at sixes and sevens, we have contented ourselves with beginning to prepare a report on Newfoundland – a not very serious proposition.[391]

---

390. These would be among the first Canadian troops to serve in the First World War. Canada's professional army began with the Permanent Force created in 1883, but this numbered only 3000 in 1914. The provinces had relied largely on the militia, totalling 60,000 in 1914, for internal order and frontier defence. With the outbreak of war the Canadian Expeditionary Force was formed, at first by volunteers but from 1917, amidst much controversy, by conscription.

391. The *Fourth Interim Report* on Newfoundland was published in 1915. The Maritime Provinces of Canada were eventually dealt with in the next report in 1917, following the final journey to the rest of Canada. On this trip, 11 days of taking evidence were formally recorded, 79 witnesses questioned.

The *Royal George* at Avonmouth.   *Postcard*

I must stop at this point as a light is reported on the port bow. Everyone is hurrying up on deck, so as to be sure to get a good view of the Germans!

London
September 2nd

Previous diary letters have generally ended on the ships. This one did not, but might easily have done so. The 'light' which I spoke of was only another passing ship. After all I shall only have the remembrance of a voyage with 'doused' lights, but without further incident. We reached Bristol[392] early this morning, and came up on a line of which all the bridges were guarded and to a London where everything has the look of a somewhat horrible dream!

Your affectionate brother
E. J. Harding

---

392. As noted earlier, Canadian Northern operated, unusually, to and from Avonmouth, where Bristol Corporation, concerned about the difficulties of navigation up river for large modern vessels and intent upon preserving the city as a major port, had constructed a large dock. Bristol was a manufacturing town as well as seaport and railway terminus, with a population of 357,048 in 1911.

Fourth Journey

To Canada,
August–November 1916

R.M.S. *Metagama*
August 27th 1916

My dear Father,

We left on Friday afternoon, and now it is Sunday evening.[393] We are running with decks lighted up and portholes open – so you will see that obviously those in authority think we are well out of the 'danger zone'. It is a strange contrast to our experiences of two years ago when we had 'lights doused' all the way across. However, they were pretty strict for the first 36 hours, and you will be interested to hear of our doings in the 'zone' itself.

The first 'sign of the times' was in the train from Euston which had no luncheon car. That difficulty we surmounted by the aid of luncheon baskets and they, with a game or so of cribbage with the Chairman, made the journey to Liverpool seem comparatively short.

At Liverpool it was obvious that there were precautions. The ship was painted dull grey – looked in fact almost like a warship, and it seemed at first sight as though one would have to sit for an hour or so on the

393. The Commission party which sailed with Harding to Canada on Friday August 25 consisted only of the Tatlows and Lorimer (representing the United Kingdom) plus Bridgman. Foster (Canada) and Bowring (Newfoundland) awaited their arrival, and Bateman and Garnett (UK), Sinclair (New Zealand) and Langerman (South Africa), plus Mitchell from the Treasury, joined them later at various stages of the journey: Campbell had been withdrawn by the Australian government, D'Abernon was committed to the work of the Central Control Board (Liquor Traffic) and Haggard, just back from a tour of the dominions he had conducted between February and July 1916, was busy writing up his report to the Royal Colonial Institute on opportunities for post-war soldier settlement in the Empire.

landing stage waiting one's turn to go on board. Only one passenger was allowed on at a time, and there seemed endless formalities over the production of passports etc.[394] Fortunately I had had previous warning that this sort of thing might happen and had got the Home Office to telegraph to the Aliens Officer, who supervises embarkation, to give us all possible facilities. After hunting about a little I found him, and the rest was easy. We got on board, settled down in our cabins and paid a fond farewell to the Chairman. Then it only remained to see what was to follow. As a matter of fact – nothing did, at least for a very long while. We cast off about 4.30 p.m. on Friday – crawled down the river for about a mile, and then anchored till about 4 a.m. on Saturday morning. I think the idea was to let us reach the coast of Ireland and skirt it during Saturday, and leave it just as the night came on. At any rate, that was what actually happened.

On Saturday morning when we got up, we found a notice stuck up that all passengers were requested to wear their lifebelts till further notice. We discovered also small cards, sitting in each of our cabins, telling us what the number of our lifeboat was, in case necessity should arise.

As to the lifebelts, I daresay Nellie told you that I did finally buy a lifesaving waistcoat, so that saved me some trouble. One merely put it on instead of an ordinary waistcoat, and walked about, fully equipped.

Those who hadn't this advantage – Mr. Lorimer among others – had to go about trailing their belts with them to their obvious disgust. Everyone was relieved when the notice aforesaid disappeared, as it did about midday today.

As to the lifeboats, I defy anyone to discover his or her own, unless they made extensive enquiries in advance. There wasn't a sign of any lifeboat drill and the numbers on the boats were so small that it needed some looking to find them.

Still nothing has happened and, as I said at the beginning, we are now well out of the zone. We came by the North of Ireland and kept very close inshore all day yesterday.[395] We saw one patrol boat, but not very much else, and so far as I could tell there was no 'zigzagging' whatever!

---

394. Historically, passports had normally been issued by governments to request safe conduct for their citizens in wartime, although the Foreign Office before 1914 had recommended and issued them for peacetime travel through certain countries: they have become a standard requirement for all overseas travellers only since the First World War.

395. On 7 May 1915 the Cunard passenger liner *Lusitania* had approached the British Isles on the normal route from New York south of Ireland and had

R.M.S. Metagama.   *Postcard*

August 31st
In the gulf of St. Lawrence

When I wrote the last lines above, I went up on deck, and there were the
lights of Ireland just fading away. This morning, when I woke up, we
were just abreast of Belle Isle – having come by the northern route.[396]
It is really a revelation how narrow comparatively the Atlantic is. This is
only a 15 knot boat, or a little more, but we have come from shore to
shore in only just over 4 days.

The weather has, of course, been very kind. That is to say there has
been no fog, and an insignificant amount of wind. But the North Atlantic
is a dreary ocean at the best of times. This being my 4th trip across, I feel
justified in saying that. It has rained a good bit and till today has always
been 'grey'. Today, though, has been beautiful, bright sunshine and a

---

been sunk by a German U-boat with the loss of 1198 lives: the ship had
also been carrying war material. Germany temporarily abandoned
unrestricted submarine warfare in the face of American protests in August
1915, but there were further sinkings of passenger vessels in March 1916
and from February 1917. Eventually such attacks helped to provoke the
United States into entering the war on 6 April 1917.

396. The Straits of Belle Isle lie between Newfoundland and the coast of
Labrador.

perfect sea, and we have been near enough in at times to the coast of Labrador to see it perfectly plainly. We expect to be in to Rimouski some time tomorrow evening, and this letter will get posted there.

We have found lots to do in the way of work, and consequently the time hasn't hung heavy. This is fortunate, as our fellow passengers are by no means an interesting lot. There is a good sprinkling of soldiers, mostly coming back wounded.[397] Of the rest – and they number well over 300 so that the ship is fairly full – most seem to be women; one gathers they are mothers, sisters and wives of the men who are serving from Canada. There are swarms of children (who presumably couldn't be left behind in Canada owing to lack of domestic servants!), mostly ill mannered and somewhat ill featured.

The most attractive people are Sir Thomas Esmond, the Nationalist whip, and a Colonel Hughes, brother of 'Sir Sam'. The latter is a great talker, and volubly explains that one of his grandmothers was French and the other Irish. Query, does this ancestry explain the idiosyncracies of Sir Sam?[398]

The ship is pretty comfortable, but suffers from having only one enclosed promenade deck which is sometimes inconveniently crowded. She is a 'one class' boat, i.e. has cabin and steerage passengers only, but the cabins are roomy and the food very good, so we do very well on the whole.[399]

---

397. During the First World War 619,636 men joined the Canadian Expeditionary Force, of whom 424,589 served overseas: 60,661 were killed. Newfoundland, too, sent its contingent: 6241 joined up, 4984 went overseas and 1251 were killed. These troops distinguished themselves in particular at Ypres in 1915, at the Somme in 1916 and at Vimy Ridge in 1917. Other men served in the navy and air force.

398. Sir Thomas Esmonde (1862–1935) was an Irish Nationalist M.P. 1885–1919. The party's political authority in Ireland was currently being rapidly replaced by that of Sinn Fein following the executions after the Easter Rising in Dublin in 1916. Sir Sam Hughes (1853–1921) had campaigned enthusiastically in Canada since the 1880s to raise volunteer colonial troops to fight in Great Britain's imperial wars. He was the Canadian Minister of Militia and Defence from 1911 until Borden felt forced to sack him in 1916 for incompetence.

399. *Metagama*, 12,420 tons, 501 feet by 64 feet, was built by Barclay Curle on the Clyde for Canadian Pacific and launched in November 1914: she was designed to carry 520 cabin class and 1200 third class passengers. Her maiden voyage began on 26 March 1915. She survived the war, but not the economic depression of the 1930s: she was laid up in 1931 and broken up in 1934.

Our own party is small – only the Tatlows, Lorimer, Bridgman and myself. But we have a valuable acquisition to our table in the shape of one Holloway, a leading metallurgist in London who is Chairman of a Royal Commission on Nickel in Ontario, and is an expert on all mining questions. He has helped us a lot, and he and Lorimer foregather a good deal.[400]

That is all my news, I think, so I will 'close down' and get on with the rest of the letters to catch the mail at Rimouski.

> Best love
> Ever your affectionate son
> E. J. Harding

Car *Natalia*
Saskatoon
Saskatchewan
Sept. 10th 1916

My dearest Mother,

Ever since my last letter was posted – and that was at Rimouski more than a week ago – I have never had an opportunity even to begin a letter much less to finish one. But today we have shaken off all well-meaning visitors for an hour or so, and there is an opportunity at any rate to start.

We ended up our voyage to Montreal without incident, and arrived there early on last Sunday morning, having done almost a record trip from Liverpool, certainly a record in war time. There were various formalities at Quebec such as medical tests, and immigration tests, which we succeeded, with a little trouble, in avoiding. We had an hour or so on shore and had a drive up to Parliament Buildings to do some business. But I have probably described Quebec before, and anyhow won't do so now.

On getting to Montreal we stayed for Sunday night at the Ritz-Carlton Hotel, a palatial building with very comfortable rooms, but indifferent service. The charges were also high! However, the conditions

---

400. George Thomas Holloway (1863–1917) began his career as an Assistant-Demonstrator at the Royal College of Science in London and then practised as a consulting metallurgist, chemist and essayer. He became a member of the British Institution of Mining and Metallurgy in 1901 and a Vice-President in 1913. The serious physical demands of the Royal Ontario Nickel Commission, of which he had been made Chairman in 1915, strained his fragile health and he died in October 1917, only a few months after the publication of its report.

Montreal, Quebec Province, View with Courthouse and City Hall.
Postcard franked 15 July 1914

were ten times better than anything we had had two years ago in the Maritime Provinces, so there was really no cause for complaint. On arrival, I found O'Hara had come down from Ottawa to meet us (he is Foster's 'permanent head of Department', i.e. the Department of Trade and Commerce, and had been making all the arrangements for our visit), and I spent practically the whole of Sunday in going through the plans and settling things with him. Our only interlude was to go down to one of the station yards and inspect this car, where we have been for one week and are to be for another. I will come to her later on. We found that the arrangements contemplated our starting westwards on Monday night, and as Monday was 'Labor Day' in Canada (i.e. something corresponding to our August Bank Holiday) and all the business houses were closed, there wasn't really very much to do. I spent the morning talking to the Canadian Pacific Railway people about the railway arrangements[401] and in the afternoon had a walk up the 'Mount Royal' which dominates the city of Montreal. It is rather a fine hill, not very

401. The building of the Canadian Pacific Railway had been a political necessity, to bring the western territories into the Canadian confederation. The decision to build was made in 1872 but the work was largely carried out 1881–86. It completed a rail link from Halifax facing the Atlantic to Vancouver on the Pacific, 5827 kilometres.

high, but laid out with walks and drives and covered with trees of all kinds and specially maples. There were lots of grey squirrels about, and one felt reminded of Regent's Park. I had also a look at the lower part of the town, and the canal down which the grain comes on its way to the sea from the west.[402] That was interesting, but somewhat technical, so I needn't worry you more about it.

We started after dinner on Monday evening – that is to say the Tatlows, Lorimer, Bridgman and I – and picked up Foster at Ottawa about three hours after starting, and Bowring two days later.[403]

The car, called the *Natalia*, is the private car of the head of the Canadian Northern Railway, Sir William MacKenzie, and has been lent to us for the journey west.[404] She has 5 sleeping saloons, with berths for one or two more, a bathroom, a sitting room, kitchens etc. So we are really very comfortable, and she fits us exactly. Two boys look after the car, one of whom is cook and the other waiter and housemaid. They both are very good, and work extraordinarily hard. Altogether the travelling, so far, has been far more comfortable than I dared to hope! Now to go back to our journey. We woke up on Tuesday morning to find ourselves travelling through a country of rivers, lakes and pinewoods, and the same country continued without any intermission till yesterday afternoon! The country is very little settled except, of course, in the mining districts which I shall come to in a minute. It is very level, no hills of any note, and not particularly exciting. But the rivers and lakes are beautiful. They would give worlds for them in Australia or South Africa.

---

402. Montreal was founded as a French mission station in the early 17th century, and was occupied by the British in 1760 during the Seven Years War. It developed as a commercial and transport centre, helped by the completion of the Lachine Canal in 1825. Mount Royal Park was laid out in 1874 by Frederick Law Olmstead, who had already designed Central Park in New York. Montreal was the largest city in Canada by the time of Confederation in 1867. In 1911 its population had reached 470,480, making it one of the major cities of the Empire. 'Montreal', wrote the poet Rupert Brooke (1887–1915), who visited in July 1913, 'consists of banks and churches. The people of this city spend much of their time in laying up their riches in this world or the next': see his *Letters from America*.
403. Foster was to act as chairman of this small party of Commissioners until Bateman joined them on 16 October.
404. The Canadian Northern Railway Company began in 1896: it planned to construct another route to the Pacific from Montreal. This was completed in 1915, but the company's financial difficulties led to its takeover by the government in 1917.

Our first break was at Sudbury, where we arrived at midday on Tuesday, leaving on Wednesday evening. Sudbury is the headquarters of the nickel industry (which is particularly interesting since Canada practically commands the world's supply), and there are two big companies operating, which we inspected on the two days available.[405] Both were very kind to us, gave us lunch etc. and showed us all over their principal works. One is an American company, and the head of the works had a charming American wife, who gave us lunch at their private house. It was a pretty house, anyhow, for a mining district, but rendered more charming by the fact that the sulphur in the nickel destroys all vegetation for miles round, so that the neighbourhood of Sudbury is a veritable wilderness of stones and dead wood.

We were hard at work inspecting and talking for both days, and were pretty tired when we left on Wednesday evening. But rest wasn't permissible, for when we got to North Bay (where the car was to be shunted for the night) about 10 p.m., the Mayor and leading citizens insisted on taking us out in motor cars, and showing us their town in the dark.[406] When we got back after this experience, we found that the car had been sent a long way down the line to be turned, and we had to wait sleepily on the platform for nearly an hour!

Next morning – that is last Thursday – found us at Cobalt which is the centre where most of the silver in Canada comes from. It is also the place where cobalt comes from which is used for colouring. The town is a typical mining camp – put up anyhow, and with mines all round for a distance of 4 or 5 miles.[407] We had the usual ceremony on arrival – Mayor – mining people – Board of Trade etc. etc. and were taken to lunch at the Cobalt Mess, a sort of mixture of Club and boarding house

---

405. Sudbury, 702 kilometres from Montreal, had a population of 4150 in 1911 (7215 by 1921). Its nickel mines were valued at $18 million in 1919 and produced about two-thirds of the world's output. Written evidence for the Commission was collected in Sudbury on Tuesday September 5 and Wednesday September 6.

406. The Commissioners had retraced their route: North Bay, on Lake Nipissing, was 580 kilometres from Montreal. It was developing as a holiday resort, a railway junction and as the centre of a mining, agricultural and lumbering district. By 1921 it had a population of 9200.

407. Cobalt lay north of North Bay on the Timiskaming and Northern Ontario Railway, completed in 1911. It had grown rapidly as a mining town since the mineral discoveries of 1903. 31½ million oz. of cobalt had been extracted when output peaked in 1911. The population in 1911 was 5638. Here, on Thursday September 7, more written evidence was gathered.

Ontario, 'Drilling
for Silver in an
80-foot level at
La Rose Mine,
Cobalt, August
1908'.
*Photograph, Fisher
Collection, 1908*

where the unmarried men put up, or at any rate have their meals. The
waiters were two Canadian soldiers just back on 4 days leave before
crossing to England. They were ex-employees of the Mess, and were
seized during their leave to go back temporarily to their old job. After
lunch we started again on the work of inspection – going to about 3 mines
between 2 and 4 p.m. The place is just mines and 'tailings' and scrub, not
much else. But it certainly has produced for a good many people a good
many millions of dollars, and is likely to produce as much again! I forgot
to add that one of the incidents of our arrival was the solemn presentation
by the Mayor of a piece of silver quartz to each member of the party.

After nickel and silver – gold. We went on from Cobalt on Thursday
afternoon to a district which rejoices in the name of Porcupine, and a
township with the equally elegant name of Timmins. There we arrived
late in the evening and were 'laid up' till Friday morning. Timmins is

very young, compared with Sudbury and Cobalt. That is to say gold was only discovered there in 1909 and the mines have only started working since 1912, the works having been destroyed by a forest fire just as they were ready in 1911. But it is really a very great place.[408] The largest mine – named Hollinger – is now producing to the tune of about £1,000,000 a year and paid last year a dividend of over 50%. Several others are coming along. We looked over the three most important in the course of the morning with the aid of their respective managers, and finally joined the car about 2.30, quite ready for our lunch.

That completed our visit to the Ontario mining districts. I must say, I was immensely impressed, not only with the present productivity, but with the prospect of more to come. At present only the fringe of Northern Ontario has been thoroughly looked into for minerals. There are probably heaps more districts as rich in minerals as those already discovered.

We were fortunate in that for the 4 days we spent there – I mean at Sudbury, Cobalt and Porcupine – we had with us one of the head mining officials of Ontario Province, one Gibson, a man whom I had met in London, and spotted as being likely to be useful.[409] He travelled with us on the car, and gave us little lectures beforehand on each of the districts. You may imagine that he and Lorimer became great pals. The latter worked tremendously hard all the time (harder, I think, than he ought to have) and when we came away our knowledge was quite extensive!

Since Friday afternoon we have, till this morning, been travelling without intermission. From the Porcupine district we went up to Cochrane (a town on the new National Transcontinental Railway) which was nearly burned out with a big forest fire 6 weeks ago, and is now largely tents.[410]

---

408. Gold had been discovered in 1896, but the real rush began in 1909. Timmins had a population of 3648 in 1921. Again, the Commissioners collected written evidence, on Friday September 8.

409. Thomas Wilson Gibson (1859–1941) was from 1906 to 1935 the Deputy Minister of Mines for the Province of Ontario, secretary of the Royal Ontario Nickel Commission and the man largely responsible for the orderly development of the mineral resurces of Northern Ontario.

410. Cochrane had suffered an earlier fire in 1911: its population then was about 2000. It was a railway junction. Here the Commissioners joined the National Continental Railway, built by the established Grand Trunk Railway from 1852. It was extended by their subsidiary, the Grand Trunk Pacific Railway, between 1905 and 1914 to form a third transcontinental route. However, the company was soon in financial difficulties, and its assets were taken over by the government after the war.

Train Crossing the Prairie, Western Canada. *Postcard*

There we joined one of the big expresses, and went straight through to Winnipeg which we reached late yesterday (Saturday) afternoon. The country was just the same as before – rivers, lakes, woods – and practically empty.[411] I fear the railway was constructed for political, and not practical reasons. Still the journey was interesting enough. There wasn't a single road, much less railway, anywhere to the north of us as far as the Pole.[412]

At Winnipeg we only stopped half an hour or so, and then came straight on here. But the prairie country, where we have been for the last 20 hours is altogether different. It is practically flat, almost treeless, with only an occasional river, wholly cultivated, at any rate within eyesight from the railway, and with wheat practically the only crop. The soil, where you can see it, is rich copper-colour for a good part of the way.

---

411. The Commission was now in the province of Manitoba. This district had originally been part of Rupert's Land, a huge region granted by King Charles II in 1670 to the Hudson's Bay Company of which his cousin, Prince Rupert (1619–82), was the first Governor. Manitoba became a province of the Dominion of Canada in 1870. In 1911 its population was 455,614 (6% of the total) and it was attracting much new settlement, reaching 553,860 in 1916 and 609,614 by 1921.
412. The vast North West Territories, one-third of Canada in extent, contained just 18,481 people according to the 1911 census.

There are occasional houses – homesteads, I suppose I should say – still more occasional villages and towns, lots of railways, and a general air of detached prosperity. I won't say more at present, as we are likely to see more of the same thing during the next few days.

We sleep here tonight (in the car) and stay most of tomorrow. Then we go on to Edmonton where we stay a couple of days, then through the Rockies to Prince Rupert. So far it has been most interesting, and everything has gone quite smoothly.

> Best love
> Ever your affectionate son
> E. J. Harding

Car *Natalia*
Prince Rupert
Sept. 17th 1916

My dear Eva,

Last Sunday the car was at Saskatoon – this Sunday it is in the yards at Prince Rupert, some 2000 miles further on. In the interval we have had about as interesting a week as it would be possible to conceive. Every day has had something, and most many things, new, and the diversity of scene has been wonderful.

When I left off last week, we had just arrived at Saskatoon.[413] It is a jolly town (very mushroom having had only 300 people, I think, in 1901) but well lighted, well laid out, and with street tramways all over the place. It lies on the banks of the Saskatchewan river which flows in curves round it.

Saskatoon was, further, our first experience of a Canadian west 'boom' town. That is to say some bright genius a few years ago proclaimed to the world that the place was an ideal town site. Everyone began to buy land – values went up sky high, vast sums were spent on roads and lights and all the rest of it. Then something happened – happened, in fact, before the war. Values went down again with a run, and someone – goodness

---

413. Saskatoon, built on both banks of the South Saskatchewan River, began as a Methodist temperance colony in 1883, but it became a substantial and rather different community with the arrival of the railway, bringing in new settlers from 1908. The population had reached 12,004 by 1911 but was double that by 1921. The Commissioners arrived on Sunday September 10 and on the following afternoon met formally in the Board of Trade Offices in the City Hall to question 7 witnesses.

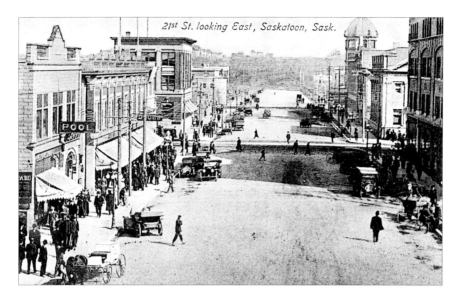
Saskatoon, Saskatchewan, 21st Street Looking East.   *Postcard*

knows who – was left lamenting with unsaleable land. Probably the British investor was let in as much as anybody.

Saskatoon still smiles, however. It has the consolation that it hasn't been hit as far as others farther west!

Meanwhile, it goes on as best it can, and hopes for another boom soon. And its people were quite charming and very hospitable. We spent Sunday morning more or less in peace. Then in the afternoon we were called for by the Mayor, and the President of the Board of Trade, and the local M.P. and such like, and were taken round the town in motor cars. The chief things to remember are the river and the University. The latter is really extremely well built – almost in the Oxford manner. But its activities are more extended in that it has an experimental farm of 80 acres or so attached, also horses and cattle and sheep etc., all of which we saw and admired. Incidentally, we found out that it had a faculty of engineering, but that that was temporarily closed down, all the teachers and all the students having gone off to the war! Saskatchewan believed apparently in coeducation. The University is a residential one, I gathered, both for boys and girls.[414]

---

414. The University of Saskatchewan had been founded in 1907: it had included the Provincial Agricultural College since 1912.

Our inspection ended, we went off to tea and conversation at the house of the local M.P., Macraney by name, one of Foster's opponents, i.e. on the Liberal side.[415] Included in the party was the Conservative candidate. Possibly they are on speaking terms, as no Dominion general election is pending at the moment. At election times, I should imagine, they would not be. Such is the force of politics in this country.

We ended up with dinner in the local hotel, and went to the local theatre afterwards to hear a speech by Sir George Foster. That he is a natural orator is undoubted, that those who are with him for 2 months get rather bored with his speeches is equally undoubted. However, he spoke for an hour or more, to the apparent delight of his audience, and we – well, we managed to stick it out without too obvious yawns.

On Monday morning we had a repetition of Sunday afternoon – but on a larger scale. That is to say, we first made a further inspection of the town (including a visit to a registration booth where the women of Saskatchewan were registering themselves in view of impending women's suffrage),[416] then we went to a big elevator erected by the Dominion Government for handling and storing grain, and went all over it – in fact mounted to the top of the roof and had a splendid view of the prairie all round – then we went for a drive round twenty miles of country or so, and had a good look at the wheat, which stretches for miles, and the various interludes such as oats, clover etc. which make up the rest.

The wheat is really delightful to look at – most of it was in sheaves, and only a little uncut, but with the sun on it, as was the case when we saw it, and with great stretches, as far as one could see, the sight to my

---

415. George Ewan McCraney (1868–1921) was a lawyer by profession and served as Liberal M.P. for Saskatchewan 1906–08 and for Saskatoon 1908–17: he was one of the representatives of the Canadian House of Commons at the coronation of King George V and Queen Mary in 1911.

416. A lengthy campaign led to the granting of votes to women in provincial elections in Saskatchewan, Manitoba and Alberta in 1916, and in Ontario and British Columbia in 1917. The other provinces had conformed by 1922, except Quebec where women were denied the provincial vote until 1940. Votes in Federal elections were granted first to women in the armed services and relatives of enlisted men in 1917 and to all women in 1918. Other settler societies of the British Empire had made such concessions earlier, beginning with New Zealand in 1893 and South Australia in 1894, followed later by Western Australia in 1899, and then by the Commonwealth of Australia in 1902 and other Australian states. But in the United Kingdom only women ratepayers enjoyed a limited vote in local elections before the Representation of the People Act in January 1918 gave the vote to women over the age of 30 (over 21 from 1928).

mind was extraordinarily beautiful. The point which struck me particularly was that the prairie isn't flat even in Saskatchewan, as I had expected it would be. It 'rolls' very slightly, that is, there are small valleys and hills. Also there are patches of woodland, either natural or planted.

> S.S. *Prince Rupert*
> Sept. 18th
> On the way to Vancouver

I had got so far when I was interrupted, and couldn't find time to finish this letter last night. So I must finish it here and send it off from Vancouver.

To go back to Saskatoon, we went back from our drive straight to the Hotel, had a 'Canadian Club' Luncheon there – i.e. a cold lunch with the inevitable speeches – took evidence afterwards at the City Hall, and left for Edmonton just after five p.m.

There is nothing worth recording about the later proceedings, except that in the room at the hotel where we went to wash for lunch we found a notice on the door: 'Gentlemen are requested not to strike matches on the walls'. Yet it was the best hotel in the place. That reminds me that, on the evening before, we found 'combination cuts', *anglice* 'cold meats', figuring on the dinner menu.

We reached Edmonton early next morning – that is on Tuesday. Taking warning from our experiences in Australia, I telegraphed to the local Board of Trade not to come to the car till 9.30 a.m. So we had breakfast in peace.

Edmonton is the capital of Alberta – the furthest west of the Prairie Provinces.[417] It is like Saskatoon, only more so. That is to say, it had a tremendous boom in land a few years ago. It has built magnificent Parliament Buildings costing two million dollars. It has a still more magnificent hotel, costing much the same. It has planned its streets,

---

417. This district was formerly part of the North West Territories, itself an amalgamation in 1876 of part of Rupert's Land and other territory of the Hudson's Bay Company. In 1905 the southern portion of this huge area was separated out into two more provinces, Alberta and Saskatchewan, and incorporated into the confederation. The population of Alberta in 1911 was 374,663 (5% of the total), growing to 496,525 in 1916 and to 661,663 in 1921. There were fur trading forts at Edmonton by the late 18th century, but significant growth occurred only with the arrival of the railway, the rush to the Klondike goldfields in the 1890s, and the town's selection as the provincial capital. The population in 1911 was just 24,900 but by 1916 it was 53,846.

Edmonton, Alberta, Jasper Avenue, East from First Street.

Photograph c.1910–12

trams, drains, telephones etc. for a population of at least a million, and has about 70,000 inhabitants. We were told that the municipality alone has a debt of 30,000,000 dollars. Judging from the general appearance of the place, the people have some difficulty in paying the interest.

However, we found the place comfortable enough, and the Macdonald Hotel, run by the Grand Trunk Pacific Railway, was excellent.[418]

We spent most of Tuesday taking evidence in the luxurious Parliament Buildings.[419] The arrangements had been very ill made by the local Board of Trade Secretary, and we had some little difficulty in getting started. However, when once we got going, things went all right. At lunch time we had a little variation, in the shape of a lunch given by the Board of Trade. But though the hosts were different and the proceedings varied slightly, there were speeches all the same. You never get out of them for long in Canada.

---

418. The MacDonald Hotel boasted 200 rooms: many of the major hotels were constructed by the railway companies.

419. Each new province needed its provincial legislature. Alberta's yellow sandstone Parliament Buildings in Edmonton were opened in 1912. The Commission here questioned 15 witnesses on Tuesday September 12 and Wednesday September 13.

In the evening Bowring and I had quite a long walk through the outskirts. Edmonton, like Saskatoon, lies on the banks of a river (the north Saskatchewan) and the surroundings are quite impressive. After dinner I retired early and had a hot bath, a very necessary luxury after nine continuous nights in the train.

On Wednesday we continued, and finished, our evidence in the morning. It wasn't highly important, but interesting enough. Then the majority of the party went off to lunch with the Lieutenant Governor. As a sidelight on the way things go in Canada, he is a doctor and ex-head of a Sanatorium at Banff, nice enough but by no means a man to set the Thames on fire. However, he has a very comfortable job, and a delightful house and garden. I judge only from seeing the latter, and the porch of the former, as I personally had lunch with three or four people who were interested in the question of settling soldiers on the land,[420] and I only went out afterwards to the Governor's house on the way to a drive in the country.

We got away by three, and were motoring almost continuously till 7 p.m., so we had a good look at quite a lot of country. Alberta, as we saw it, differs a lot from Saskatchewan. It is more 'rolling' – in fact there are some quite fair sized hills and the people go in much more for mixed farming, instead of confining themselves to wheat. However, the homesteads look equally flourishing in both Provinces, and at one big farm, where we called for tea, the property of one Bremner, an upstanding, hard headed Scotchman, we were shown a big wheat field averaging 50 bushels to the acre, of which its owner was tremendously proud. Incidentally, he possessed stock of various kinds including a thoroughbred horse which had never been beaten either racing or at a show. So perhaps his house (which might well have been an English country house) wasn't a fair specimen.

We left Edmonton for the Rockies and Prince Rupert at 10.30 on Wednesday evening. None of us thought either it, or its people, quite up to Saskatoon. None the less it enlarged our impressions, even if it didn't make them more favourable, of a boom town in the west.

Thursday morning found us nearing the Rockies. At breakfast time we had almost reached the top of the Yellowhead Pass through which the Grand Trunk Pacific Railway goes, and by lunch time we were well

---

420. The prairie provinces were keen to increase their populations. The D.R.C. recommended in its *Final Report* the migration of ex-soldiers from Britain, and this was partially satisfied by a British govenment-financed scheme launched in 1919.

Farm near Edmonton.   *Photograph, Fisher Collection, 1908*

down on the other side. The Pass itself is very low, only 3700 ft. or so, and the gradient on both sides is very small. So one doesn't get the same impression of immensity as one does in crossing the Alps. Mount Robson, which we passed and saw perfectly soon after getting on to the 'Pacific slope', is quite as perfect as any of the big peaks in Switzerland, and its absolute loneliness (there can't be 100 people within a circle of as many miles) is astonishing.[421] But generally speaking I was rather disappointed in the main ridge of the Rockies – nor were one's impressions improved by finding that the country flattened itself soon after we were across. By lunch time, we had got into quite a wide undulating valley through which the Fraser, one of the big rivers of British Columbia flows, and the same type of country continued for the rest of the day.

What was surprising was to find that the scenery on the next day, Friday, when we were getting near the coast, was much more picturesque,

---

421. Constructing railways over the Rockies was one of the major engineering achievements of the previous half century. The Yellowhead Pass, 3723 ft. or 1145 m., runs below Mount Robson, 3954 m., the highest peak in the Canadian Rocky Mountains. It had only recently been climbed, on 31 July 1913. Further down the track the railway divided, with one line cutting south-west to Vancouver, and the other, taken by the Grand Trunk Pacific, heading north-west to Prince Rupert.

taken as a whole, than anything we had seen. The railway creeps down two more river valleys, first the Bulkley, then the Sceena,[422] and each rushes down either in a gorge or in a comparatively narrow valley, with snow capped peaks on each side. The whole country is thickly wooded – mainly with spruce, larch and cottonwood, and there is very little sign of agricultural land. But occasionally there are patches of cultivation, and one is reminded of Swiss pastures. In fact for hundreds of miles on Friday, I should have thought we were in the Ticino valley, if it hadn't been that there are no villages perched up on the heights.

Population is very sparse. The country is much too thrown about to make it accessible, and the timber is another obstacle. Only occasionally is there a little town, and sometimes an Indian hut or village.[423] Even the mountains, for the most part, have no names, and we found that Haggard who had been along the route in June, had induced the railway authorities to give his name to quite an outstanding one.[424] No doubt we could have done ditto if we had been so disposed!

We got to Prince Rupert on Friday evening just before dinner time.[425] The scenery gets finer and finer the nearer you get to the coast, and at the end the railway is really running along a fiord with mountains at each

---

422. Correctly, the Skeena.
423. A rare reminder in Harding's account that North American Indians still occupied parts of the country which Europeans had come to call the Dominion of Canada. By 1917 it was officially estimated that 105,998 Indians remained, mainly in reservations, perhaps half the number of those present when Europeans first arrived.
424. On the other hand, Haggard recorded in his diary that the proposal came from the Grand Trunk Pacific Railway Company. The Sir Rider Mountain and the accompanying Haggard Glacier were names accepted by the Geographical Board of Canada. He had travelled across the continent from west to east, pursuing his enquiries about soldier settlement.
425. Evidence was collected in the City Hall from 11 witnesses on Saturday September 16. Prince Rupert is Canada's most northerly Pacific Coast city. The site was selected as the terminus for the Grand Trunk Pacific Railway, which arrived in 1912. The name was chosen in 1906 after a public competition. It lies close to the border with Alaska at 54° 40'. The entire region south of this latitude had once been claimed by the United States: the dispute with Britain threatened war but was settled by a treaty of partition along the 49th parallel in 1846. The Hudson's Bay Company administered the territory until 1858, when gold strikes on the Fraser River, renewing fears of American control, led to the formal establishment of the colony of British Columbia. In 1866 it was merged with the colony of Vancouver Island, and in 1871 the region became a province of the Dominion of Canada. In 1911 British Columbia had a population of 392,480 (5% of the Canadian total).

Prince Rupert, British Columbia, Dry Dock, City and Harbour.
Postcard dated 16 December 1916

side some thousand of feet high. Every now and then the train stops so that you can get out, take photographs, and admire the scenery. Once we stopped 20 minutes at an Indian village. One old man was pointed out to us – stepping out gaily along the street – who was 107 years old. But the main object of interest is a long string of totem poles, all along the river front. They consist of a series of grotesque figures – quite indescribable here but I hope to bring back a specimen or two – setting out the history of the family or tribe.

Prince Rupert is *the* boom town of the West. I described my impressions of it in a letter to the Chairman. To save myself trouble, I send you a copy. I will only add to this very long letter that we arrived in the throes of a Provincial election, to which, to all appearances, far more local interest attaches than to the most exciting incidents of the war. The protagonists are Bowser and Brewster (at the moment I forget which is which). Anyhow the Conservatives have been well beaten, and Foster is correspondingly depressed.

Best love
Ever your affectionate brother
E. J. Harding

DOMINIONS ROYAL COMMISSION
Prince Rupert, B.C.
17th September, 1916

Dear Lord D'Abernon,

We have been here since Friday evening and leave for Vancouver to-morrow morning. You asked me to let you know what I thought of the place and what its prospects were. I will tell you to the best of my ability.

The harbour is wonderful. It has a depth close in of 30ft. You get 60 ft. by going out ten feet or so. We are told that really the only objection to it is that shipowners do not like anchoring because they have to use up so much anchor. There is a floating dock just finished 600ft. by 100ft. by 28ft. with complete ship repairing and ship construction plant and a foundry. At present it does no business nor has it any regular work in prospect. It looks now as though the machinery might well be antiquated before the business comes. The town lies alongside the harbour with the railway between itself and the foreshore. It is built upon what are supposed to be a series of terraces blasted out of the rock. It extends for five miles or so along the inlet. Almost all the roads are made of wood and are carried over a number of small canyons by means of trestle bridges. We are told that the British Columbia Government expended 250,000 dols. on these roads and recouped itself by the sale of the town lots in its share of the township. It is said that the Government made a profit of 1,250,000 dols. over the whole transaction.

The boom must have been a wonderful thing. Just in the middle of the town there are two lots each 25ft. by 100ft. To the observer they look like two twin rocks guarding the entrance and there is a half made road between them. One of these lots sold at 18,000 dols. and it is said that it would cost 11,000 dols. to level it. There will be, further, the expense (amount unknown) in carrying away the debris.

We walked out to-night to the south west end of the town. There we found a small house at least two miles out from the centre in a lot measuring 25ft. by 300ft. We talked to the householder who told us that it and the neighbouring lot had cost him 1,110 dols. each some four years ago. At the height of the boom he was offered 2,500 dols. for one of the lots. Unfortunately for him he did not take it.

The town is full of land agents most of whom appear to be doing no business whatever. Amongst them are a firm called the Prince Rupert Financiers Limited, Pattullo, the just elected Liberal candidate at the Provincial elections, and MacCaffrey, the present Mayor. The latter met us when we arrived and has been with us on and off since then. He is a fat and bleary man with a plaintive and somewhat surprised look.

Bowring says that he obviously woke up one morning thinking that he would make money enough to buy a little public-house in Boston or elsewhere (he comes from the United States) but finding that the bottom had dropped out of his investments and that he could not unload. The expression has been with him since then.

I made enquiries about Harrison, Gamble, and Co. Harrison, it appears, has been killed at the front, Gamble has just gone there. I was told that the firm's solicitor would, no doubt, answer any enquiries, but I thought it best not to pursue the matter.

The fact is that as far as one can see no one at the moment is making any money whatever except people on salaries, and on the face of it, these are very few.

Prince Rupert I feel sure has a big future but not for the next few years.

> Yours very truly,
> E. J. Harding

Since writing the above, I have found out that the highest price paid for a town lot (60 x 100 ft) was $58,000. That was at the first sale, and was not a speculation. It was paid for a Government lot by a prospective hotel keeper. This site is absolutely empty now. $45,000 were paid for several lots nearby – also empty.

> Car *Lake Agnes*
> Sicamous
> Sept. 26th 1916

My dear Father,

Since I closed my last letter, I haven't had a moment to write. We have been very hard at work, trying to crowd several days evidence into one, and so on. But now we have left the British Columbia cities and have a comparative rest (except for travelling) until we get to the Prairie towns. I will start again, therefore, this evening. We are lying in a siding at a little station up in the mountains, having left Vancouver at 8.30 this morning.

I think my last letter left off as we were coming down in a steamer from Prince Rupert.[426] It was really a wonderful journey all the way to Vancouver. Most of the way is along narrow channels between small islands, or between Vancouver Island and the mainland. At times there

---

426. The steamer *Prince Rupert*, 3379 tons, 306 feet long, was built to carry 250 passengers by Swan, Hunter and Wigham, Richardson Ltd at Newcastle upon Tyne in 1910.

The Season's Greetings from Vancouver Frontiersmen

Vancouver, British Columbia.   *Postcard dated 9 December 1913*

are 'Narrows' with very strong tides, and practically all the way along the mountains come down very steeply into the sea. Just before you get in to Vancouver, the gulf widens out, and there is a good stretch of sea with snow-clad mountains in the distance. We saw this under ideal conditions – bright sunshine and a windless sea – and altogether I shall look upon the voyage down as among the most delightful of our travels.

Vancouver has a splendid harbour, somewhat marred by a rather narrow, and not very deep, entrance. Compared with Prince Rupert, it is a Metropolis – both as a town and in the amount of shipping it has. But it has clearly modelled itself on San Francisco, and isn't therefore the most artistic of cities. There are one or two skyscrapers and in close proximity not a few unbuilt-on 'corner-lots'.[427]

We found the usual crowd waiting when the boat got in, President of the Board of Trade etc., and, as we had about 2 hours to wait before the boat went on to Victoria, were taken off in motor cars and shown round. The chief show feature of Vancouver is a really magnificent public park –

---

427. There was little settlement in Vancouver until the 1860s and no significant growth until its selection in 1885 as the terminus of the Canadian Pacific Railway terminus. The site was then incorporated in 1886 and named after George Vancouver (1758–98) who surveyed this coast in 1792. The population was then around 800: by 1911 it was 100,401 and by 1921, with its suburbs, an estimated 180,000.

Victoria, British Columbia, The Palm Room of the Empress Hotel.
Photograph, Fisher Collection, 1908

surrounded on three sides by salt water, and left so far as possible in a natural state. We saw this, and also the hotel where we were to stay later on, a palatial building in the C.P.R. best style. Then we did a little business in the way of arrangements against our return, and went back to the boat.

It takes about 4 hours to get across to Victoria. We didn't get in till 10.30 p.m. – that was on Tuesday Sept. 19th – and went straight to the hotel (another C.P.R. one) and to bed.

Sept. 27th

I will go on with this while we are waiting – by the Lakeside – to start.

The usual rush began at Victoria.[428] In the morning of last Wednesday we were met in the Hotel by the ordinary people (with a sprinkling of B.C. officials as well) and taken off to see farms, poultry yards, shipbuilding yards etc. etc., for the whole of the morning. However, the trip was pleasant enough and Victoria is certainly a very jolly town – more homelike, indeed, than most of the places which we have come across. It has nice houses and beautiful gardens, and its public buildings are not too huge or gaudy. This seems the place to say that one feature about British Columbia would please you all at home exceedingly. All the favourite English flowers – sweet peas, asters, chrysanthemums, hydrangeas and so on – were blooming luxuriantly and with the most brilliant colours. In fact I have never seen anything to compare with the blaze of flower colour in some of the gardens. We were told too that Vancouver Island is a great place for growing bulbs – likely indeed to rival Holland. From personal observation, I think there is a lot in it.

To go back to our doings – we finished our inspection of Victoria, went back to a public lunch at the hotel (from which, I am thankful to say, I escaped just before the speeches) and afterwards settled down to a couple of days very strenuous taking of evidence. We must have had at least 30 witnesses before the full Commission – to say nothing of all and sundry who came to see Lorimer on mining questions. You can imagine that by the time we left – that is last Friday afternoon – I was pretty well exhausted.

The net result was that with the exception of the first morning one saw scarcely anything of Victoria. We had, however, two interludes from work – the first was on Thursday at lunch time when we went to a lunch, given by an institution called the 'Rotary Club', at which all the members present (not we I am thankful to say) had to introduce themselves in rhymes of not more than 4 lines, with a penalty of 25 cents for not doing so. The result was amusing, and in some cases very good. One of the rules of the Club is that there is only one representative of each profession, so that there is no fear of repetition. This incident was followed by a speech from a 'Cinema' man, touring British Columbia in search of a suitable 'movies' school, and the speech in turn by some 'patter' from two members of a touring music hall party. Altogether a refreshing episode.

The second interlude was on Thursday evening. We went out by launch to have a look at the harbour, and then on to Esquimault, the naval base, three miles or so away, where there were two submarines

---

428. The Commissioners, meeting in the Board of Trade Offices, packed the questioning of 37 witnesses into three days, Wednesday September 20 to Friday September 22. Victoria, the capital of British Columbia, began as a Hudson's Bay Company trading post in 1842 and named as a defiantly loyal (and anti-American?) gesture. It was boosted by gold finds in the colony in the 1850s and 1860s. By 1911 the population had reached 31,660, and about 65,000 by 1921. Its Parliament Buildings were locally designed and built in grey stone in 1894–98. Vancouver Island had been formed into a British colony out of Hudson's Bay Company territory in 1849, prior to its merger with the mainland into British Columbia in 1866.

Esquimault Harbour, British Columbia, H.M. Ships at Naval Station.
Postcard dated 27 March 1912

visible, and a light cruiser repairing – also some 9.2 inch guns on the forts outside which recalled Milford Haven![429] Otherwise there is not very much except a little shipbuilding yard, run by Yarrows, the Clydeside firm, and, just outside the Dockyard, a public house on the English model – oddly reminiscent of an English village. We landed at Esquimault, and walked back to Victoria – at least I did. It was the first considerable exercise for some weeks.

Friday afternoon saw us on the move again. We finished off the evidence with rather a rush, and went off to Vancouver by boat, the first move in the homeward direction. We got to Vancouver on Friday evening, just in time for dinner and bed, and started the same old game of evidence on Saturday morning, not even having the respite of Saturday afternoon.[430] Again, though, we had an interlude. We had a look at the harbour by launch after the sittings were over on Saturday

---

429. Until 1905 Esquimault had been the base of the Royal Navy's Pacific Squadron, but this had been closed as part of the strategical reorganisation required by the growing challenge from other European fleets. It became instead the Pacific headquarters of the Royal Canadian Navy, such as it was. (Halifax was its Atlantic base.) Milford Haven was a port in south-west Wales whose forts commanded the entrance to Pembroke and a Royal Navy base.
430. Meeting in the Board of Trade Offices, 11 witnesses were questioned on Saturday September 23 and 10 more on Monday September 25.

afternoon. One's impressions of the goodness of the harbour were confirmed, but it suffers from two things. First, most of the frontage belongs to the C.P.R. – so that it can practically control development, and very naturally looks after its own interests first. Secondly, the Harbour Commission, which is supposed to supervise, is a body, it seems, whose members owe their appointment to politics. Consequently its value is by no means what it might be. The Chairman, to whom I talked a good deal, seemed distinctly 'doddery'.

Monday was a repetition of Saturday, so far as evidence went – but on Sunday I did get away for a little. Having disposed of all the members of the party, I went off 'on my own', had a look round the outskirts of Vancouver, and then went by electric tram to the mouth of the Fraser River, the celebrated river of British Columbia, which comes out some ten miles to the south of the city. There is a 'delta' there, and very fertile country – largely, as far as one could judge, looked after by Orientals.[431]

I went on to New Westminster, a few miles up the river, a town which wanted to rival Vancouver as the biggest city in British Columbia, but unfortunately failed. The result is rather sad. There is no doubt a certain amount of trade and shipping but the place looks dead. There is an Opera House, for instance, shut up. There are several biggish houses, standing deserted. There are 'town lots' innumerable waiting occupants.[432]

I got tea in the town, and returned to Vancouver by another car, a journey which revealed the fact that the site of Vancouver has been planned with streets, parks etc. for a distance of say 12 miles by 12. True, most of the streets don't yet exist, or, if they do, are grassgrown! Still, no doubt the speculators sold endless 'lots', miles out from the present centre, and retired on the proceeds.

Altogether one can't but feel utterly disgusted at the Western Canadian boom and its results. I don't think, in all our travels, we have seen a country so naturally beautiful as British Columbia. I am certain

---

431. Chinese immigrants had been attracted to British Columbia first by the gold strikes on the Fraser River (many moved up from California) and then by employment prospects on the railways. Several remained as farmers and market gardeners. There were about 2000 Chinese in British Columbia by 1871. But further Oriental immigrants to this Anglo-Saxon settlement were not welcomed: on arrival they were subject to a $500 head tax from 1904. However, it required the Chinese Immigration Act of 1923, not repealed until 1947, to stop their entry altogether.

432. New Westminster, now incorporated into Greater Vancouver, was founded in 1859. It even served briefly in the 1860s as the capital of British Columbia. In 1911 it had a population of just 13,199.

that we have not found one more deplorably dealt with by man. I suppose the Province will recover in time. Gradually the land will ease down to its proper value or something like it, and the 'concessions' will revert to the Government because they haven't been worked. Meanwhile, the Government is practically bankrupt, the cities are burdened with debt, and full of unsuccessful speculators. If British Government can't do better than this, one wonders whether it is really any better than German!

> Best love
> Ever your affectionate son
> E. J. Harding

DOMINIONS ROYAL COMMISSION
Banff Springs Hotel
Banff
Alberta
October 1st 1916

My dearest Mother,

It seems but yesterday that I finished my last letter. However, here is Sunday again, and I suppose I must begin another. We have been having what is supposed to be an 'off' day here today, but as you may imagine it has been spent very largely in work.

I think I brought my last letter down to the time when we left Vancouver. I omitted to mention one incident, which constitutes an addition to our experiences. On Monday we had to go to a 'Canadian Club' lunch at Vancouver, given in one of the big rooms in the Hotel. It is a ceremony where you eat indifferent food for one half hour, and listen to more indifferent speeches for another. Imagine my (if not our) horror at finding that the Commission as guests of honour were to be seated at a long table raised up high – about 6ft above the level of the rest of the hall. I never knew what it felt like before to be a beast being fed. Now I have more than an inkling. I even heard whispers of a comparison with a famous Leonardo picture – but I will leave you to guess at that.[433]

At Vancouver our numbers got swelled. Sinclair turned up from New Zealand, and Langerman and his wife from South Africa. Result, more

---

433. *The Last Supper* by Leonardo da Vinci (1452–1519) was painted in the 1490s as a fresco in the dining hall of the monastery of Santa Maria delle Grazie in Milan: it had much deteriorated by Harding's lifetime, but it was known also from several early copies. The figures are seated around a raised table.

trouble for the already overworked staff. However, neither member is really troublesome, and we have got on all right so far.

We had enough to 'split up' slightly at Vancouver. Lorimer took the route to the south, through the mining districts of British Columbia. If you will look at the map you will find places, almost on the United States border, called Greenwood and Grand Forks and Trail. He visited all those, in company with one of the mining officials of the Province, and according to his account had a very interesting time. He returned up the Arrow lakes and joined the main party at Revelstoke, just west of the Selkirks.[434] His chief disability seems to have been the condition of the hotels. It is one of the districts where you don't put out your boots for cleaning at night if you are really anxious to see them again in the morning!

The rest of us left Vancouver on Tuesday morning, bound for the Okanagan valley, the chief fruit district of British Columbia. We have a baggage car, as we had coming out, also a private car, the *Lake Agnes*, which is to take us all the way to Toronto. She is quite comfortable, having 'seven compartments and a drawing-room': in other words, eight separate living and sleeping rooms instead of the horrible arrangements which you generally find in the Trans-Canadian Trains. But she hasn't a kitchen or a dining room such as we had on the *Natalia* – nor has she those extremely intelligent white boys whom we had as servants going out, only a rather solemn black porter.

However, we are pretty happy on the whole. Our first day's journey took us as far as Sicamous, where we arrived at 10 p.m. on Tuesday and were 'unhitched' and put in a siding for the night.

It is a most interesting journey – first up the lower Fraser valley – then up the Thompson river – and so to a many tentacled lake (Lake Shuswarp), *vide* the map on which is Sicamous.[435]

For a good deal of the way the country is extremely bare, in fact it would be exactly like South Africa if it weren't for the rivers flowing down. There are occasional 'oases' of cultivation, and now and then a little settlement, but for the most part only grandeur and solitude.

Sicamous is nothing but a junction on the lake with a mountain hotel. But the lake is very pleasant – and the hotel comfortable, and we enjoyed both.

---

434. A railway linked these mining towns with the Canadian Pacific Railway at Hope in the west and at Revelstoke in the north. Lorimer gathered written evidence during his tour, Monday September 25 to Wednesday September 27.
435. Shuswap Indians occupied a reservation to the west of the lake.

Wednesday morning saw us on the move again, but we had only a 2 hours' journey, and reached Vernon, near the head of the Okanagan valley, by lunch time. There we put up for the night at the best local hotel (though 'very moderate' is the best) had a look round in the afternoon and held a session in the Court House in the evening.

The Okanagan valley is very surprising. It looks quite barren – yellowish soil on the 'ranges', i.e. the hill sides, and very little vegetation. But when irrigated (and there are irrigation ditches lying all the way along the valley sides) the soil becomes extremely productive, and grows apples to perfection. There are thousands and thousands of acres (including the big Coldstream estate first started by Lord Aberdeen) all planted in apples. Our visit was just at the picking time, and we found operations in full swing.[436]

Vernon, the town, is also of interest because it possesses an internment camp and is also a military centre. We had a look at the internment camp – chiefly notable perhaps because 12 prisoners escaped the other day, and only three were caught! It looked well kept enough, and I saw one small 'apartment' away from all the rest where a professional pianist was keeping his hand in! We also paid a visit to the Camp, and were shown over by the Commandant, exercises in physical drill, bayonet fighting, and even bombing, being given for our benefit. The atmosphere was not unlike Lydd, and the men looked particularly healthy.[437]

The 'session' in the evening wasn't particularly exciting. The main item of interest was the President of the local Board of Trade, who kept a hardware shop in the town, and was blessed, or cursed, with only one good eye. He had signed a Memorandum on the Fruit Industry which was being put in as evidence, but was, apparently, desperately afraid of being hauled in to answer questions on a subject of which he knew

---

436. The Okanagan Valley was much favoured by 'Gentlemen Emigrants', often of English public school background, who often tried, and often failed, to reproduce the idealised lifestyle of the English country gentlemen. Lord Aberdeen (1847–1934) had been Canada's Governor-General 1893–98: he bought property in the valley in 1890, led the shift from cattle ranching to fruit growing which others followed, and launched a company in 1906 designed to attract upper-middle-class Britons to this tasteful form of farming.

437. During the First World War enemy aliens in Canada were interned if they were thought to pose a threat to national security: 8579 people, mainly from Austria-Hungary and Germany, were gathered into 24 camps. Lydd, in Sussex, England, close to Hastings, contained a military camp: the explosive 'lyddite' was developed at its experimental ranges.

nothing. He, therefore, flitted disconsolately in the passage outside occasionally giving the good eye a look in.[438]

We spent Thursday in travelling down the Okanagan valley – partly by motor car, partly by lake steamer. It was really a delightful day, and we were blessed with very good weather. We inspected orchards and packing houses, canning factories and what not. I, personally, even did a little manual labour for once and assisted in dismantling an exhibit at a just finished agricultural show.

The whole valley is as pleasing as any place we have seen. It has the advantage of lake and hill scenery as well as of extensive cultivation. If you were to substitute apple trees for vines on the shores of the Lake of Zurich, there would be quite a good analogy.

We spent the night – at a place called Penticton at the lower end of the valley – on the lake steamer which was to bring us back to Vernon next day. Friday, at lunch time, saw us back in Vernon. Thence we motored to Armstrong, a place rather further north, and famous for its vegetables. There we visited another Agricultural Show – and Foster was persuaded (or rather not much persuading was needed) to make a speech which lasted so long that the train had to wait for him.

We got back to Sicamous at 5.30 p.m., had dinner there, and slept again in the *Lake Agnes*. At 5 in the morning we were hitched on to the east-bound train, and started on our journey through the Selkirks and Rockies to Banff.

Car *Lake Agnes*
Regina Station
Oct. 7th

I haven't had a moment to complete this letter – and it is now Saturday, and another one will be due to begin tomorrow! I will try to finish this off (we are just waiting to start for Winnipeg) by describing our journey through the Rockies to Banff last Saturday.

It is a wonderful journey, much more wonderful than the outward journey through the Yellowhead Pass. We also had a good day for it – not a perfectly clear one, but a mixture of snowstorms, clouds and bright sunshine. So sometimes we could see the Peaks, and sometimes only guess at them.

---

438. Altogether, 7 people gave evidence in the Court House in Vernon on Wednesday September 27.

The route first climbs up the Selkirks – it has some trouble to do so, and has to make several turns of this kind to get up to the top. Then it drops quite a lot to the Columbia River – and a place called Golden upon it – rather an attractive name I think. Then it climbs again up the Kicking Horse River to the top of the Rockies. Here it goes through two circular tunnels à la St. Gothard. Finally it reaches the Great Divide again which is suitably marked – and plunges down again towards the prairies, Banff being a station on the east slope.[439]

One's impression going westward was that the Rockies were an incident. Coming east they certainly seemed an obstacle and a very serious one. I am not surprised that for a good many years it seemed inconceivable that a railway could get across. We got down to Banff at about 6.30 p.m. – to find bitter cold and quite a lot of snow. But our experiences there I will leave for the next letter.

> Best love
> Ever your affectionate son
> E. J. Harding

> DOMINIONS ROYAL COMMISSION
> Car *Lake Agnes*
> Fort William
> Oct. 12th 1916

My dear Eva,

Our arrival at Banff ended my last letter. Today we are at Fort William right through the Prairie Provinces, and the Rockies are almost forgotten! I must hurry up – or else they will be quite crowded out. Well, Banff is an extremely jolly place for a Sunday. It is well on the East slope of the Rockies – that is within an hour or two of the foothills on the prairie side – but it has high snow mountains all round, a river (the Bow) forcing its way through a remarkable cleft, a National Park – i.e. some thousands of square miles sacred to game and denied to the hunter – and a collection of Buffaloes, Yak, Rocky Mountain goats, and other queer animals which aren't usually seen on our side. Last, but not least, it has hot sulphur springs with a natural temperature at the source of 115° – and suitable baths for enjoying the water to the full. In fact the place, including the odour, is distinctly reminiscent of Rotorua.

There is a big C.P.R. Hotel, where we stayed, rather tired out (the hotel, I mean, not necessarily ourselves!) after a full and long season, but

Banff, Alberta, C.P.R. Hotel and Sulphur Mt.   *Postcard from 1921 collection*

still comfortable enough. The weather was bad – it snowed a good deal, and was cold to thawy. However, we bathed in the hot baths (the experience being that one's body was hot and one's head cold, as the baths are not covered in). We visited the buffaloes, we admired the mountains, and generally enjoyed our Sunday.[440] On Monday we were on the road again. Really our party now is something between 'Commercial travellers' and 'Movies'!

At Calgary, our next stop, the weather was disgusting, but the people very pleasant. The two facts counterbalanced, as owing to the weather one didn't mind so much being entertained. We had a dinner from the Board of Trade on Monday, another Canadian Club lunch on Tuesday (more talking by Foster – you can assume that that happened five or six times at each place, if I don't mention it again) and various other entertainments or would-be ones. A good deal of work – but not excessive,

---

439. The pass reaches a height of 1639 m. The spiral tunnels, eliminating earlier steeper gradients, were completed in 1909.

440. Banff remained a tiny settlement, only about 1400 people in 1921, but it boasted C.P.R.'s magnificent Banff Springs Hotel. The hot springs had been noted by the explorer Sir James Hector (1834–1907) in 1858, just before he made the first European crossing through the Kicking Horse Pass. The C.P.R. president George Stephen (1829–1921) called the spot Banff after his native county in Scotland. The Rocky Mountains Park was dedicated in 1887.

Calgary, Alberta, Eighth Avenue looking West, from First Street East.
Postcard franked 24 November 1909

fortunately, and what there was well prepared beforehand. That is about the tale except that on the day we left, when the sun had returned, we had a motor drive round the town and the outskirts, and visited a big dam where the water is impounded to irrigate districts nearby, a home for returned soldiers, a Government elevator, and a stock-yard and canning plant. A variegated afternoon, in fact.

Calgary is a pleasant town – not remarkable except for the wonderful view of the Rockies from the top of the Palliser Hotel where we stayed. That really is worth seeing. It is exactly the same kind of view as you get from Ste Croix of the Alps.[441]

As Western towns now go, Calgary seemed fairly prosperous. Of land booms we heard not very much. Of the oil boom of 1914 a good deal. Oil is suspected in the neighbourhood. It may or may not be there. Anyhow, none has been found yet in quantity. Yet in the early part of 1914, people were flinging money through brokers' windows in the effort to get oil-shares – with no name attached. I was told of one company whose shares were originally 25 cents each. They went up, within a week, to 75 cents. They are now, at a high estimate, worth 1½ cents.[442]

Truly, the west must have been a great place three years ago.

We had intended to make a stop at an Indian Reserve village on our way east from Calgary to Regina, but the weather was too much for us. The snow got thicker as we came east, and on the prairie there were 4 inches at least. Consequently the roads were impassable.

Not daunted, however, we got the C.P.R. to drop us at Medicine Hat for an hour or two, so that we could see the natural gas wells there.[443] It was an interesting experience, but meant turning out at 7.30 a.m. for an hour's motor drive with a temperature in the neighbourhood of 20°. The wells are 3 miles or so from the town. The gas comes out with a pressure of, I think, 550 lbs to the square inch, and when they uncork it the noise is like several engines 'blowing off' at once. One wonders if some day Medicine Hat will blow off too. Meanwhile, as you may imagine, gas is cheap. The streets are kept lighted all day – because that is cheaper than the labour of turning them out.

Medicine Hat was our last stop in Alberta. By Thursday evening (that is October 7th) we were in Regina, the capital of Saskatchewan. Our prairie journey to reach it, which was made in daylight, was perhaps a trifle monotonous. One cannot keep continued enthusiasm over 150 miles of flat country covered with a pall of snow. But I am glad to have seen the prairie under snow. One gets an inkling of what it is probably like in winter.

Queen's Hotel
Toronto
Oct. 15th

I go on with this letter after the conclusion of our heavy travelling. We are here, we hope, for a week or thereabouts. But the work promises, as usual, to be heavy, so I will make an attempt to finish up this evening.

---

441. Calgary began as a North West Mounted Police post, but became truly established when the C.P.R. chose to route their line through the settlement. A rush of settlers followed. The population reached 43,704 in 1911 and 65,514 in 1916. The Palliser Hotel, 298 rooms, was built by the C.P.R. The Commission gathered evidence from 17 witnesses during its three days Monday October 2 to Wednesday October 4: sessions were held in the City Council Chamber.

442. Oil deposits near Calgary certainly did exist. They had been modestly tapped for about thirty years before major discoveries in 1947 turned the region between Calgary and Edmonton into Canada's principal oil-producing district.

443. Medicine Hat's natural gas wells were its principal claim to fame, discovered in the 1880s, although Baedeker (1907) prefers to note that 'Picturesque Indians haunt the station, selling buffalo horns and other curiosities'. The population in 1911 was just 5608, in 1916 9272 and in 1921 it was 9575.

Regina, Saskatchewan, South Street and King's Hotel.

Postcard from 1921 collection

We reached (or nearly reached) Regina to find that the hotel, to which we had been recommended as the best, was quite unknown and did not appear in the Hotel Books. So we had to change at the last moment, and finally went to the hotel which was *said* by the locals to be the best in the place. Its level may be gauged from the Rules hung up in the rooms, a copy of which – if I can persuade Bridgman to make it – I shall add to this letter. Here I will only say that it was ultra commercial-travellery. By the way, the scale of prices in Western Canada may be roughly gauged by the fact that the cost at the King's Hotel, Regina, $4 per day – the lowest we have yet struck in Canada – is roughly the same as at the Oriental Hotel, Melbourne, the best hotel in Australia.

Regina itself is the Capital of Saskatchewan. It has beautiful Parliament Buildings, erected at immense expense, and no doubt not yet paid for, about 1½ miles from the town. It has a Grand Trunk Pacific Hotel in embryo, of which only the foundations now exist. (Tightness of money prevents progress.) It has an enormous oil refining plant now being put up by the Imperial Oil Company of Canada (the Canadian Branch of the Standard Oil Co.). Otherwise it is not much but a western country town – the centre of an immense wheat-growing district and an important distributing centre.[444]

The people were moderate to fair – not so nice as at Calgary. We had one amusing witness – a member of the Provincial Government who preferred not to be cited as such! We had one man (fortunately dealt with entirely by Lorimer) who was prepared to make bricks out of any kind of straw, in other words to harness any form of natural resource from clay to the wind, and turn it to commercial use. Otherwise the citizens whom we came across were 'inconspicuous' (I think that is the proper term). There was a desperately dull reception at the City Hall on our arrival, there was a Canadian Club lunch the following day. For the rest – the usual crowd of witnesses – unpacking – packing and off.

One incident, however, to relieve the monotony. On the last afternoon Lorimer and I were taken out by motor car to see the Imperial Oil Company's works aforesaid. As I said, there had been snow to a considerable depth on the prairie, and this was just melting, adding inches of mud to an already very soft road. We reached the works with difficulty, the mud sometimes coming up to the hub of the wheels, inspected them, and in returning tried to come along a newly laid tram-line to avoid further trouble. Unfortunately, just as a tram was approaching, our wheels got stuck between two sleepers, and we could move neither forwards nor backwards. We only got out finally by borrowing a large chain from a passing railway engine, hitching one end to the car springs and the other to the tram, and making the tram back till we reached a level road. We upset the local tram service somewhat but fortunately caught our train.

We left Regina on Saturday evening October 7th, travelled all night, and were in Winnipeg on Sunday morning. There we stopped till the following Wednesday evening.

Winnipeg is a beautiful town, and we had the best of weather for it, crisp air, bright sunshine, warm days and coldish nights. It has the advantage of two rivers, the Assiniboine and the Red, which meet just

---

444. Regina was entirely a creation of the C.P.R., marking the point where the line crossed a creek and chosen, just possibly, because the Lieutenant-Governor of the then North West Territories owned land there. The railway arrived in 1882. Princess Louise, wife of the Governor-General, rechristened the settlement after her mother, Queen Victoria. In 1901 the population was only 2249, but it rose to 30,213 by 1911, fell to 26,127 in 1916 but recovered to about 40,000 by 1921. It was selected as the capital of Saskatchewan, the other province created out of the division of part of the North West Territories in 1905. The Parliament Buildings, built in limestone, went up 1908–12, at a cost of $1½ million. In 1911 Saskatchewan had a population of 492,432 (7% of Canada's total), but this had risen to 687,835 in 1916 and to 843,450 by 1921. The Commissioners met in the City Council Chamber in Regina and saw 23 witnesses during Friday and Saturday, October 6 and 7.

C. S. Co. 7 —

MAIN STREET, WINNIPEG, LOOKING NORTH FROM PORTAGE AVENUE.

Winnipeg, Manitoba, Main Street, looking North from Portage Avenue.

Postcard

above it and flow down to Hudson Bay. A good many of the private houses are built on the banks of the Assiniboine and very nice they look. (Winnipeg itself is on the left bank of the Red River – opposite it, on the right bank, is St. Boniface, a French settlement with a Cathedral, Convent etc. of quite respectably good architecture.) The mercantile houses, banks etc. are really remarkably fine considering the age of the place – hardly 30 years, I suppose.[445]

Winnipeg had the usual land boom, but the effects are not so apparent – I suppose because the whole of the prairie provinces are really tributary to it, that is, practically the whole of the grain trade outwards, and the stores inwards from and to the prairie provinces go through the place. It certainly looked more prosperous than any of the cities we had seen for some time.

---

445. Winnipeg began as the centre of the struggling early 19th-century Red River Settlement, but in 1870 it became the capital of the province of Manitoba. As elsewhere, future prosperity and an enlarged population were dependent upon the arrival of the railway. It became a C.P.R. maintenance and repair centre, an increasingly important commercial focus for the marketing of wheat and a distribution centre for new immigrants to the prairies. The population in 1881 was only 7985, but it grew to 136,035 by 1911, about 163,000 by 1916 and to 178,364 by 1921.

Winnipeg, 'The Fort
Garry, Grand Trunk
Pacific's New Hotel'.
Postcard

Our time in Winnipeg was not unduly strenuous – mainly because the local Board of Trade (which was supposed to have the arrangements in hand) was clearly an effete body, and had taken very little trouble. One result of this was, however, that we had to create a good deal of the evidence ourselves – and this we did rather successfully by arranging to have a sitting at the Winnipeg Grain Exchange, i.e. the place where all the dealings in wheat go on. We first visited the 'pit', i.e. the room where all the sales are made. The noise was hideous, and one was glad to get out of it. Then we adjourned to the Council Chamber of the Exchange, and there the actual evidence was heard. This was really interesting.[446]

There was a dinner or so to be attended, and one or two more functions which I managed to avoid. In fact I actually found time to get my hair cut, a process weeks overdue! Otherwise there is not much more to be recorded, except that the hotel (the Fort Galsy)[447] was particularly

446. In fact, the Commissioners managed to see 35 witnesses in Winnipeg from Monday October 9 to Wednesday October 11, meeting first in the Legislative Council Chamber and later in the Grain Exchange.
447. Harding means Hotel Fort Garry (300 rooms), which took its name from the early frontier post on the site.

comfortable and quiet, and that we had a good look, as usual, on the day
of leaving, at the city and surroundings in general and particularly at the
Immigration Depot, through which pass all the immigrants from Europe
on their way to the west.

The arrangements are admirable – that is for the British who are kept
apart. As for the others, Eastern European and what not, the place is not
what you would call luxurious. Just bare boards to lie down on, and
something that might quite well be a hose pipe for ablutions. From what
I hear though, and from what one has seen, and smelt, in the colonist
cars on the railways, the limitations are necessary and advisable! [448]

Another night's journey, on Wednesday, took us to Fort William. It was
very shaky, and nobody slept very well. However, we were in for a full
day's work on Thursday. To Fort William, and Port Arthur its neighbour,
comes all the grain from the west. There it is unloaded into elevators, and
loaded again (most of it) into steamers for the Great Lakes. [449] All the
unloading and loading arrangements were duly inspected by us – also the
harbour (it seems queer to think of big harbours – but then look at the size
of these lakes!) and one of the grain ships. Then we were hurried off to a
lunch given by the Mayor of Fort William – where incidentally the
waitresses were the ladies of the place, a new form of entertainment to a
jaded Royal Commission. Then there were other festivities which, as I
escaped them on the plea of work, I needn't particularize further.

Only one small story to show how things go in Canada. Fort William
and Port Arthur, as befits neighbours (and rivals), are furiously jealous
of one another. To avoid bitterness, all the arrangements for our visit
had to be put into the hands of a third party, the Board of Grain
Commissioners, which is a Dominion Government concern!

---

448. The encouragement of other than British immigrants was highly
controversial: it was demanded by population-hungry prairie communities
and those hostile to the Imperial connection but deplored by British
Canadians further east who were more settled and more committed to the
Empire. In fact, in 1913, immigrants to Canada totalled 402,432, of
whom only 150,542 (37%) came from the United Kingdom: 107,530
entered from the U.S.A., 24,722 were Italians, 30,107 came from Russia,
and many others arrived from Eastern Europe. The Canadian government
ran the Immigration Depot at the C.P.R. station in Winnipeg.

449. Fort William (population 16,499 in 1911) and Port Arthur (11,200)
began as key staging posts by Lake Superior on the fur trade route to the
north west, but they became more important to the wheat business with
the settlement of the prairies. The two rivals were combined in 1970 into
the city of Thunder Bay.

'Fort William, Ogilvie Flour Mills Co. Ltd., grinding floor, sifting from coarse to fine'. *Photograph, Fisher Collection, 1908*

We left on Thursday night, and travelled practically continuously till we got to Toronto on Saturday morning. For details of the country, I refer you to my letter (I have forgotten which) describing our journey from Cochrane to Winnipeg on the National Transcontinental. There is nothing to add or take away. The country (till close in to Toronto) is exactly the same – pinewoods, rivers, lakes.

And so we reached the last Capital of the last Province of the last Dominion to be visited by the Commission, and I feel just a little proud that I have seen them all!

> Best love
> > Your affectionate brother
> > > E. J. Harding

King's Hotel, Regina.
H.W. Shore, Manager
Rate of this room is 4.00 dollars per day
single.
Strictly American plan.
No credit on meals missed.
Any party staying after 8 p.m. will be charged for the night.

1. The proprietors will not be responsible for baggage left in rooms. Guests will give notice at the office of their departure and their baggage will be taken care of.
2. Guests are respectively notified that money or valuables can be left at the office for safe keeping, otherwise the management will not be responsible for their loss.
3. Persons engaging rooms will be charged from the time they are placed at their disposal, whether they are occupied or not.
4. Dogs are not allowed in bedrooms or any other part of the hotel.
5. All damage done to furniture or articles in the room, other than reasonable wear, will be charged to the occupant of the room.
6. Loud talking, dancing, loafing in halls and rooms positively forbidden.
7. All bills must be paid weekly.
8. Guests will please turn out lights on retiring or leaving room.
9. No lady or gentleman is allowed to have friends of the opposite sex in their rooms, a parlour being provided for that purpose.
10. No cooking, washing, or ironing allowed in rooms.
11. Guests will please lock their doors on retiring or leaving their rooms, and on departure leave the key at the office.
12. Guests without trunks or baggage are required to pay in advance.
13. Any neglect on the part of the employees should be reported to the manager.
14. There are lavatories and public baths on each floor, and any violation of customs will not be tolerated by the management.
15. Please do not put unclean parcels or lie on the bed with your shoes on.

DEAD BEAT ACT

'407b. Everyone is guilty of an offence and liable upon summary conviction to a fine of one hundred dollars and costs or three months imprisonment who fraudulently obtains food lodging or other accommodation at any hotel or inn, or at any lodging, boarding, or eating house.'
'2. Proof that a person obtained food, lodging or other accommodation at any hotel or inn, or lodging, boarding, or eating house, and did not pay therefore, and made any false or fictitious show or pretence of having baggage, or had any false or pretended baggage, or surreptitiously removed or attempted to remove his baggage or any material part thereof, or absconded or surreptitiously left the premises or knowingly made any false statement to obtain credit or time for payment, or offer any worthless cheque, or draft or security in payment of such food, lodging, or other accommodation, shall be prima facie evidence of fraud.'

The Clifden Inn
Niagara Falls
October 22nd 1916

My dearest Mother,

This letter will have to be a short one – first because I haven't much time to write, secondly because we have been comparatively quiet for the last week (that is except for the last two days) we have been at Toronto since I ended my last letter.[450]

The Queen's Hotel, Toronto, where we stayed, was very 'Victorian' compared with the palatial hotels put up by the C.P.R. and Grand Trunk. That is to say, it had started as a small place 50 years ago at least, and had been added to gradually. But it was comfortable enough (except that for the first two nights I had a room which faced all the trams of the city and had to change it because of the noise) and the service, compared to the hotels of the West, pretty good. I found that one of the waiters in our room was an ex-subporter of Balliol.[451] That reminds me to tell you of a story of the hotel at Vernon B.C. which I think I omitted before. The waitress at dinner enquired of Lady Langerman, after she had had her soup, what she would like next, and on hearing (I have forgotten what she ordered) further enquired whether she wanted a 'starter' or a 'filler'. I leave it to you to interpret – but perhaps it would have been even more appropriate if she had added a third category viz a 'stretcher'.

To go back to Toronto, we had four days' sittings at the City Council Chamber presided over by Bateman whom we found on our arrival from the West. It is pleasant to have him for some reasons – chief amongst them that speeches are reduced to a minimum! – but as a Chairman he is distinctly inferior to Foster. With Bateman came Mitchell, and he has

---

450. Toronto was founded in 1793 on land purchased from the local Indians and was settled particularly by United Empire Loyalists. It changed its name from York to Toronto in 1834, and developed rapidly as a major port on Lake Ontario, as a commercial centre and as the capital of Upper Canada, later Ontario. Its pink sandstone Parliament Buildings were erected 1888–92, at a cost of $1,300,000. Not even a massive fire in 1904 could arrest the city's progress. By 1911 it had a population of 376,538, making it second only in size to Montreal, and by 1921 of 512,812. According to Rupert Brooke, it was 'a clean-shaven, pink-faced, respectably dressed, fairly energetic, unintellectual, passably sociable, well-to-do, public-school-and-'varsity sort of city'. Ontario was one of the founding provinces of the dominion: by 1911 it was also the most populated, 2,523,274 (35% of the national total).

451. Difficult to escape from Oxford: Balliol is a college of the university.

Hamilton, Ontario, James Street looking South.
Postcard dated 23 September 1914

Otherwise, the city is a pleasant, and obviously prosperous, one – built between a ridge some 200 ft. high (locally known as the Hamilton Mountain) and Lake Ontario. We found an excellent hotel (American I regret – but then so are a good many of the factories), a very kindly reception from Mayor and City Council – and (I need scarcely add) the inevitable Civic Lunch.

Chateau Laurier
Ottawa
Oct. 24th

I find an English mail is said to be leaving today – so I will hurriedly close up this letter – leaving Niagara for the next one. You will see, though, from the address, that we have completed yet another stage of our journey!

Best love
Ever your affectionate son
E. J. Harding

Ritz Carlton Hotel
Montreal
Oct. 29th 1916

My dear Eva,

Whether or not I sent a previous diary letter from this address or not, I can't remember. Anyhow, here we are back again, and all our railway travelling over unless we choose, as likely enough we may, to go down to

'Ontario Fruit, St. Catherine's, Local Horticultural Society'.
Photograph, Fisher Collection, 1908

Quebec by rail instead of water. I am not a little relieved – now that the major part of the work is over, I confess to feeling that it has been rather a strain!

When I stopped the last letter – in a hurry I remember – we had just left Hamilton and were on the way to Niagara. There we journeyed through orchards of pears, peaches and vines (vineyards, as you would understand the term, is not really the word to be used). It occurs to me to mention that though grapes do grow, and grow well, in the district, they have a most unpleasant flavour. The whole country was very pleasant-looking, and rather reminiscent of Kent – closely settled (very closely, indeed) in comparison with most of Ontario.

I suppose most people expect to reach Niagara Falls station and find themselves unable to speak for the noise of the water. At any rate that was rather my idea. The reality is a rather unpleasant-looking town station, and a distinctly second rate street near by! The only sign of a world's wonder is a cantilever bridge just beyond the station, below which there appears to be a gorge. In fact, the gorge is the St. Lawrence (or rather the St. Lawrence flows in the gorge) and on the other side is the United States.

Niagara, Ontario, The Iron Bridge and *Maid of the Mist.*
Photograph, Fisher Collection, 1908

Some of us decided to walk up to the hotel – which turned out to be 1½ miles away.[457] Even the walk was not very exciting. True, there was the river flowing 150 ft. or so below. But it was perfectly placid, and the only sign of activity was several preposterous factories away on the American side of the river. What they produce I don't know.

Even the first sight of the Falls is not very impressive. There is the drop (but only 160 feet), and the mass of water, and the mist coming up from the pool, but one didn't feel particularly enthusiastic. The hotel (modelled on an English Inn and very comfortable indeed) was more attractive for the time being. After tea, I paid a visit to the United States (i.e. I crossed the bridge and came back again). Again, one was not impressed. On the other side is merely a tourist resort with all its unlovely appurtenances.

You will think that I, or in fact that we all, were disappointed. That isn't quite true. On Sunday we were taken (by various methods of conveyance including an aerial car) to see the whole gorge and its wonders. Only then did one realize how stupendous is the force coming over the Falls and through the chasm. We went down on the Canadian

---

457. He was perhaps wise to walk: Baedeker (1907) warns the unwary of 'the ... extortionate charges and impertinent behaviour of the Niagara hackmen'.

side on the top of the cliff, we came back on the American side, quite close down to the Rapids. We crossed the Whirlpool where the water makes a complete circle and then changes its direction thus (It takes half an hour, we were told, to complete the circle.) We saw the water coming down at various speeds – up to 27 miles an hour. Then we saw the mass of water above the falls proper, which perhaps is more striking even than that below. And finally – this was in the afternoon – we were shown over one of the power houses, which produces electricity by means of power generated by the river and then conveys it in various directions up to 200 miles.

By the time we had seen all these wonders, we were really impressed, and sorry to go.[458] If we had been asked the evening before what we thought of Niagara, and had felt at liberty to say what we thought, it would not have been complimentary! I won't worry you with unpleasant figures, but I think I am right in saying that 56,000 cubic feet of water *per second* are taken from the St. Lawrence above the falls, and used in developing power – and that already the users are crying out for more! True there are 1,000,000 cubic ft. or so per second left to come over still, but the experts say that if much more is taken the beauty of the Falls will be seriously impaired.

Who is to settle where to draw the line? I confess that where waterpower is concerned my sympathies lie mainly with the man who wants to use it. It is such a clean and nice system.

That's as may be. Meanwhile, the Canadians, anyhow, are doing their best to preserve the natural beauty of the place. They won't allow unsightly power stations near the Falls. They will allow no factories whatever. They have reserved a strip of land for national purposes for the whole length between Lake Erie and Lake Ontario. And at various points along this line they are constructing National Parks.

We left Niagara on Sunday evening. Monday morning found us in Ottawa. There we had three pretty strenuous days' sittings.[459] Then a morning 'clearing up', and off to Montreal on Thursday afternoon.

---

458. Harding was not alone in being forced to admit the impact upon him of the sight of the Falls. They had been known to Europeans since 1678, and this was now well-beaten tourist country. Nevertheless, Rupert Brooke wrote in July 1913: 'I'm so impressed by Niagara, I hoped not to be. But I horribly am'.

459. Between Monday October 23 and Wednesday October 25 the Commissioners dealt with 40 witnesses: sessions were held in the Carnegie Library.

At Ottawa, I was at work from 9 a.m. to midnight practically every day. There were rather long sittings, and when they were over, there were certain people in the Government service whom I simply *had* to see in connexion with the work of the Commission – Immigration Department and so forth. The consequence was, and rather an unfortunate one, that one really got very little of the atmosphere of a place which must be largely stocked with civil servants and politicians.[460] One could only judge by surface indications that things (I mean amongst the civil service) are much as at home only more so. Want of coordination, jealousy of Departments and Sub-Departments and all the rest of it were only too apparent. One job I had was to smooth two officials of the same Department, who each had prepared to come before the Commission without knowing that the other was coming too. They only found out the position when they arrived in the room, and stood glaring at one another!

There was a Ministerial lunch in honour of the Commission, and that was the only time that I saw any of the Ministers. On the whole they looked of fairly high class. I found myself between the Minister of Labour (who had spent the past 24 hours in settling a railway strike) and Dr. Roche, Minister of the Interior, with whom I had a long talk on immigration. Certainly the latter seemed sensible enough.[461]

On the last evening Mitchell and I had dinner with O'Hara, Deputy Minister of Trade and Commerce and our 'local officer'. We owe a good deal to him, and certainly he is very capable. He has a very pleasant wife and an attractive house. Altogether we really enjoyed ourselves.

Here I must stop again – Montreal must wait till next time.

> Ever your affectionate brother
> E. J. Harding

> DOMINIONS ROYAL COMMISSION
> *R.M.S. Missanabie*
> Nov. 14th 1916

My dear Father,

I had no time to write at Quebec, and I have been more or less on the sick list ever since we left there – that is to say, two days out, I developed a chill on the liver, and have been in bed on and off, and in the doctor's hands, ever since.

However, I hope that I am now getting over it. Today I am up and dressed, though somewhat weak. If this letter is more than usually dull, please ascribe the cause to physical debility!

We went back, as my last letter will have showed you, to our old quarters in Montreal. I remember that when we were there at the beginning of September the place seemed stuffy and the service bad. The second time, as the result no doubt of our experiences elsewhere, the hotel seemed quite fresh and the waiting quick!

But it was far too gay for war time – dances every night, card parties and the like. Which reminds me to say, if I haven't said it before, that the social atmosphere right through Canada is quite different to what it is at home. 3000 miles' distance and the newspaper conditions (the latter form a long story which I won't go into here) make all the change in the world.

As I think I told you before, the Ritz Carlton Hotel lies on the slopes of Mount Royal round which Montreal circles. The business quarter is some way away, and our sittings were held down there.[462] One consequence of that was that we had quite a respectable walk each day – a great change, and a considerable relief!

There was nothing of great note about our sittings in Montreal. We came across the heads of the big railways – who were interesting people, and one or two of the leading manufacturers, also attractive enough – but otherwise the witnesses were of a normal type. The Secretary of the Board of Trade was getting rather *passé* and anyhow was of a highly nervous temperament. We didn't think much of him. On the other hand he had a very pleasant and capable assistant – one Cook – with whom, I found, Cowell had fraternized when he was out in 1909.[463]

We spent our Saturday afternoon very pleasantly in going round the harbour and *inter alia* in inspecting the work and dry dock put up by Vickers not so very long ago. There they were repairing the *Carnarvon*,[464]

---

460. Rupert Brooke detected 'an atmosphere of Civil Servants about Ottawa'.

461. The Minister of Labour was Thomas Wilson Crothers (1850–1921): a lawyer by training, he was first elected in 1908 and served as Minister of Labour 1911–19. William Roche (1859–1937) practised medicine in Manitoba, was a member of the House of Commons 1896–1917 and served as Minister of the Interior 1912–17.

462. Sessions were held in the Board of Trade Council Chamber. Over four days from Friday October 27 to Tuesday October 31, 37 witnesses were called.

463. H.R. Cowell had been to Canada as the Colonial Office secretary of the Royal Commission on Trade Relations between Canada and the West Indies 1909–10.

464. *H.M.S. Carnarvon* was a Devonshire class armoured cruiser, 10,850 tons, 450 feet long, capable of 22 knots, armed with 7.5 inch and 6 inch guns and some smaller weapons, and carrying a complement of 655 officers and men. She was built in 1905–06, at a cost of nearly £900,000.

Montreal, Quebec Province, Harbour from Custom House.
Postcard dated 19 September 1912

a light cruiser. They were also making munitions on some considerable scale. Finally they were turning out 'submarine searchers', little craft for, I imagine, submarine work inshore, at the rate of one a day, and they had also a big plant for shipbuilding, though the only craft in evidence on it at the moment was a special type of dredger. We were told, though, that they had just completed an icebreaker for the Russian Government, then down the river on her trials.

You may be interested to read the following notice which we found put up – printed if you please – in the shops. Whether it does least credit to Vickers' tact, or to Canadian habits, I won't argue, but will just give it you as it is.

'If you spit on the floor at home, spit on the floor here; we like you to feel at home.'

I made friends with the Engineer of Montreal Harbour, Cowie by name, and went to dinner with him one night at his house, or rather flat, which I found to be full of old prints and maps of all kinds. Obviously, indeed, his taste in these directions was almost too much for his wife and family, not to say for the flat. They talked of moving for the sake of the prints! I had a very pleasant evening there, and met one of the heads of the Grand Trunk Railway and one of the partners in the Dominion

Recruits Learning Rifle Drill, Valcartier Camp.   *Postcard*

Bridge Company (another firm manufacturing munitions on a large scale), each with their respective wives.[465]

Incidentally one learned there (now I come to think of it, it was the first dinner at a private house in Canada that I had been to except at the O'Hara's house at Ottawa) that the casualty list of the C.E.F. is beginning to make its force felt in Montreal. One certainly would not have suspected it just by staying at the hotel.

We had an official dinner from the Board of Trade one evening which lasted till nearly midnight, and involved at least 7 different kinds of drinks! (This was the first occasion on which we felt the full effect of having got to the Province of Quebec! All the others are now 'dry' except British Columbia, and even that was practically dry so far as we were concerned, no doubt out of respect to Foster!)[466] We had also to go to a final Canadian Club lunch and hear yet another speech from Foster, this time for three-quarters of an hour! So our time was, as usual, fully

---

465. The manufacture of munitions was a substantial and lasting stimulus to Canadian heavy industry. During the course of the war some 66 million shells were produced. Production was organised by the Imperial Munitions Board, a branch of the British Ministry of Munitions which Lloyd George had created and inspired as its first minister in 1915–16.

466. As noted earlier, prohibition spread during the war.

occupied! The only other incident worth mentioning was a walk with Garnett, his daughter and a friend over Mount Royal on Sunday afternoon during which we inspected the local 'crematorium', a golf course and several suburbs.

Did I mention before that Garnett turned up for the last fortnight's sittings commencing at Ottawa? He came over to New York by (I think) an American boat, and is returning the same way. His daughter (one of the younger ones) was about 18, her friend a few years' older. Both fairly goodlooking, neither intensely attractive otherwise!

We left Montreal on Wednesday morning November 1st, and travelled down to Quebec on the right bank of the St. Lawrence. That is to say, we crossed the river at Montreal by bridge, and crossed back again at Levis (opposite Quebec) by ferry. It rained hard for most of the journey (about 5 hours) and anyhow the country was mostly flat and didn't look inspiring. The French *petite culture* was apparent throughout.[467]

We had heard before leaving Ottawa that the *Missanabie* was to be three days late in starting back. In fact, she hadn't reached Quebec on her way to Montreal when we arrived there.

So we were in no anxiety lest the time for our work at Quebec should be too short. As a matter of fact, we had done all we had to do (and that wasn't very much) by Friday evening. We spent the rest of the time (till Tuesday evening November 7th when the boat sailed) clearing up, making new acquaintances, and generally looking about.

Nov. 15th 1916

I will go on with this tonight – as I am still 'upstairs' or in other words in my cabin, and there isn't much to do. Still I think I am improving slowly!

We had to face in Quebec what we had never anywhere else – that is witnesses whose knowledge of English was very sketchy! We had to have a French shorthand-writer handy, though in fact his services weren't wanted.[468] Also at the various functions which we went to, the people

---

467. The term *petite culture* refers to the system of landholding which by the late 19th century was characteristic of French agriculture: small-scale farms owned and operated by peasant proprietors. This model was much referred to in Britain during the interminable discussions on the Irish land question. In French Canada, such farms often stretched down to narrow fronts on the banks of the St Lawrence.

468. The Commission met in the Provincial Parliament Buildings on Thursday and Friday November 2 and 3, and questioned 31 witnesses. With these

were mostly French, and Bateman had to essay making French speeches at which he is none too good.

Personally I found most of the people delightful, and so I think did we all. There is an air of leisureliness, and also indeed of culture, about Quebec and its citizens which we had found nowhere else in Canada.

Fortunately we only had one dinner to attend, and that was at the very old and very comfortable Garrison Club, the old Army Club of Quebec, which would in any case have made it bearable. But there was the further excitement that one or two of the speeches had a distinctly 'racial' flavour, and it looked at one moment as if there might be a storm. Racial feeling runs very high in Quebec![469] Fortunately, however, it blew over, and the only real episode was that of the man who, when the speeches came on, leaned over the table and commenced to snore – a great tribute to the Commission's oratory! I didn't say, but you will no doubt have understood, that Quebec, like Montreal, is not dry!

We went out on Sunday afternoon to pay a visit to St Anne de Beaupres, the Lourdes of Canada and about 20 miles from Quebec by electric railway down the St. Lawrence. The atmosphere of the place – it is just a village with big church, monastery etc. – was very French and very Catholic, and we found the church itself much more attractive and less tawdry than might have been expected. In fact parts of it are really beautiful – though discarded crutches are, perhaps, too apparent for the cynic or the connoisseur.[470]

---

sessions, dutifully recorded as Days 156 and 157 in the official record, the Dominions Royal Commission concluded its formal gathering of evidence. On this final journey, evidence had been obtained from 323 witnesses over 31 days. In addition, much written information had been collected and numerous visits of inspection made: Lorimer and Langerman, for example, were in Southern Quebec on November 3, inspecting the asbestos mines at Thetford.

469. Quebec, of course, still retained its French language, its distinct culture and its different loyalties, in spite of English annexation over one hundred and fifty years earlier. For example, Henri Bourassa (1868–1952), politician and newspaper editor, was actively encouraging French Canadian nationalism, campaigning against Canadian support for Britain in the war and opposing the introduction of conscription.

470. A shrine dedicated to Ste Anne de Beaupré had been founded by Breton seamen about 1620, a church was built in 1658 and a basilica in 1876. This became the most magnetic place of pilgrimage in North America, attracting an estimated 200,000 people in 1905. Their journey had been eased by the construction of a railway from Quebec city.

Quebec, Chateau Frontenac and Citadel.   *Postcard dated 11 May 1907*

Another glimpse of French atmosphere which we had was at a private lunch to which Bateman and I went at one of the French houses in Quebec. The host, by name Tessier, was head of a big savings bank business in the City and altogether charming. He had a son and daughter-in-law as charming as himself, and the house was full of old silver, books, ivories etc. which would have made you jealous to look at, the gem of the collection being, probably, an original letter from Longfellow written in rather stilted French. We enjoyed our lunch very much, and would have liked to stay all the afternoon! I also made friends with the Superintendent of the Arsenal at Quebec, who was in the Canadian Regular Army and had been over at Woolwich for several years. Possibly he took an interest in me as having a dim knowledge of Artillery (it is *very* dim now!), his own line. Anyhow he was very kind, and showed me the whole of the processes of manufacture of rifle ammunition and 18 pounder shell, including the actual filling with cordite and the other explosives.

It was all most fascinating – the more so as the Superintendent had had to evolve practically all the machinery personally, and then show the Canadian manufacturers of munitions what was wanted. And all the processes had to be carried on in a number of ramshackle and rather ancient buildings – part of the old Quebec Arsenal – which ordinarily would certainly have been condemned as insanitary!

I was also taken up into the barracks for the present garrison, and saw all the old buildings there, including the 'King's Bastion' whence there is a magnificent view over the City and River, and what is called the 'Governor General's quarters' which the G.G. uses when he comes to Quebec.

The only other incident at Quebec worth recording is that I celebrated the end of the Commission's sittings by going to a prize fight – very interesting (I can't remember ever seeing one before) but very probably the cause of my subsequent disorder! The wind, I remember now, was biting cold!

Nov. 16th

All being well, we should be in Liverpool by daybreak tomorrow, so I will end up this letter now. Of the voyage I need say nothing – except that it has been unpleasant in all ways. There are far too many passengers (428 cabin passengers and 6/7th women and children), bad food, unpleasant weather (our Marconi apparatus was carried away by a gale one night!) and a variety of unpleasant smells, even to the healthy.[471] I shall be thankful to be on shore and back.

> Best love
> Your affectionate son
> E. J. Harding

---

471. Harding might have counted his blessings that on this last stage of his final journey for the D.R.C. he arrived home safely: *Missanabie* was torpedoed and sunk by a submarine on 9 September 1918 with the loss of 45 lives. She was the sister ship of the *Metagama* on which he had crossed the Atlantic in August.

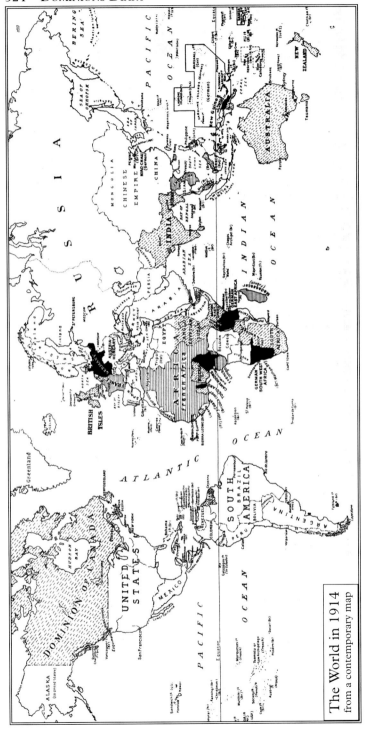

The World in 1914
from a contemporary map

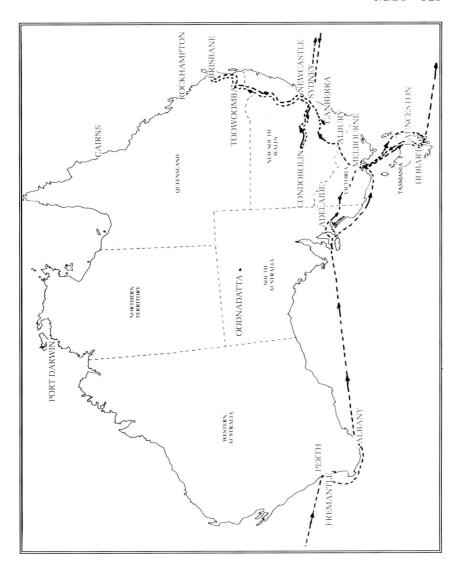

Outline map indicating Harding's travels in Australia.

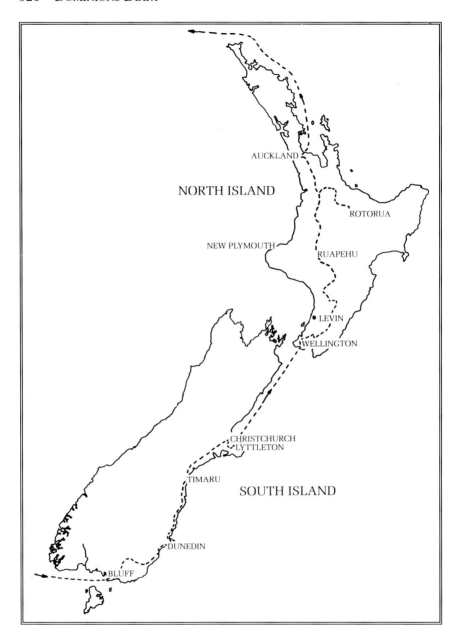

Outline map indicating Harding's travels in New Zealand.

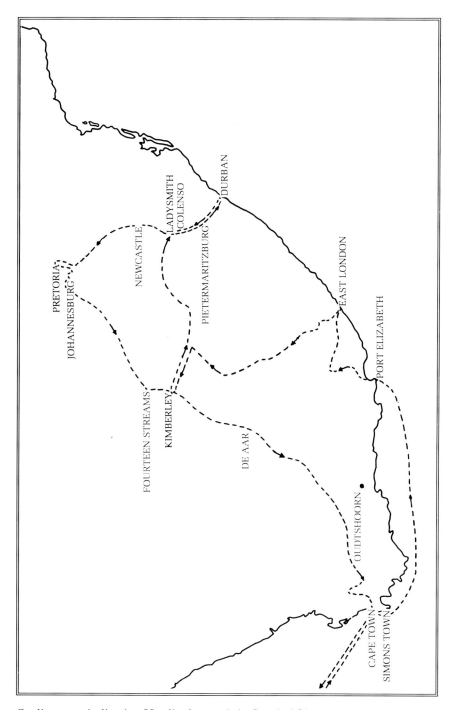

Outline map indicating Harding's travels in South Africa.

Outline map indicating Harding's travels in Newfoundland.

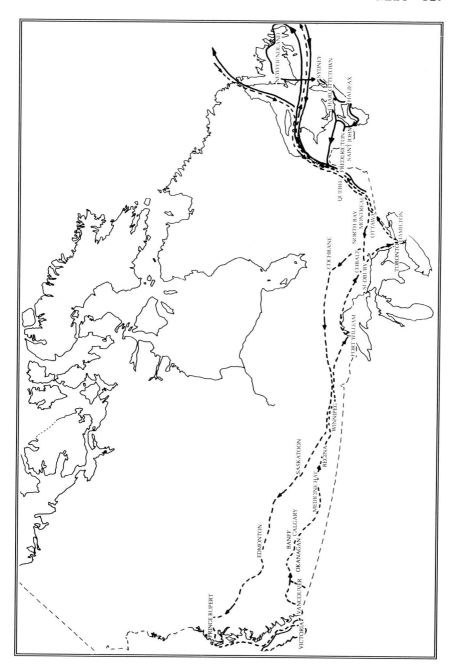

Outline map indicating Harding's travels in Canada.

INDEX

References to illustrations are in italics